P9-CRO-163

Fundamentals of Programming Using Java

FASTTRACK

Fundamentals of Programming Using Java

Edward Currie

THOMSON™

Australia · Canada · Mexico · Singapore · Spain · United Kingdom · United States

THOMSON

Fundamentals of Programming Using Java
Edward Currie

Series Editors	**Publishing Partner**
Walaa Bakry, Middlesex University	Middlesex University Press
Alan Murphy, Middlesex University	

Publishing Director	**Commissioning Editor**	**Managing Editor**
John Yates	Gaynor Redvers-Mutton	Celia Cozens

Senior Production Editor	**Manufacturing Manager**	**Marketing Manager**
Alissa Chappell	Helen Mason	Mark Lord

Production Controller	**Text Design**	**Cover Design**
Maeve Healy	Design Deluxe, Bath	Matthew Ollive

Typesetter	**Printer**
Keyline Consultancy, Newark	C&C Offset Printing Co.,Ltd.China

Copyright

© 2006, Middlesex University Press

Reprinted 2006 twice by Thomson Learning

The Thomson logo is a registered trademark used herein under licence.

For more information, contact
Thomson Learning
High Holborn House
50-51 Bedford Row
London WC1R 4LR

or visit us on the World Wide Web at:
http://www.thomsonlearning.co.uk

ISBN-13: 978-184480-451-1
ISBN-10: 1-84480-451-8

British Library Cataloguing-in-Publication Data
A catalogue record for this book is available from the British Library

All rights reserved by Thomson Learning 2006. The text of this publication, or any part thereof, may not be reproduced or transmitted in any form or by any means, electronic or mechanical, including photocopying, recording, storage in an information retrieval system, or otherwise, without prior permission of the publisher, with the exception of any material supplied specifically for the purpose of being entered and executed on a computer system for exclusive use by the purchaser of the publication.

Disclaimer
The publisher reserves the right to revise this publication and make changes from time to time in its content without notice. While the publisher has taken all reasonable care in the preparation of this book, the publisher makes no representation, express or implied, with regard to the accuracy of the information and cannot accept any legal responsibility or liability for any errors or omissions from the book or the consequences thereof.

Products and services that are referred to in this book may be either trademarks and/or registered trademarks of their respective owners. The publisher and author/s make no claim to these trademarks.

Contents

The FastTrack Series

Thomson Learning and Middlesex University Press have collaborated to produce a unique collection of textbooks which cover core, mainstream topics in an undergraduate computing curriculum. FastTrack titles are instructional, syllabus driven books of high quality and utility. They are:

- **For students**: concise and relevant and written so that you should be able to get 100% value out of 100% of the book at an affordable price
- **For instructors**: classroom tested, written to a tried and trusted pedagogy and market assessed for mainstream and global syllabus offerings so as to provide you with confidence in the applicability of these books. The resources associated with each title are designed to make delivery of courses straightforward and linked to the text.

FastTrack books can be used for self-study or as directed reading by a tutor. They contain the essential reading necessary to complete a full understanding of the topic. They are augmented by resources and activities, some of which will be delivered online as indicated in the text.

How the series evolved

Rapid growth in communication technology means that learning can become a global activity. In collaboration, Global Campus, Middlesex University and Thomson Learning have produced materials to suit a diverse and innovating discipline and student cohort.

Global Campus at the School of Computing Science, Middlesex University, combines local support and tutors with CD Rom-based materials and the Internet to enable students and lecturers to work together across the world.

Middlesex University Press is a publishing house committed to providing high quality, innovative, learning solutions to organisations and individuals. The Press aims to provide leading-edge 'blended learning' solutions to meet the needs of its clients and customers. Partnership working is a major feature of the Press's activities.

Together with Middlesex University Press and Middlesex University's Centre for Learning Development, Global Campus developed FastTrack books using a sound and consistent pedagogic approach. The SCATE pedagogy is a learning framework that builds up as follows:

- **Scope:** Context and the learning outcomes
- **Content:** The bulk of the course: text, illustrations and examples
- **Activity:** Elements which will help students further understand the facts and concepts presented to them in the previous section. Promotes their active participation in their learning and in creating their understanding of the unit content
- **Thinking:** These elements give students the opportunity to reflect and share with their peers their experience of studying each unit. There are *review questions* so that the students can assess their own understanding and progress
- **Extra:** Further online study material and hyperlinks which may be supplemental, remedial or advanced.

Fundamentals of Programming Using Java

This book introduces you to computer software development, using the Java programming language. You will learn to interpret and understand programs written by others, and to write your own programs. You will gain knowledge and experience of sound programming practice by writing lots of simple programs.

The book covers the areas of:

- The programming environment – compilers, integrated development environments, the Java software development kit (SDK)
- Structured and object-oriented problem solving
- The software development process, specification, design, implementation and testing
- Foundations of computer programming (data types, variables, input, output, arithmetic and logic operators, sequence, selection, iteration)
- Subprograms – methods, parameters
- Objects and classes
- Composition of classes
- Inheritance and polymorphism.

Using this book

There are several devices which will help you in your studies and use of this book. **Activities** usually require you to try out aspects of the material which have just been explained, or invite you to consider something which is about to be discussed. In some cases, a response is provided as part of the text that follows – so it is important to work on the activity before you proceed! Usually, however, a formal answer will be provided in the final section of each chapter.

The **time bar** indicates *approximately* how long each activity will take:

short	< 10 minutes
medium	10-45 minutes
long	> 45 minutes

Review questions are (usually) short questions at the end of each chapter to check you have remembered the main points of a chapter. They are a useful practical summary of the content, and can be used as a form of revision aid to ensure that you remain competent in each of the areas covered.

Where computer code is encountered, it is displayed in a different typeface and, where practical, is also provided online (see *About the Website*) – so you are not required to key in very long pieces of code. Do note, however, that the act of keying code is a useful discipline, and your keying errors are a valuable lesson in their own right. If your code does not run, do check the obvious – there is often little visual difference between l,1, I (small 'L', figure one, capital letter 'I' or between 0 and O.

About the author

Edward Currie

Edward Currie is the Academic Group Chair for Computing and Multimedia Technology at Middlesex University. His interests include object-oriented programming, functional languages and formal specification. He is the author of a number of journal and conference papers, and has acted as reviewer for papers and books for publishers including the Computer Journal, Macmillan and Pearson. He is the author of the book *The Essence of Z* (Prentice Hall, 1999).

Visit the accompanying website at **www.thomsonlearning.co.uk/fasttrack** and click through to the appropriate booksite to find further teaching and learning material including:

For Students

- Activities
- Multiple choice questions for each chapter

For Lecturers

- Downloadable PowerPoint slides

CHAPTER 1

Solving problems with computers

OVERVIEW

Java is one of the most popular programming languages in the world. It is popular partly because it can be used to solve a wide variety of problems in different domains.

Using Java is a great way to begin a programming career or lifelong interest in using computers to solve problems. This chapter will cover some basic contextual material about the programming process and the nature of programming languages. Start with the basics; build solidly; enjoy!

Learning outcomes On completion of this chapter you should be able to:

- Discuss the evolution of programming languages

- Discuss the main reasons why Java has become popular

- Discuss the basic ideas behind object-oriented software development

- Describe the program development cycle and the software associated with it

- Explain the concepts of compilation, interpretation, virtual machines and program portability

- Enter, compile and execute a simple Java program.

1.1 Computers and programming

What is a computer?

A computer is a general-purpose device that behaves according to the sets of instructions and data it is provided with. Computers execute instructions to process data. Each computer has at its core a central processing unit (CPU) – these days CPUs are built as a single microprocessor chip. Each microprocessor is associated with a set of instructions (machine code) which it can execute. The instructions and the data are stored as binary bit patterns; that is, strings of 1s and 0s. Any given computer can only execute instructions in the machine code language of its microprocessor.

What is a computer program?

Every computer is associated with a set of 'machine code' instructions that it is designed to recognise and execute. A machine code computer program consists of a sequence of these instructions which might look like this

```
1001010010010010
0010100100001001
0010100010010010
1110010100101010
etc.
```

The instructions, like all information stored by computers are sequences of ones and zeros (binary bit patterns).

This program can be stored on a disk. To execute the program, it is loaded from the disk into the computer's internal memory, then the instructions are fetched one by one by the CPU and executed.

In the early days of computers, the programmer would write all programs in the native machine code of the processor.

So: what is bad about writing programs in this way? Well, think about these points:

- Writing machine code is extremely time-consuming and therefore costly in terms of staff time(effort) and financial cost
- Machine code is meaningless to a human reader, which makes programming more difficult and more error-prone
- Machine code programs are not portable – that is, they cannot be taken from one type of processor to a different type of processor, because the instruction sets of each will be different
- When the processor becomes obsolete, the program can no longer be used. Note that hardware has developed very quickly, and some processors have become obsolete.

Assembler language

To overcome the problem of writing programs using binary bit patterns, *assembler language* was invented. In this, little words (mnemonics) are used, each of which corresponds to one of the machine code instructions. Data can be represented using decimal numbers instead of binary.

Thus an instruction to load the number 5 into a CPU register might look like

LD 5

instead of

0010010001001101

The names given to instructions are more meaningful to a human than their machine code equivalents. This assembler language program could be stored in the computer's memory, using a binary character code to stand for each character in the program, but the program could not be executed by the processor. (Remember: a processor can only execute programs written in its own machine code.) Therefore, a program is required to translate an assembler language program into machine code. This program is called an *assembler*.

The assembler must be an executable program, so it must be written in machine code.

Assemblers made programs easier to read for humans, and programming less error-prone, but did not overcome the portability problem or the fact that programs would eventually become obsolete along with the processor they were written for. Given the huge effort required to write programs and the fast pace of hardware development, this was very unsatisfactory.

High-level languages and compilers

The shortcomings of assembler programs led to the development in the 1960s of so-called 3rd generation programming languages, which were independent of any particular processor. These 'high-level' languages had more abstract, problem-oriented instructions that captured common patterns of instruction usage found in assembler languages. This meant that a single instruction from a 3rd generation language might correspond to several assembler language instructions, so that programs became shorter and more succinct. Programming languages became more oriented towards *solving problems* and less towards machine architecture.

We say that a 3rd generation language operates at a higher *level of abstraction* than the assembler program. Examples of 3rd generation languages include

- 1960s: ALGOL   FORTRAN   COBOL
- 1970s: SIMULA   PASCAL   ADA
- 1980s: MODULA-2   C++
- 1990s: MODULA-3   JAVA

These problem-oriented languages made programming less error-prone and more productive, but again, they could not be executed on a computer – they had to be stored as character codes, then translated into the machine code of the required processor. A program called a *compiler* is used for this purpose. This first checks the *syntax* (spelling and grammar) of the high-level program, and reports any errors. If there are no errors, it creates a machine code version of the high-level program. Once this is done, the machine code program may be executed on the host machine as many times as required, without the compiler being present.

The compilation process

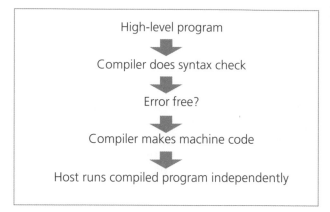

In order to run on a computer, a compiler must be written in machine code, but a compiler is a complex program, hard to write in a low-level language. Therefore, the compiler will be written in a high-level language (often the one which it is designed to compile!). We then have to compile the compiler, for which we require a compiler written in machine code! Of course, initially, someone had to write a machine code (or more likely, assembler) version of the compiler, but anyone subsequently writing a better compiler could use the existing compiler to compile it. Once a machine code version of the better compiler is available, this can be used to compile the high-level version of itself, to obtain an optimised version. This process is called *bootstrapping*.

Compilation of Java programs

With most programming languages, for example C++, the compiler produces a form of machine code that can be executed directly by the computer's hardware; no further software is needed. Once the program is compiled, the resulting machine code is completely self-contained and can be distributed on its own. This machine code is made up of the native instructions associated with that particular computer (every computer processor is associated with a set of machine-code instructions which it can understand and therefore execute). Java does not work like this. To make it possible to run the same compiled program on any computer, the Java program is compiled to something called *Java byte code*. This is machine code, but it is machine code for a computer called the Java Virtual Machine (JVM). The JVM is actually a piece of software which simulates a computer. The byte code instructions are processed by the JVM, which is also known as the *run-time interpreter* or the *run-time engine*. This 'interpreter' takes each instruction in turn, converts it into the host machine code, and executes it. This extra level of processing makes Java programs somewhat slower than the equivalent C++ program, but they are more portable. The Java byte code program can run on any machine with the run-time interpreter.

About Java

Java is a relatively new programming language developed by Sun Microsystems, Inc. Java started out in 1991 as a project code-named Green and the language was at one stage called Oak. Java is thought by many to have been a compromise between what its two inventors, James Gosling and Bill Joy, wanted.

- Java is a *high-level* language

- It has built-in graphical user interface support
- It is intended to be *platform-independent*
- Its syntax (structure) is similar to C++, but it is simpler than C++ in some important areas.

A high-level language is one that is much more abstract than the computer's machine code. In a high-level language, things like text, windows, buttons and files have a meaning. In machine code only numbers have any meaning. Java is very much more like C++, Pascal, or FORTRAN than it is like machine code. One thing that sets Java aside from these other languages is the built-in support for the graphical user interface. There is no standard way of handling a menu, for example, in C++ that would work the same on any computer. The Java language was developed from C++ by a process of simplification; Java has fewer features than C++, not more. The Java designers argue that they have removed the features that caused the most problems, but there is no universal agreement about this. In any event, if you master Java you will have little difficulty getting to grips with C++ if you wish to.

1.2 Constructing and running Java programs

In this section you will:

- Enter program text using a text editor
- Translate Java text into byte code
- Run code using a run-time interpreter.

You will find that the detailed procedure depends on the development software being used.

A Java program is just a text file: it contains letters, numbers and symbols. This is often called a *source code file*. You can create the source code file using any text editor. You can even use a word processor if you wish, but you should be careful to avoid using any text formatting, as this won't make sense to the compiler. Commercial Java development packages normally have an editor built in. However, if you are using Microsoft Windows, then the *Notepad* program makes a perfectly useful alternative to a commercial editor. More powerful integrated development environments (IDEs), which combine an editor with menus to invoke the Java compiler and run-time interpreter, are also available. An example is *JCreator*, available free from **www.jcreator.com** or *TextPad*, available from **www.textpad.com**. The Java compiler will require the filename of the Java source file to end in '.java'.

The program text is then fed into the Java compiler. If there are no errors in the program, the output will be a file containing the compiled byte code program, ready to run. The name of this file is the same as the source code file, but with the extension '.class'. If there are errors, the compiler will tell you *what* they are, and will try to tell you *where* they are. However, it will not always do this very well. To run the program, the '.class' file is fed into the run-time interpreter. Depending on how well you have written the program, it may work, or it may not. The process of finding out why a program does not work – or does not work as expected – is called *debugging*.

Using the Sun Software Development Kit

The Software Development Kit (SDK) is distributed free of charge by Sun Microsystems. You can download the entire system from Sun's website – if you have plenty of time, as it is a huge package. Choose the standard edition rather than the enterprise edition which contains features you do not yet need. The SDK is a no-frills system for producing programs in Java. It does very little to help the programmer, and assumes that the programmer knows what he or she is about.

There is very detailed documentation, supplied in the form of Web pages, but no step-by-step guidance.

Here is the URL for the SDK downloads:

http://java.sun.com/downloads/

Specifications

All the programs in this book will work with both the older 1.3 SDK and J2SE – SDK 1.4.2 versions and with the newer Java 1.5. However, you must have a version of Java installed on your machine.

The most basic way to use the SDK software is by typing commands at a command prompt. With the rapid rise of graphical user interfaces, most people have got out of the habit of doing this, so now is a good time to re-learn (or learn, if you grew up with Windows). Here is how to compile and run a Java program called *First*, using the SDK on a Windows NT system.

Start a command line session. (Look for something labelled *DOS prompt* or *command prompt*. If all else fails, from the *Start* menu select *Run...* and enter the word *command*.) You should end up with a Window containing a prompt (e.g., C:\WINNT>) where you can type commands.

Use the *cd* command to change to the directory where you want to store the Java program by typing, for example:

    cd \work\java

Use the *Notepad* program to edit the Java program by typing:

    notepad First.java

Keep the *Notepad* program running from now on. You will need it to edit the program later. Compile the Java program using the 'javac' program, by typing

    javac First.java

If there are no errors, this will produce a file called *First.class*. If there are errors, go back to *Notepad* and fix the errors, then try to compile again. You may have to go through this cycle lots of times at first when learning to program!

Run the program by typing:

    java First

However, if you have the *JCreator* or *TextPad* programs, compiling and running your Java programs is achieved by simply clicking menu options.

Activity 1.1

Compiling and running a Java program

Type the following program into Notepad, Text Pad, JCreator or your favourite editor and take a look at it.. Then compile and run it. Make some changes, re-compile and see what errors are reported by the compiler. Don't worry too much about understanding how the program works; all will be explained soon!

```java
// Prints 'Hello world!' on the screen in a dialog box
import javax.swing.JOptionPane;

public class Hello
{
    public static void main(String[] args)
    {
        JOptionPane.showMessageDialog(null, "Hello world!");

        System.exit(0);
    }
}
```

Note that the punctuation is important and { is not the same as [or (

Learning to program

- The best way to learn is by doing it
- You should not be afraid to try different things to see if they work
- A faulty Java program will never damage the computer.

As you start programming you will often find that your programs do not work! This is inevitable. If you have an instructor, he or she may help you to fix the errors in your programs. However, you will learn more if you first put a good deal of effort into making them work yourself. Often you will not have enough information to do this very effectively, and you will have to rely on a process of trial and error. This is perfectly normal in programming. At first, people make trivial errors with the syntax of the language.

Eventually the syntax will become second nature to you, and you will not even have to think about it. Then you will be able to spend more time looking for the logical errors, that is, places where the program tells the computer to do something that is not really what is required. The computer will follow the program's instructions slavishly, and cannot be blamed when the program is incorrect!

Interactive development environments (IDEs)

- IDEs combine the edit-compile-run stages
- They may also provide user interface design tools and interactive debugging
- The language and facilities are the same.

Interactive development environments (IDEs) are useful for automating some of the steps in production of a program. Most people who program extensively use an IDE, but IDEs do not allow anything different to be achieved, compared with using the basic SDK. The advantages of using the SDK for development are that it is free and that it exposes the operations that would be 'behind the scenes' when using an IDE.

An elementary Java program

Here is the program from Activity 1.1.

```java
// Prints 'Hello world!' on the screen in a dialog box
import javax.swing.JOptionPane;

public class Hello
{
  public static void main(String[] args)
  {
    JOptionPane.showMessageDialog(null, "Hello world!");

    System.exit(0);
  }
}
```

This is just to give an idea of what a Java program looks like. The details will be covered later. Some things to note are:

- Any text following '//' on a line is a **comment** – an explanation of what the program does. More on this in Chapter 3.

- Braces { } group sections of the program

- The program consists of English-like words

- The program is long, for what it does. Beginners are often surprised at how long computer programs have to be, to accomplish even the most trivial tasks. This is because the computer is so much less intelligent than people think. The program tells the computer exactly what to do, in great detail.

Classes

The fundamental unit of organisation in an object-oriented program is the *class*, which structures and organises a program. Classes are self-contained and autonomous.

Some things to note:

- One class must have the same name as the program file itself. In this case, the program file must be called *Hello.java*

- This class should have a method called *main()*; this is where the program starts

- All program **instructions** must be inside **methods**, which are inside **classes**.

In this program, the instruction

JOptionPane.showMessageDialog(null, "Hello world!");

prints (i.e. outputs) *Hello world!* to the screen in a dialog box. The only method is *main()*, which is in class *Hello*.

Most of the programs in this book will have only one class.

A program must know where to start. It is a common misconception that a program starts at the top, and continues downwards. Java programs start by executing the method called *main()*. So at least one class must have a *main()*. After this, execution is controlled by the programmer. The *main()* method can execute any other methods from any other classes in any order. These methods can, in turn, execute other methods, and so on. The only thing that is imposed by the language is the starting point of the program. In the class Hello, there is only one method, *main()*, which gets executed when the program runs.

However, classes can also be used to specify **objects**, which will be described in more detail later in this book. Objects are representations of the elements of the problem domain for which a software solution is being created.

Note that:

- There may be many objects of the same class
- A large program will have many classes, and many objects of each class.

The idea is best illustrated with an example. *War and Peace* is a novel; *Great Expectations* is a novel; *Wuthering Heights* is a novel. These three *objects* are members of the class 'novel'.

They all have things in common: they are all works of fiction, and they are all published in the form of a book. Of course they have differences as well; however, they are more similar to one another than they are to, say, a hatstand or a cheese sandwich.

Object-oriented analysis is the process of breaking down a system into the classes it contains, and finding how these classes are related. Object-oriented programming is the process of writing sections of program that correspond to each class.

In this book, your programs will mostly be using objects of predefined classes, but later you will be creating programs with multiple classes, and you will cover most of the building blocks to enable you to create more sophisticated multi-class programs in the future.

Attributes and operations

- **Attributes** (also called 'data' or 'variables') represent the relevant characteristics of the object
- **Operations** (called 'functions' in some languages and called 'methods' in Java) are what an object does, or has done to it. They represent the behaviour of the object.

Pause for a moment and consider the example *novel* class described above. What **attributes** does a novel have?

Some possibilities are: author, date of writing, date of publication, number of pages, text. All these things distinguish one novel from another. For a particular novel (that is, for an object of the *novel* class) the attributes will have values. For example, the object *Great Expectations* has the value *Charles Dickens* for its *author* attribute.

Similarly, consider the **operations** which the *novel* class has.

This definition rather depends on the application. The things that a library does with a novel will not be the same as, say, a publisher (e.g. reviewing or marketing or selling).

These ideas may seem a bit strange at first but you will not need to worry about them for a while, as your programs will not be complex enough to need more than one class. We will lightly touch upon object-oriented concepts, but we will lay the foundations for further study of this ubiquitous and powerful software development technique.

Applications and applets

- An *application* is an independent program, with a useful function, such as Hello
- A Java *applet* is a program that is usually part of a Web page, and can run on any computer with no software required except a Java-enabled web browser
- Programming principles are the same for applications and applets.

Most computer programming is concerned with the production of *applications*. An application is something that does something useful outside the context of the computer itself, like a word processor or a spreadsheet.

An *applet* is a 'mini-program', one that relies on other software to support it. The term is usually, but not always, used to refer to programs that are embedded in web pages.

The Java programming language can be used to produce applications and applets. The programming techniques required to produce an application are not much different from those used in applets. In this book we will concentrate on application programming.

1.3 Software development

Levels of abstraction

The production of a computer program can be seen as a progression through successively more detailed *levels of abstraction*.

- In its most abstract form, a program is an idea in someone's mind, or perhaps a specification on paper. This is abstract because it does not concern itself very much with the details of the computer, or exactly what the computer has to do. The specification probably says *what* the program should do
- The next level of abstraction is the *model*. This is more detailed than an idea or specification, but much less detailed than a program. If the program is a simple one, or the programmer is very experienced, the model may only exist in the person's head; nevertheless, it is more structured and 'computer centred' than a specification.

Expert programmers are those who can form a model of the application in their minds, and keep the model in mind when programming. If the program is large and complex, or if a number of people are working on the same program, it is almost always better to formalise the model, either on paper or using computer software for this purpose.

The computer program itself is much more detailed than a model. The programmer must tell the computer exactly what to do, and when to do it.

However, the high-level language program is still too abstract for the computer to understand. Computers understand machine code, and nothing else.

All the transitions between these different levels of abstraction occur in the minds of software engineers, except the last one. The translation from a program in Java, say, to a program in machine code is sufficiently well defined that it can be done by a computer program (a compiler). There is some limited computer support for translating a model into a program, but at present it requires too much human intuition to be automated. The conversion from a specification or idea into a model will probably never be automatic.

Software development activities

Software systems do not come from nowhere, and computer programmers do not simply sit down at a computer and start writing code. Each software system goes through its own *life cycle*. Although every system's life cycle is unique, there are certain activities that tend to take place in some form for most systems.

In the case of object-oriented systems development, activities are often repeated in a cyclical fashion, since problems and limitations of models may not be identified until the design or implementation stages. Or perhaps the system users, when presented with a prototype of the system, identify new features of their real-world system that need to be integrated into the software system model and design. Examples of activities occurring in software systems life cycles might include:

- **Analysis and modelling**
- **System design**
- **Implementation**
- **Testing and evaluation**
- **Maintenance and enhancement**.

Let's look at these in more detail:

- **Analysis and modelling:** an analyst or team of analysts perform a study of the real-world system that a computer system is to be developed to support. There may be an existing real-world system, there may also be an existing computer system, or the project may be the development of a new computer system to support some new department or organisation that does not exist at present. One important task in modelling is the identification of the boundaries of the system to be modelled and what the system is to include. Models are created by looking at any existing system and analysing the data, tasks, communications etc that it needs to make with other systems. This analysis creates the model for the new system that adds in all the things you wanted the existing system to do but which it could not. In other words, you start by drawing what exists and improve the drawing to show what needs to be added to make a new system work. This is usually done at a high (overview) level as the practical detail is added later at the system design stage.

  Analysis and modelling involve activities where you try to concentrate on abstract views of the system; you should avoid making assumptions about detail. So analysis is what we do when we try to produce a model of a system free of any internal technology. The enclosing system context may set technology constraints; for example, automatic teller machine (cash point) software may have to be analysed in the context of current machine and debit card technology. Hence you do not have choices during analysis, but you do at the next level down (in terms of detail and precision), and this is called *design*

- **System design:** based on some form of model and analysis, a design for the computer system can be created. Such a design is often, but not always, focussed by having chosen the programming language in which the system is to be implemented

- **Implementation:** a system design is implemented in a particular programming language (or several, for complex systems). Part of a system implementation may involve integrating existing computer sub-systems, and perhaps designing communication with external computer systems and databases. Often, one or more prototypes are implemented, to test ideas, and perhaps to enable users to help in an improvement of the system modelling and design. Often the term *coding* is used to describe the exercise of actually writing computer programs. The term *programming* is usually used in a more general way, to describe all the activities of software development. One part of programming a computer system is the actual coding during implementation

- **Testing and evaluation**: the complete implemented system, or parts of it, are tested with real data. These software (sub)systems can also be tested by the real-world users, or perhaps staff playing the roles of the eventual real-world system users. The results of testing and evaluation often direct the software development team to perform one or more previous activities again. In such a way, systems may be developed incrementally

- **Maintenance and enhancement:** studies have shown that at least 70% of the costs associated with software projects are incurred *after* the system has been deployed. The work done after deployment is usually called maintenance. However, this term is misleading as it suggests that the software might degrade in functionality or performance if not 'maintained'. Software is not like mechanical artefacts that perform less well if not, for example, cleaned and oiled. While software maintenance is most often associated with fixing bugs, in reality the major difficulties and costs are encountered when changes or enhancements must be made. Object technology is supposed to help here because it allows software to be better designed and implemented to simulate the world it is designed for. Hence, when changes appear in the real world, such as changes in tax laws or network arrangements, the software can be straightforwardly changed or enhanced.

In the case of object-oriented systems development, the modelling, design and implementation are performed from an object technology perspective. The various techniques and programming languages of object technology should help in all these aspects of software development.

Types of software development

There are three main types of software development:

- **Totally informal**. The programmer gets an idea in his or her head about how the program should work, and sits in front of a computer typing a program
- **Structured** (semi-formal). A step-by-step design procedure is followed, often involving modelling the system to be constructed. Using a combination of rules and intuition, the models are transformed into a program
- **Formal** (mathematical). The system is modelled mathematically, then transformed in a rigorous way into a program. The result is a program which is provably correct.

Object orientation is usually part of a semi-formal, modelling-based development process. In practice, most software engineers working in the commercial and industrial arenas use semi-formal techniques, although a vast amount of informal development still goes on. Other semi-formal techniques concentrate on the data managed by a system (e.g. data flow modelling) or on the operations the system carries out (e.g. functional decomposition).

What is object orientation?

Object orientation is a *philosophy* and a *modelling technique*. It is useful for:

- Improving the quality of computer software production
- Reducing the cost of computer software production
- Understanding and designing complex systems
- Planning and managing corporate data and databases.

Object orientation is not limited to computer programming. Fundamentally, object orientation is a system for *modelling* in terms of the objects (entities) which make up a system. It is based on the idea that software systems are best thought of as a set of interacting parts, *objects*, that do the work of the system by sending messages to each other. (Although the Internet is not an object-oriented system, it is quite useful to think of object-oriented systems as working in a similar way.) Object technology has particular strengths because it allows developers to move in a relatively smooth fashion from that part of the world that the software has to simulate, to the software itself. For example, in an object-oriented implementation of a banking system (i.e. in the code) you should find *customer* objects that directly and straightforwardly represent how actual bank customers behave.

Most software development technologies evolve after a language has emerged that best represents the ideas. The programming languages Simula and Smalltalk were the starting points for object technology. Then came C++ and Java. C++ has support for object concepts and became hugely popular because of its relationship with C. Java has given a further boost to object technology because of the Web, not to mention its superficial relationship with C++ and its inclusion of many ideas from Smalltalk.

A strength of Java is that it implements most of the concepts of object-oriented systems. Object technology encourages and facilitates both software reuse, and the development of programs that allow computer systems and computer programs to be conceptualised and worked with in a flexible and powerful way.

At the processor level (i.e. machine code languages) many thousands (sometimes hundreds of thousands) of instructions must be executed in any useful piece of software, but high-level languages that are more suited to human expression are used so we have to write significantly fewer 'instructions'. Java has 'class libraries', which contain pre-written chunks of program code which can be reused or extended, so that we write even fewer instructions than with traditional high-level programming languages such as Pascal.

Writing simple pieces of software can be straightforward – even easy, and fun. However, when pieces of software become large or have to fit into a complicated system, complexity becomes hard to deal with. In this book, the examples will often be small and not representative of full-scale software development. However, in further study you may be asked to examine more complex software. Indeed, as you explore Java and its classes, you will have to get used to trying to learn about pieces of a whole that nobody can fully understand. This is what makes software development both hard and exciting!

A fundamental problem in software development is making a match between the 'declarative' knowledge that people have (i.e. knowing *what* behaviour is required of a system) to the 'procedural' knowledge of the computer (i.e. knowing *how* to do something). The development of techniques to assist the translation between declarative and procedural knowledge is one of the major advances in the software industry in the last twenty years or so. Object technology has made a significant contribution here. It encourages a declarative approach, using procedural techniques for the detail of how to implement behaviour.

1.4 Summary

The main points of this chapter may be summarised as follows:

- To learn about programming, you must write lots of programs!
- Java is an elegant, portable high-level programming language
- Java programs must be compiled to byte code
- TextPad is an integrated development environment in which you can easily edit programs and launch the Java compiler and run-time interpreter
- Byte code programs are executed by the Java Virtual Machine.

1.5 Review questions

P **Question 1.1** What are the characteristics of high-level languages, as opposed to assembler language?

P **Question 1.2** How does a computer run (execute) a high-level language program?

P **Question 1.3** How does Java differ from other high-level languages in this respect?

P **Question 1.4** What is an integrated development environment (IDE)?

P **Question 1.5** What is meant by 'levels of abstraction'?

P **Question 1.6** What is object orientation?

P **Question 1.7** Answer *true* or *false* to each of the following:

1 A computer can understand the Java programming language.

2 Java is more similar to C++ than it is to Pascal.

3 The Java Software Development Kit (SDK) is software for compiling and running Java programs.

4 The command to compile a Java program called *Prog.java* to bytecode is *javac Prog*.

5 The command to run a compiled Java program called *Prog.class* is *java Prog*.

6 Java programs are described as portable because they will fit onto a small, lightweight disk.

7 In the software development life cycle, roughly 70% of the life cycle is spent in maintenance of the software.

8 A class is a category of programming language.

1.6 Answers to review questions

Question 1.1 Assembler instructions have a 1-1 relationship with the machine code instructions of the computer, whereas high-level languages support more abstract, problem-oriented instructions, each of which may subsume several assembler language instructions, capturing a common pattern of usage of assembler instructions.

Question 1.2 It does not do so! Computers can only execute machine code, and a program called a *compiler* is required to translate the high-level language program into machine code.

Question 1.3 Java programs are compiled to *byte-code*, which is effectively machine code for a virtual computer, simulated by the Java Virtual Machine (JVM) software. This means that the byte-code program can run on any computer which has the JVM software, making Java programs extremely portable.

Question 1.4   It is a piece of software which supports the editing, compiling and running of programs all within one graphical user interface. In theory, this makes software development easier, but often IDEs are quite sophisticated, and novice programmers are likely to spend most of their time getting to grips with the IDE rather than writing programs! The alternative is to use a basic editor such as Notepad, with the javac (java compiler) and java (run-time interpreter) commands, which operate in a simple command line mode.

Question 1.5   This refers to the different levels of detail at which a solution to a programming problem may be viewed. These range from the initial specification of a solution on paper (high level of abstraction), through more detailed descriptions, to the final highly detailed and precise description of what the computer must do, written in a programming language (low level of abstraction).

Question 1.6   Fundamentally, object orientation is a system for *modelling* in terms of the objects (entities) which make up a system. It is based on the idea that software systems are best thought of as a set of interacting parts, *objects*, that do the work of the system by sending messages to each other. In object-oriented programming languages, the *class* construct is used to specify objects. Thus, for example, we could define a class to describe the characteristics of a sheep, then create numerous sheep objects for a program to simulate a sheepdog trial (competition). Object orientation is one of the most important features of Java.

Question 1.7 (true/false)

1   **False** Computers only understand their own native machine code.

2   **True** Java has many of the features of C++.

3   **True** Often supplemented by Integrated Development Environments.

4   **False** The extension *.java* is required. i.e. *javac Prog.java*

5   **True** This time, the file extension is not required.

6   **False** They are so described because they will run on any computer that implements the Java Virtual Machine.

7   **True** That is why it is very important that programs are easy to understand by people other than the programmer who wrote them.

8   **False** A class is a means of giving structure to object-oriented programs.

CHAPTER 2

Algorithms and programs

OVERVIEW

In the last chapter, you learned a little about the development of programming languages, and the process of software development. In this chapter, you will undertake a swift travelogue through some of the main programming concepts that are supported by most modern programming languages. Later in the book, we will revisit each of these concepts using the Java programming language, but here we will start without a specific computer language and look at the concepts through the international medium of pizza. Really, you can learn a lot from thinking about the decisions needed in creating a pizza.

Learning outcomes   At the end of this chapter you should be able to:

- Explain what algorithms are, and their relationship to programs

- Discuss the problem-solving process and explain how it relates to programming

- Explain the need for programming languages and their relationship to pseudocode and natural language

- Describe non-computing examples of each of the main concepts of structured programming.

2.1 Problem solving

Programming is all about solving problems. A program is just a set of instructions that describe how to solve a particular problem, written in a language that a computer can understand (or more often, a language which a compiler can *translate* into a language (machine code) which the computer can understand.

There are usually four steps to solving a problem:

- Understand the problem
- Work out a plan
- Sort out the details
- Test and evaluate.

The same also applies to writing a program!

Understanding the problem is a vital step in solving the problem. You need to ask:

- What information do you know?
- What do you want to happen?
- How can one lead to the other?

In software development, this is the *analysis* phase described in the last chapter. It involves talking to customers in order to establish *precisely* what they want the program to do. However, this is not as easy as it sounds, as often the customer does not *know* precisely what they want; or they are unable to express their requirements precisely enough for you to go away and write a program. This process of establishing a precise specification of what the program should do, and if possible expressing this as a contract between you and the client, is absolutely vital.

Writing a program is very time-consuming, and if it turns out that the program does not do what the client wanted it to do, then the process of rewriting or changing the program can be extremely expensive! Even for the relatively short programming exercises in this book, it is still important to ask yourself:

- Do you understand what you are required to do?
- Do you understand the programming constructs you will need to use?

You should not start to write a program until you have fully understood the problem.

2.2 The pizza eater's problem

Before looking specifically at computer programming, consider the problem-solving process as applied to an equally important problem; that of satisfying the desire to eat pizza. To improve your understanding of this problem, you need to ask lots of questions.

You'll probably be amazed at the range of questions that you consider even on something as simple as eating a pizza:

- You know that you want to eat pizza – but when?
- Are you desperately hungry? ... or can you wait for a while?
- Do you prefer the taste of a home-made pizza?
- Do you have the time or inclination to make a pizza yourself?
- Do you have the ingredients?

- If not, can you be bothered going to the shops to get them?
- Do you have a pizza in the freezer?
- Do you live near a take away? ... and do they deliver?
- Would you prefer the ambience of a restaurant?
- Do you want an upmarket place (independent restaurant, Pizza Express) or a popular chain (Pizza Hut etc)?
- If you would prefer an upmarket place, do you need to travel far to get to it?
- Is it worth it?
- If you are cooking, do you have a suitable recipe book?
- Do you want a thin or thick base?
- Is it just for you, or for friends too? .... and if so, do your friends like the same type of pizza as you?

You should 'brainstorm' in the above manner until you fully understand the problem and have some alternative strategies for solving it. This should enable you to decide upon a suitable plan for achieving the goal.

From this you can conclude:

- There are often several different ways to achieve a task
- One must consider the trade-off between the advantages and disadvantages of each
- What is best depends on the situation
- Given a plan, there are still different ways to achieve it.

Programming is about devising plans; the above processes all apply equally to programming problems.

From the Pizza exercise, alternative plans should emerge, such as:

> Plan 1: Go to a pizza restaurant
> *Issues:*
> Pizza Express or Pizza Hut?
> City centre or local restaurant?
>
> Plan 2: Buy a frozen pizza
> *Issues:*
> Buy one with toppings?
> Add your own toppings?
>
> Plan 3: Make your own
> *Issues:*
> Which recipe?

Brainstorming

Do a similar brainstorming exercise for devising a plan for travelling to work, where you are in possession of a bicycle, a car and an umbrella.

Problem solving is an iterative (i.e. cyclic) process. The first step is to understand the problem. Never rush in with a solution until you have collected and organised as much information as you can about the problem. Then rough out the general outline of the solution. Only when you are happy with the outline do you fill in the details. Finally, always test and evaluate your solution. You will probably discover problems or things that could be done better, so go back to the understanding phase as the first step in improving your solution. Each time round the loop you will improve your solution.

Activity 2.2

Problem solving

What would you do in each of the phases of the problem-solving cycle if the problem was:

1 An essay

2 An exam question

3 A program to write

4 A presentation to prepare and give?

2.3 Algorithms

An algorithm is a set of instructions for solving a problem; it consists of the *actions to do* and the *order in which to do them*. In general an algorithm should, at least, be:

- **Complete** (i.e. cover all the parts): it shouldn't be possible to get into a situation where the algorithm does not tell you what to do
- **Unambiguous** (there is no doubt about what it does): everyone should agree on what each instruction means and the order in which they are to be carried out – there should be no dispute
- **Deterministic** (only one possible result): if the same data is input, the same result should be obtained. For example, tossing a dice is non-deterministic, as you get different results each time
- **Finite** (it should finish): when following the algorithm, you should eventually finish and not end up following instructions for ever.

Some examples of algorithms are:

- A set of directions for getting from one place to another
- A musical score
- A recipe
- The instructions you learned about how to do long multiplication
- A set of instructions for solving a Rubik's Cube
- A set of instructions to tell a computer to perform a given task; i.e. a computer program.

The following exercise gives you some practice in writing algorithms to solve problems.

Activity 2.3

Algorithms

You have two containers, one of which has a capacity of 5 litres, and the other 3 litres. You have access to a water tap. These are no markings on either container. Devise an algorithm to place 4 litres of water in the 5-litre container, without using any other equipment.

An algorithm is a solution to a problem written in such a way that, if its instructions are followed blindly, the problem will be solved. The actions to be performed and the order in which they should be performed must be clearly given. Writing an algorithm involves not just being able to solve the problem, but knowing exactly how you solved it, so that you can write it down. One way to solve a problem involves coming up with a rough solution, evaluating it and then refining it into a more detailed solution from the lessons learned. Programming is often done in a similar way.

2.4 Developing algorithms by refinement

One solution to the 'eat pizza' problem was to make a pizza, using a recipe (i.e. algorithm) from a book of pizza recipes. Let us assume that you are writing a book of pizza recipes, and have already written a recipe for a pizza base. How would you develop a new pizza recipe (algorithm)?

Often when devising an algorithm, you will first express it using instructions at a *high level of abstraction*, that is, in quite general terms, without great detail. For the pizza recipe, a first attempt might be:

1 Make the base
2 Make the topping
3 Put the topping on the base
4 Cook it.

This algorithm has only four instructions, each of which represents a sub-problem of the original problem. So you now have four smaller problems to solve, but each of these should be easier to solve than the one big original problem. The instructions are not yet sufficiently detailed to enable a cook to make the pizza by following them, but they do enable us to begin the process of *stepwise refinement* which will, hopefully, eventually lead us to an algorithm at a sufficient level of detail for a cook to follow. The detailed algorithm is said to be more *concrete*, or at a *lower level of abstraction*, than the original attempt.

You examine the highly abstract algorithm, and establish that it does indeed appear as if it could lead to a solution to your problem. You then take each instruction in turn and break it down into a series of smaller steps. Each of these may then be examined to see if they need to be broken down into still more detailed instructions, until eventually you arrive at an algorithm comprising instructions sufficiently detailed for our processor to follow. The measure of this in the recipe will be whether or not a cook can follow the instructions. When developing a computer program, the 'high-level' instructions will probably be written in *pseudocode*, a structured English notation resembling a programming language, which you can use to express your ideas, and the final refinement of the algorithm will be written in the notation of a particular programming language, and therefore ready to use with a computer. You will return to this notion of pseudocode shortly.

Now think about trying to improve upon the initial attempt at the pizza recipe. You need to create a list of ingredients (data) for the algorithm to operate on. Suppose you choose all your favourite things to make the topping. Assume also that you already have a pizza base recipe on, say, page 15 of your book, but you want a big pizza for your friends, so you double all quantities associated with the pizza base recipe.

Ingredients

Topping:

8oz mozzarella, sliced	8 plum tomatoes, chopped
1 tbsp tomato puree	1 onion, chopped
3 cloves garlic, finely chopped	2 tbsp olive oil
3 tbsp fresh basil, torn	1 tbsp capers
50g anchovy fillets, chopped	2 tbsp green olives
4oz Milano salami, thinly sliced	Salt and pepper
2 fresh green chillies, deseeded and chopped	

Base:

350g flour	2 tsp salt
2 tsp dried yeast	1 tsp caster sugar
2 tbsp olive oil	240ml water

You also have to decide what to do with each of the four instructions:

1 Make the base
2 Make the topping
3 Put the topping on the base
4 Cook it.

They could be refined as follows:

Instruction	Refinement
1 Make the base	Make the base according to the recipe on page 15 of your recipe book. **Note:** quantities given for the base are double those given on page 15.
2 Make the topping	Heat the oil in a frying pan. Add the onion, garlic and chillies topping and fry for 5 minutes. Add tomatoes, puree, anchovies and capers and fry until the sauce has reduced to a thick paste. Add the basil and salt and pepper to taste.
3 Put the topping on the base	Spread the sauce evenly over one base. Arrange the mozzarella evenly on top of the sauce. Arrange the salami and olives evenly on top of the cheese. Drizzle some olive oil over the top of the pizza.
4 Cook it	Bake for 20 minutes directly on the oven shelf.

Sometimes you notice something wrong with the initial breakdown of the problem, and you have to go back and add or change instructions. In your initial algorithm, suppose you notice that you have forgotten to preheat the oven, which should have happened before the other four instructions.

Adding this instruction, the complete recipe becomes:

Pizza Java

Topping:

8oz mozzarella, sliced	8 plum tomatoes, chopped
1 tbsp tomato puree	1 onion, chopped
3 cloves garlic, finely chopped	2 tbsp olive oil
3 tbsp fresh basil, torn	1 tbsp capers
50g anchovy fillets, chopped	2 tbsp green olives
4 oz Milano salami, thinly sliced	Salt and pepper
2 fresh green chillies, deseeded and chopped	

Base:

350g flour	2 tsp salt
2 tsp dried yeast	1 tsp caster sugar
2 tbsp olive oil	240ml water

Method
1 Preheat oven to 200ºC
2 Make the base according to the recipe on page 15 of your book
   Note: the quantities given for the base are double those given in the book
3 Heat the oil in a frying pan
4 Add the onion, garlic and chillies and fry for 5 minutes
5 Add tomatoes, puree, anchovies and capers and fry until the sauce has reduced to a thick paste
6 Add the basil, and salt and pepper to taste
7 Spread the sauce evenly over the base
8 Arrange the mozzarella evenly on top of the sauce
9 Arrange the salami and olives evenly on top of the cheese
10 Drizzle some olive oil over the top of the pizza
11 Bake for 20 minutes directly on the oven shelf

The above algorithm has much in common with a computer program.

Data

There is a set of items which are operated on by the algorithm. In the recipe algorithm, these are the ingredients. In a computer program algorithm, these will be, for example, integers (whole numbers), floating point numbers (i.e. with decimal points), characters (for example, representations of each of the keys on the keyboard, such as the letter 'A'), and strings of characters such as 'Hello and welcome to the show'. These items are the **input** to the algorithm.

Process

There is a list of instructions which, if carried out ('executed', in programming parlance), will achieve the desired result.

Output

There is an **output** from the execution of the algorithm. In the recipe algorithm, this is of course a delicious pizza; in a typical computer program algorithm, it might be numbers or strings as above.

For example, a program to compute the **average** (mean) of a set of input numbers might have:

- Input: 2 4 6 8
- Output: 5.

A program to **count** how many times the word 'had' occurs in a given input string might have:

- Input: 'Janet, where Paul had had *had*, had had *had had*. *Had had* had had the approval of the tutor.'
- Output: 11.

An algorithm being executed is generally known as a *process*, and the thing that is executing it is called a *processor*. For the recipe, the processor is the cook; for a computer program, the processor is the computer. Another analogy is that of a play; the text of the play being the algorithm, and the performance of the play being the process.

2.5 Subprograms

The recipe algorithm also illustrates another important feature found in computer programs; that of **subprograms**. You will have noted that the instruction:

'Make the base according to the recipe on page 15 of your recipe book. Note: the quantities given for the base are double those given in the book.'

is actually asking the cook to execute *another* algorithm, the one 'on page 15' for making a pizza base. When a cook gets to such an instruction, they are being asked to stop executing the algorithm currently being followed, remember where they are up to in the algorithm, and perform another algorithm. When they finish the other algorithm, they must return to where they left off in the original algorithm, and continue with its execution.

This idea that instructions in an algorithm may themselves stand for algorithms is *very* important in writing computer programs.

Before reading on, you might like to pause and consider what the advantages of sub-algorithms such as this might be.

By writing sub-algorithms:

- The main algorithm will be more **succinct**
- The main algorithm will be **easier to understand**, as the code for the sub-algorithm is not cluttering it up
- The sub-algorithm can be used over and over again (**reuse**).

What do you think would happen if an instruction in an algorithm told the processor to execute the algorithm *of which the instruction was itself a part*?

Well, the same mechanism applies as with any other subprogram. The processor is being asked to stop executing the algorithm currently being followed, remembering where it is up to in the algorithm, and start executing the same algorithm again at the first instruction. When it finishes the current execution of the algorithm, it must return to where it left off in the original execution. However, if the algorithm is just a sequence of instructions, it will eventually reach the instruction that told it to execute the algorithm again, and so on. The processor would just keep doing the algorithm until it reached this instruction, over and over, forever! This idea of an algorithm 'calling itself' is called *recursion*, and can actually be very useful, although it may not appear so from this example! You will meet recursion again later in your study of programming.

Parameters

The **'make the base...'** instruction in the pizza recipe also demonstrates another important concept in computer programming; that of *parameterisation*. The instruction tells the cook to follow the base-making instructions on page 15 of the recipe book, but using the quantities of ingredients (input) listed in the current recipe, causing a double quantity of the base to be made.

The same instructions can be followed to make any required quantity of the base, by simply specifying different quantities of ingredients (provided the ratios between quantities of each ingredient are the same).

The quantities of ingredients are *parameters* to the sub-algorithm. An example in a computer program might be a subprogram to compute the square of a number. You could write a subprogram to compute the square of four, but it would be much more useful to write one to which you could give *any* number, as a parameter, and it would compute the square of that number.

What do you think the advantages of parameterising an algorithm might be?

By parameterising, the same algorithm instructions may be told to operate on different data, making the algorithm much more general, versatile and useful.

Reuse of algorithms

Note that sometimes an instruction needs very little refining, if any – note, for example, instruction number 4 in the pizza recipe, 'Cook it'.

Sometimes, each more abstract instruction is refined into several more detailed instructions (e.g. instructions 2 and 3 in the pizza recipe). However, sometimes it turns out that an instruction can be implemented by simply *reusing* an algorithm which you already have available, as with instruction 1 in the pizza recipe.

This idea of reuse is also extremely important in computer programming. Most modern programming languages come with extensive libraries of pre-written subprograms (algorithms) which may be used by programmers in their own programs. This can potentially save the programmer a lot of work, the maxim being:

- **'Don't reinvent the wheel!'**

The library that comes with the Java programming language is called the Applications Programming Interface (API). In fact, the Java API is far more sophisticated than simply a collection of algorithms, and this is discussed in more detail a little later. So when you have an initial algorithm for solving your problem, you should first check, for each sub-problem, whether there are any existing algorithms in the API or elsewhere, which you could reuse. Even if one of these might require some modification to meet your specific needs, this will usually be easier than writing it from scratch.

2.6 Pseudocode and structured programming

The final version of the pizza recipe is probably sufficiently detailed for a cook to follow. However, a lot of details can be left out of the recipe algorithm, in the knowledge that any decent cook can work these out for themselves. For example, you wouldn't break down the 'Heat the oil...' instruction into:

1 Strike a match
2 Turn the gas knob
3 Put match near gas ring
4 Blow out match
5 Place frying pan on gas ring
6 etc.

Such detail would be boring and unnecessary. However, with a computer program, you *do* require a much greater level of detail than with the recipe – simply because a cook is intelligent, and a computer is not. You must be absolutely precise in your instructions to the computer, as it does not have the ability to make judgements about what you 'really mean' if you have not been precise enough.

For example, if you spelt the word 'pizza' as 'piza' somewhere in your recipe, any human would know what you meant from the context in which the word appeared, but a computer would not surmise that you really meant 'pizza'. Such misspellings are known as *syntax errors* in a computer program, and will prevent the program being understood by the compiler, which will not consider it to be a valid program.

The English language has enormous expressive power and subtlety, and enables great literature and poetry to be written, but this very power and openness to interpretation can mean that it is often hard to be precise when using English to describe something accurately. Think of the sentence

'He drove her round the bend.'

This could mean driving someone, in a car, around a bend; or, colloquially, that he made her go crazy; or it could be, also colloquially, that he simply drove the car round the bend (we often refer to cars, especially sports cars, as 'she'); or it could mean that he was a farmer, and made the sheep or cow go round the bend in the road. This is one of the reasons why we use formal computer programming languages, a feature of which is that each instruction written in such languages has precisely one meaning. This is also why you will often use pseudocode to express your algorithms before final translation into programming languages.

Pseudocode

So what is pseudocode? It is a combination of English words and so-called control structures similar to those found in programming languages, which we can use to sketch out algorithms prior to implementing them in a programming language. To illustrate this, think about further refining the pizza recipe algorithm towards the kind of precision that is required for a computer program algorithm. Of course, this is a rather artificial example, as the pizza recipe is already fit for its purpose, but it will serve to introduce the kind of constructs you will come across in programming languages. You will look at examples of *sequence, repetition* and *selection* which are the basic constructs of pseudocode – and indeed programming languages which facilitate what is known as *structured programming*.

Sequence

For brevity, we will only consider the following instruction from the initial, abstract version of the pizza algorithm at this stage:

Make the topping

You will remember that this was refined into the following sequence of instructions, perfectly adequate for most cooks to follow:

3 Heat the oil in a frying pan
4 Add the onion, garlic and chillies and fry for 5 minutes
5 Add tomatoes, puree, anchovies and capers and fry until the sauce has reduced to a thick paste.
6 Add the basil and salt and pepper to taste.

The above piece of the algorithm comprises a *sequence* of instructions, which are intended to be carried out by the processor one by one in the order in which they appear. The sequence of instructions is the most basic structured programming construct. However, it is not sufficient to express any algorithm which one might want to write as a computer program.

Repetition

Let us refine the first instruction from our sequence:

3 Heat the oil in a frying pan

How can one be more precise about this? Well, for example, for how long should the oil be heated? An accepted test for correct temperature for oil to be used for frying is that it sizzles when a piece of onion is added to it. You might well ask 'how loudly should it sizzle?', but don't – sometimes refinement can be taken too far!

You can express this part of the algorithm using a pseudocode construct called a *while loop*, as follows:

1 Put oil in pan
2 Light gas
3 Place small piece of onion in pan
4 WHILE onion doesn't sizzle
    Wait 30 seconds

The first three of these instructions need no further explanation. The fourth one in the sequence has the general form:

WHILE <test>
    <do something>

The <test> is a *boolean* expression; that is, an expression which can have only one of two possible values, *true* or *false*.

The <do something> is actually one or more instructions, and the way that the processor must behave when dealing with a while loop is as follows:

1 Evaluate the test
2 If the test is false, then go on to the instruction following the while loop (i.e. do not do the <do something>!)
3 If the test is true, do the instructions in <do something> (the *body* of the while loop), then go back and evaluate the test again
4 Continue evaluating the test and doing the loop body instructions until the test evaluates to false.

So, in the above example, you check the piece of onion. If it's not sizzling, you wait 30 seconds, then you check again. If it's still not sizzling, you wait another 30 seconds and so on, until the onion is sizzling, whereupon you drop out of the loop, and continue with the rest of the algorithm.

The above is an example of another structured programming construct, that of **repetition**.

The while loop is only one example of a construct for implementing repetition; most programming languages have several types of loop construct. Loops are one of the things that make computers powerful; a computer does simple instructions, but loops allow the computer to do lots of these simple instructions very quickly!

Before you continue, pause and consider which of the following are valid boolean expressions (i.e. expressions which have the value 'true' or 'false').

1 It is raining	2 Is it raining?
3 Eat my shorts	4 Doh!
5 I am cold and I am wet	6 2 + 2
7 2 = 2	8 2 > 8.

In the above list, numbers 1, 5, 7, and 8 are valid boolean expressions. The others are not. 2 is a question, 3 is an instruction and 4 is an exclamation. None of these can be associated with a value. 6 is associated with a value, but it is an integer expression with the value 4, not a truth-valued Boolean expression.

Selection

Look at another of the recipe instructions:

- Add the onion, garlic and chillies and fry for 5 minutes.

This is really four separate instructions:

1 Add the onion
2 Add the garlic
3 Add the chillies
4 Fry for 5 minutes.

However, not everyone has a taste for spicy hot pizza! Some would rather do without the chillies. To take account of this in your algorithm, you need to introduce the third structured programming concept: *selection*. With this, you need to be able to do a test, and depending on the truth value of the test, you either carry out some instructions or you do not. In other words, you implement the concept of *choice*. The most common way of doing this is with an IF statement. (Note that *statement* is another word used in programming to mean *instruction*.) The above sequence might then become:

1 Add the onion
2 Add the garlic
3 IF eater likes hot pizza
        Add the chillies
4 Fry for 5 minutes.

The general form of the IF statement is:

IF <test>
    <do something>

The final instruction in the above sequence

4 Fry for 5 minutes.

is fine, but some people prefer their onions more brown than others. You could refine this instruction into

IF eater likes very brown onions
> Fry for 10 minutes.

ELSE
> Fry for 5 minutes.

This version of the IF statement has an ELSE part; in other words, rather than choosing between doing something or doing nothing, it chooses between doing something and doing something else.

> The general form of the IF-ELSE statement is
> IF <test>
> > <do something>
>
> ELSE
> > <do something else>

All modern programming languages implement the IF-ELSE construct or something similar.

With the pseudocode constructs of sequence, repetition and selection, you can express your algorithms in a notation very similar to the final programming language to be used. This is an important technique in the development of a computer program.

Test and evaluate

When you have your algorithm, it is important to test it, to improve your confidence that it does what it should. You must:

- Step through the solution
- Make necessary changes
- Check the results: Are they valid? Is the algorithm a solution to the original problem? Is it what was wanted?

You can test your pizza algorithm by using it to make a pizza, then asking yourself how satisfactory the process was:

- Does the pizza taste as you wanted it to?
- Is it quick and easy to make?
- Are the ingredients appropriate? Could one or more have been left out?
- Does it cost too much to make?

With a computer program, you can step through it on paper (this is called *performing a dry run*) where you 'pretend' that you are the computer executing the program. If the program passes this test, you can then run it on the computer, trying lots of different test cases.

2.7 **The drawing hedgehog**

Imagine you have a robot animal, a hedgehog. The hedgehog carries a pen, and walks about on a large sheet of paper. You can program the hedgehog to carry out a sequence of actions by feeding it any combination of the following instructions, which will be executed by the hedgehog in sequence. The hedgehog *only* understands these instructions.

Left   Causes the hedgehog to turn left 90 degrees
Forward(n)   This causes the hedgehog to move forward *n* centimetres in the direction in which it is facing

PenUp	The pen is lifted clear of the paper
PenDown	The pen is placed in contact with the paper
DefineInstruction	Defines a new instruction built from existing instructions

For example, to get the hedgehog to draw a square of side 2 centimetres, you could feed it the following program:

```
PenDown
Forward(2)
Left
Forward(2)
Left
Forward(2)
Left
Forward(2)
```

Note that the *Forward* instruction has a *parameter*; a number which tells it how far forward to move.

Note also that the above specification of the semantics (meaning) of the hedgehog instructions is not very precise. For example, what would be the effect of the PenDown instruction if the pen was already down? Let us assume that PenDown and PenUp have no effect if the pen is already down or up respectively. The semantics of the instructions of formal programming languages such as Java are precisely specified so that such ambiguities cannot arise.

The *DefineInstruction* instruction enables us to create new instructions to use in our programs. For example, the above program could be made into an instruction as follows:

```
DefineInstruction Draw2cmSquare
PenDown
Forward(2)
Left
Forward(2)
Left
Forward(2)
Left
Forward(2)
```

We now have an instruction called *Draw2cmSquare*, which can be used in future programs in place of the 8 instructions shown earlier.

The following program uses this to cause the hedgehog to draw two 2cm squares, 4cm apart:

```
Draw2cmSquare
PenUp
Forward(4)
Left
Draw2cmSquare
```

The program therefore contains five instructions, two of which were defined by the programmer. This idea of creating new instructions using existing ones is an example of the concept of *subprograms* discussed earlier.

Take a pen and a piece of paper, pretend you are the hedgehog and follow the instructions to satisfy yourself that the above program does indeed draw the correct picture.

Activity 2.4

The drawing hedgehog

Use *DefineInstruction* to create a new instruction for the hedgehog called *Right*, which causes the hedgehog to change its orientation so that it is facing 90 degrees to the right of its current orientation.

Now write a program to cause the hedgehog to draw a square of side 2cm positioned centrally within a 4cm by 6cm rectangle.

In the answer given at the end of the chapter, the program draws the square before it draws the rectangle. You could just as easily write a program to draw the rectangle first, and there are lots of different potential programs that would do the same job. How does one know which program is best?

To evaluate any given solution to the problem, you might look at how many instructions it takes. In general, fewer instructions should mean that the program executes more quickly. However, some instructions may be faster to execute than others; remember that instructions defined using *DefineInstruction* actually represent several basic instructions, so will be slower. There are often many different algorithms that can be used to solve a given problem, some of which will be faster than others. Try to gradually improve the above solution, each time evaluating it for further improvements.

2.8 Summary

The main points of this chapter may be summarised as follows:

- You solve a problem with a computer by devising a plan (an algorithm)
- You break the plan down into steps the computer can do (a program)
- There are many plans and many ways of breaking them down
- Which is best will depend on the situation.

2.9 Review questions

Question 2.1 What is the difference between pseudocode and programming languages?

Question 2.2 What is an algorithm?

Question 2.3 Compare and contrast the terms *ambiguous, deterministic* and *complete* as applied to algorithms.

Question 2.4 Give an example fragment of pseudocode that is *not* finite. Explain why it is usually desirable for algorithms to be *finite*. Explain also why it might be desirable for certain kinds of computer programs not to be *finite*.

? **Question 2.5**   Answer *true* or *false* to each of the following:

1   An algorithm is a plan for solving a problem by following a sequence of instructions.

2   Breaking down an abstract algorithm into a more detailed one is called stepwise refinement.

3   Programmers always have to write every instruction that forms part of their final program.

4   Parameters are a way of making subprograms more generally applicable and useful.

5   English is always an appropriate language in which to express algorithms.

6   A question can be a boolean expression.

7   'It is raining' is a boolean expression.

8   The following loop construct will execute forever:

   WHILE you haven't scored a goal

      Get a ball

      Kick the ball into the stands

9   The instruction 'Eat the grass' will never be executed in the following IF statement:

   IF the grass is red

      Eat the grass

   ELSE

      Mow the grass

10 It is important to test and evaluate a computer program.

2.10 Answers to review questions

Question 2.1   In pseudocode, the control structures (such as while and if) of a programming language are combined with statements in a natural language such as English (i.e. it is a form of structured English). The aim is to provide a language for writing algorithms without worrying about the detailed syntax of a programming language. This can be done at different levels of abstraction as appropriate to the task and helps a programmer to get the program logic correct by working at a high level and gradually filling in details. An example of pseudocode is:

```
WHILE throw is not 5
   Roll dice
   Add to total
```

A programming language is a language (such as Java, C++ or Pascal) that is used to give instructions to a computer. It is defined by formal rules that specify the grammar of the language. Programming languages are designed to be easy to process and to avoid the ambiguity of natural languages. Different languages have features suitable for solving different kinds of problems.

Question 2.2 An algorithm is a sequence of instructions that, if followed, will result in some problem being solved. It is a set of actions together with the order in which they are to be performed. For example, an algorithm to search through a pile of CDs (written in pseudocode) would be:

> Look at top CD
> Check if it is CD searched for
> WHILE it's not the required CD AND there are more CDs
>   Move to next CD

Question 2.3 All the terms are properties that algorithms should have in order to be effective. The first two (unambiguous and deterministic) are important to ensure that the same result occurs whenever an algorithm is followed.

- **Ambiguous** means that there could be multiple interpretations to an instruction. One person could think an instruction meant to do one thing; someone else, that it meant to do a different thing. The result could be that, in following the algorithm, the two people got different results, as with a non-deterministic algorithm. However, the reason for this happening is different

- **Deterministic** means the algorithm does the same thing every time. If it is non-deterministic, then even if everyone agrees what should be done (i.e. it is unambiguous) different results can still occur (e.g. throwing a dice – everyone may agree on what this means but when we do it we get a different result so it is unambiguous but non-deterministic)

- **Complete** means all cases are covered: there is no situation that can arise where the algorithm does not tell you what to do. This could occur if a branching instruction told you what to do if the test was true, but gave no indication of what to do if it was not. Note, however, that the single branch if statement (as in the brown onions example earlier) *is* deterministic because in the false case you are told what to do – nothing. This is similar to ambiguity, in that it is concerned with knowing what to do, except there is no instruction at all. It is similar to non-determinism in that it is concerned with getting into a situation where the result is unknown, but with non-determinism you are told how to get the result; is it just that in doing that, several different answers are possible.

Question 2.4 Example:

> 1 Put an egg in the bowl
> 2 WHILE there are eggs in the bowl
>   Put another egg in the bowl

This is not finite – by following the instructions blindly you would never finish! Instruction 1 is executed, then instruction 2 executes over and over again. This is an *infinite loop*; it never ends, in the sense that once you start following the rules you never stop. Note that if there was *any* possible way out then it would be finite – even if that way out was not guaranteed to be taken on every iteration.

It is useful for algorithms to be *finite* as they are to be followed blindly and if they do not finish, they may not deliver a result. Algorithms are intended to be followed to achieve some result so in this sense it would be pointless if it was never delivered. If the first part of an algorithm was infinite, you would never get to follow the later parts so there would be no point having them. It would also be a waste of resources to keep going if the result had already been obtained.

Some programs are not finite as they are designed to run continuously; for example, control programs such as those embedded in a clock – you do not want the program to stop, you just remove the power to finish.

Question 2.5

1 **True** This describes what an algorithm is.

2 **True** This method of adding more detail is also known as top-down design.

3 **False** It is often possible to reuse existing programs as subprograms, thus saving a lot of development time.

4 **True** Yes, parameters make it possible to write a subprogram able to behave differently for different parameters, making them more general and more likely to be reusable by different parts of the same program, or by different programs.

5 **False** English can be ambiguous, and must be used very carefully. It is better to give some structure to the English used, by means of pseudocode constructs such as IF-ELSE, and WHILE.

6 **False** Boolean expressions must have the value *true* or *false*; questions do not have a value.

7 **True** This will have the value *true* or *false*.

8 **True** Since the actions to be executed (kicking a ball into the stands) will never result in the test (scoring a goal) changing. This highlights an important rule when designing repetition (loops) statements – if the test is initially true, then if the loop is to be finite, an **instruction inside the loop** must be able to **change the outcome of the loop test** (if what is being tested can never change, such as our football example, the loop will continue forever).

9 **True** The instruction 'Eat the grass' will never be executed, because the test 'The grass is red' is a contradiction (i.e. a boolean expression that is always false).

10 **True** – especially if it is to control a nuclear power plant or life-support machine!

2.11 Feedback on activities

Activity 2.1: Brainstorming   You should consider the factors that would influence your choice:

- Length of journey
- Must you use main roads or is there a nice park to ride through?
- Cost
- Proximity of a tube or train station
- Availability of buses
- Weather – is it raining?

- Do you need exercise?
- Is there a car or bike park at work?
- Is the journey hilly – would you get sweaty if you used the bike?
- Is there a shower at work?
- etc.

The relative weighting/ importance of each of these would influence your choice of mode of transport.

Activity 2.2: Problem solving   This is a little subjective, as different people would tackle each problem in different ways. However, to take the presentation problem (**4**) for example:

- **Understanding the problem** might include knowing the audience you are aiming at, what AV technology is available, the acoustics of the auditorium, how much time you have available, etc
- **The plan** might include deciding upon the main topics to be covered, and in which order
- **Filling in details** will include production of slides or PowerPoint presentation, deciding on what use to make of flipcharts, etc
- **Test and evaluate** might include a dry run of the presentation for your friends, in order to obtain appropriate feedback.

Activity 2.3: Algorithms

Fill the 5-litre container
Fill the 3-litre container from the 5-litre container
   (This leaves 2-litres in the 5-litre container)
Empty the 3-litre container
Pour the 2 litres from the 5-litre container into the 3-litre container
Fill the 5-litre container
Fill the 3-litre container from the 5-litre container
   (This takes 1 litre from the 5-litre container, leaving 4 litres in it, as required.)

Note: the words in brackets are not instructions, but *comments*, the purpose of which is to *explain* the instructions. Comments are an important part of every computer program.

Given your algorithm, anyone can now solve the puzzle, without doing any problem solving of their own – they just have to follow your instructions.

Activity 2.4: The drawing hedgehog   The aim of this exercise is to prepare you for using a restricted, structured notation to express solutions to problems, which is an important part of developing computer programs.

You can use DefineInstruction to create a new instruction for the hedgehog called Right, which causes the hedgehog to turn right by 90 degrees, as follows.

DefineInstruction Right
   Left
   Left
   Left

Here is a program to cause the hedgehog to draw a square of side 2cm positioned centrally within a 4cm by 6cm rectangle:

```
Draw2cmSquare
PenUp
Forward(2)
Right
PenDown
Forward(1)
Right
Forward(6)
Right
Forward(4)
Right
Forward(6)
Right
Forward(3)
```

Again, take a pen and paper and follow the instructions to verify that the program does what it should. This 'dry running' of a program is an important and useful technique.

CHAPTER 3

Outputs and calculations

OVERVIEW

By now you should understand the main algorithmic concepts supported by most modern programming languages; but, as yet, you have not written a program. Now is the time to rectify that. This chapter shows you how to write programs in Java that carry out simple numerical computations and produce output on the screen. As first steps to real-life application, you will learn how to write programs that have more than one method and examine the types of error that can occur in computer programs. You will also find out how the errors can be detected!

Learning outcomes	On completion of this chapter you should be able to:

- Write simple programs that display information on the screen, controlling both the information that appears and its position on the screen

- Explain the features of a simple Java program

- Write programs that use more than one method

- Write programs that can do simple numerical computations

- Utilise the concept of assignment in your programs

- Write programs that store data internally for later processing

- Compare and contrast different classes of errors.

3.1 The structure of a Java program

We will investigate the structure of Java programs with reference to the following simple Java program:

```java
// Prints Hello! on the screen in a dialog box
import javax.swing.JOptionPane;
public class Hello1
{
   public static void main(String[] args)
   {
      JOptionPane.showMessageDialog(null, "Hello!");
      System.exit(0);
   }
}
```

This program displays a dialog box with the text *Hello!* and an *OK* button – when the dialog box is closed, the program then stops executing:

At the heart of this program is a simple sequence of two statements:

```java
JOptionPane.showMessageDialog(null, "Hello!");
System.exit(0);
```

The program should look familiar – we saw a similar one in Chapter 1. The first thing you may notice is that, although a program is made up of instructions (statements), this program contains a lot of other code besides the two statements above.

We will now look at the program in more detail.

Comments

Comments are pieces of text that are ignored by the compiler. They are usually included by the author of a program for two reasons, to:

- Provide useful notes or explanations for a human reading the program
- Prevent (temporarily, perhaps) statements from being executed – maybe during lazy debugging or program development.

The following are comments in our Hello program:

```java
// Prints Hello on the screen in a dialog box
// import class JOptionPane
```

Comments begin with '//', which tells the compiler that all text from this point until the end of the line is to be ignored when translating the Java program into byte code.

In other words, as far as the compiler is concerned, comments have no useful function. Comments are included in order to explain the program to a human reader, and well-chosen comments are an important part of every program. You should always place a comment at the start of the program to state:

- The purpose of the program
- An outline of how it carries out its task
- Who wrote the program and when
- A list of any changes to the program and when they were made
- Anything else which might help a reader to understand the program.

Each subprogram method (see later) should have a comment stating what it does, and any tricky bits of code should have comments explaining them to the reader. Declarations of variables (see later in this chapter) often benefit from comments to provide brief explanations. Comments are often used to indicate the ends of methods, classes and loop bodies, although this is not strictly necessary if the program is well laid out.

Comments should not be used to explain the obvious; if you have too many comments, they will obscure the program itself. However, too few comments will leave the reader guessing as to how the program works.

Other kinds of Java comments

Although the above style of comment is perhaps the most commonly used, comments can also be defined in other ways in Java. Another form of comment you may come across is one that starts with '/*' and ends with '*/'. This kind of comment can spread over two or more lines, for detailed notes, or to 'comment out' statements (i.e. make statements into comments) to prevent them, temporarily, from being executed while debugging.

There is also a special kind of comment that helps Java programmers automate the process of creating documentation about new classes. These types of comments are part of the *javadoc* documentation standard; but you do not need to worry about such issues at this stage.

Importing (reusing) code from other files

The line:

```
import javax.swing.JOptionPane;
```

is an *import statement*. You may remember from Chapter 2 that Java has a library of predefined program chunks (the Java Applications Programming Interface, or API) that can be used within our own programs, much as the pizza base-making algorithm was used in the pizza recipe. These program chunks are called classes (the concept of a class was discussed in Chapter 1), and related classes are grouped within the API into so-called *packages*. However, in order to use any of these API classes within your program, you must instruct the Java compiler to include them – this is done with 'import' statements such as in our Hello program. Thus *javax.swing* is a package (a collection of reusable Java code), which contains classes for providing graphical user interfaces for programs, and *JOptionPane* is a class within that package, which provides facilities which enable one to display a message dialog box.

When writing Java programs that reuse pre-written classes (such as *JOptionPane*), you will need to know how to write the appropriate import statement for each class. Having hundreds of pre-written classes saves programmers lots of time, but the downside is that you have to learn about these existing classes, and remember which 'package' they are defined in, in order to tell the Java compiler where the classes you are reusing are defined.

Classes

Our simple program consists of a single *class*, defined as follows:

```
public class Hello1
{
   <CONTENTS OF CLASS>
}
```

Every Java program will contain at least one class defined by the programmer. The words *public class* are Java keywords which must be included (they will be explained later), followed by the name you give to the class, in this case *Hello1*.

Class names start with a capital letter, by convention. For the time being, you may regard the class definition as something which gives a name to your program, and encloses your program algorithms (methods) between open and closing braces – the '{' and '}' symbols (sometimes informally called 'curly brackets'). Note that the name of the file containing your program must be the same as that of the class (i.e. the *Hello1* class must be in a file called *Hello1.java)*.

The filename should always be the class name (spelt with the same mixture of upper- and lower-case letters) followed by *.java*. So if the class name is *Chap03Program01*, the filename would have to be *Chap03Program01.java*

Coding style tip

Although blank lines and extra spaces are generally ignored by the Java compiler, you (the programmer) and others will have to read through the program, so it makes sense to lay out the program statements in a neat and tidy fashion.

- One rule of thumb is that related opening and closing curly brackets – shown as { and } – should be aligned one above the other
- The lines of text between them should also be aligned with each other, and indented a few spaces from the position of the enclosing { and }. This is *very* important for producing programs which are easy to understand for the human reader. Look at some of the programs in this book and think about how the different brackets are aligned.

If you follow the style of program layout used in the examples in these chapters, you will pick up good habits to make life easier for you (and others) working with your program code.

Methods

The *methods* which implement each algorithm in your program are placed within the class definition. Classes can have many methods (subprograms). To understand this better, think back to the pizza example: the recipe book could be thought of as the class and each recipe as a method or subprogram. In this simple example program *Hello1*, however, there is only one method, called *main()*:

```
public static void main(String[] args)
{
 <STATEMENTS GO HERE>
}
```

In fact, *every* Java program must contain a method called *main()*. As the name suggests, this represents the main algorithm of the program. The execution of the program will begin with the first statement in *main()*. In *Hello1*, *main()* is the only method.

public static are Java keywords, which must be present in the simple *Hello1* program. The significance of these keywords will become clear later. *void* is a keyword which indicates that the main method does not return a value. You will learn what returning a value means in Chapter 8.

Every method name is followed by open and closed parentheses '(' and ')'. Between the parentheses there may or may not be *parameters*. The *Hello1* program main method has one parameter called 'args'

```
main( String[] args )
```

This allows us to pass *arguments* (data) to the main method of the program on the command line, but we will not be using this technique in this book.

You may be thinking that the explanation of rather a lot of things about the simple Java program has been deferred until later! This is true, but intended to help you get started quickly. For now, whenever you write a program of your own, simply load an existing one into the editor, save it under another name, and edit it to produce your new program. This will save you from having to type in all the extra statements required to convert a list of instructions into a complete Java program.

3.2 Output statements

The most basic sort of program implements a single sequence of instructions in the *main()* method, each of which tells the computer to do something. Remember that program instructions are also called *statements*. The *main()* method of the *Hello1* program contains two statements:

```
JOptionPane.showMessageDialog(null, "Hello!");
System.exit(0);
```

The second statement:

```
System.exit(0);
```

calls a method *exit()*, which is found in a class called *System*, which is part of a package of classes called *java.lang*.

System does not have to be imported, as *java.lang* is automatically imported into every Java program. This call to *exit()* is needed to terminate the program properly, when the program uses a graphical user interface.

Note that Java statements must *always* end with a semicolon. This tells the compiler when the end of a statement has been reached.

The first statement in the *main()* method is

```
JOptionPane.showMessageDialog(null, "Hello!");
```

This statement invokes the method *showMessageDialog()* from class *JOptionPane*, which was imported into the program. In other words, this statement causes a method from another class to be executed.

The *showMessageDialog()* method has two parameters. The first parameter is *null*, which is a reference value (and yes, that will be explained later!). The second parameter is the string of text that you wish to be displayed in the dialog box, in this case *Hello!*. When the program runs, a dialog box is created that displays the message, and the user makes the box go away by clicking its OK button (or the close icon of the window).

A sequence of statements such as this one would cause successive dialog boxes to appear on the screen, each displaying a string of text, and persisting until the user clicks their OK button, as in the next program.

```
// Prints greeting on the screen in 3 dialog boxes
import javax.swing.JOptionPane;

public class Hello2
{
   public static void main(String[] args)
   {
      JOptionPane.showMessageDialog(null, "Hello!");
      JOptionPane.showMessageDialog(null,
         "How nice to see you!");
      JOptionPane.showMessageDialog(null,
         "How are you?");

      System.exit(0);
   }
}
```

Note that where a statement runs to more than one line, the continuation line is indented slightly. This convention helps to make clear where one statement ends and the next begins. Note also the blank line between the output statements and the *exit()* statement. It is helpful to use blank lines to delimit the different logical groups of statements; in this case the output statements and the *exit()* statement.

When the program runs, you will notice that the string of text appearing in each dialog box is all on one line.

To make the output move to a new line, you must include in the string the escape sequence '\n', which represents the *newline* character. For example, the following program will produce the greeting of the last program; but all in one dialog box, on separate lines. Other escape sequence characters include '\t ' to print a tab and '\\' to print a backslash character.

```
// Prints greeting on the screen on three lines
// in a single dialog box
import javax.swing.JOptionPane;

public class Hello3
{
   public static void main(String[] args)
   {
      JOptionPane.showMessageDialog(null,
         "Hello!\nHow nice to see you!\nHow are you?");

      System.exit(0);
   }
}
```

The dialog displayed when this program is run is as follows:

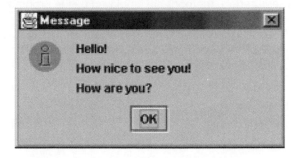

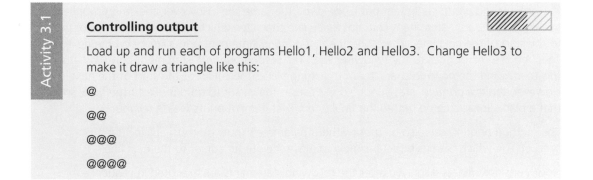

Activity 3.1

Controlling output

Load up and run each of programs Hello1, Hello2 and Hello3. Change Hello3 to make it draw a triangle like this:

@

@@

@@@

@@@@

Command line output

So far, we have used *JOptionPane.showMessageDialog()* to display output on the screen.

You can also do output in Java in the *command line window*, using the methods

    System.out.print()

and

    System.out.println()

System.out is called the standard output object. It has methods *print()* and *println()*, each of which displays a line of text on the screen. The difference is that *println()* will place the output cursor at the start of the next line, whereas *print()* will leave the cursor on the same line after printing the text. Here is a program that uses *print()* and *println()*.

```
// Prints a message in the command window

public class Hello4
{
    public static void main(String[] args)
    {
        System.out.print("Hello!");
        System.out.print("Hello!\n");
        System.out.println("Hello!");
        System.out.println("What's all this then?\n");
        System.out.println("Please tell me!");
    }
}
```

Note that this program does not require the call to the *System.exit()* method; this is only needed when graphical user interface methods are employed by the program.

Can you work out what you think the output from this program would be?

With luck, you will have decided that the printout should be:

Hello! Hello!
Hello!
What's all this then?

Please tell me!

The first *print()* statement prints *Hello!* and leaves the cursor on the same line, which means that the second *print()* statement prints *Hello!* on the same line. However, the string supplied to this second *print()* statement contains a *newline* character, which means that the cursor goes to the start of the next line. Therefore, the first *println()* statement prints *Hello!* on the next line, and the cursor goes to the following line. The second *println()* statement prints *What's all this then?*, and the *newline* character in this string places the cursor at the start of the next line. However, this is a *println()* statement, so this causes the cursor to go down a further line, so that a blank line is created before the final *println()* statement prints *Please tell me!*

The method *println()* can also be used without parameters (but you must still include the brackets), in which case its effect is simply to move the output cursor to the next line.

Now, consider what is displayed after the following statements are executed in sequence:

```
System.out.println("X...X..XXX..X");
System.out.println("X...X...X...X");
System.out.println("X...X...X...X");
System.out.println("XXXXX...X...X\nX...X...X...X");
System.out.println("X...X...X....\nX...X..XXX..X");
// the dots represent space characters.
```

The above statements will write HI! in big letters in the command line window:

Output display

Which is the best way to do output? The answer, as with so much in science, is 'it depends'. Dialog boxes look good, and are one of the building blocks of graphical user interfaces (GUIs), which have become the standard way of communicating with modern application programs. However, command line output fulfils all of the requirements for the simple programs you have written so far. It is your choice.

3.3 Subprograms

To write a bigger program, you can just add more statements to the sequence in *main()*, which is effectively the name of the algorithm which will be executed by the computer when you run the program.

However, remember the pizza recipe. This algorithm was also a sequence of instructions, but one of these instructions

Make the base according to the recipe on page 15

was an instruction to the processor (cook) to execute *another* algorithm – the pizza base-making algorithm – and then return to continue with the instruction following 'make the base...' in the main pizza recipe. This technique isolated the base-making instructions into a separate algorithm, which could be invoked from *any* pizza recipe. This separate base-making algorithm can be used many times, without having to repeat the base-making instructions in every pizza recipe. It could also be used more than once in the *same* recipe – for example, you could invoke it twice to make two bases, to make a kind of pizza sandwich!

This idea is also useful in Java, for the same kind of reasons. The name of the main method (algorithm) is always *main()*; but you can implement other algorithms as named methods, and invoke them by using their names as instructions in *main()*.

The following program has two additional methods, *spling()* and *splong()*, each of which is invoked (called) from *main()*.

```java
// Prints greetings from two separate methods
// on the screen
import javax.swing.JOptionPane;

public class Hello5
{
    public static void splong()
    {
        JOptionPane.showMessageDialog(null,
            "Hello from method splong!");
    }

    public static void spling()
    {
        JOptionPane.showMessageDialog(null,
            "Hello from method spling!");
    }
```

```java
    public static void main(String[] args)
    {
        spling();
        splong();

        System.exit(0);
    }

}
```

Note the use of () after the method names *spling()* and *splong()*. The brackets are required even though there is nothing between them. Later you will learn about parameters, which can be defined within these brackets and provide a means of passing data to a method.

In Java, any method can be invoked from any other method, by using its name as a statement. In the following program, method *splong()* is called from both *main()* and *spling()*.

```java
// Prints greetings from two separate methods
// on the screen
// Note that spling calls splong
import javax.swing.JOptionPane;

public class Hello6
{
    public static void splong()
    {
        JOptionPane.showMessageDialog(null,
            "Hello from method splong!");
    }

    public static void spling()
    {
        JOptionPane.showMessageDialog(null,
            "Hello from method spling!");

        splong();
    }

    public static void main(String[] args)
    {
        spling();
        splong();

        System.exit(0);
    }
}
```

This program will produce successive dialog boxes with the messages:

```
Hello from method spling! (called from main)
Hello from method splong! (called from spling)
Hello from method splong! (called from main)
```

There are two ways of finding out what a program does: you could load up the program, compile it and run it, and see what the output is. However, a quicker way would be to *dry run* the program. In a dry run, *you* act as the computer, stepping through the instructions in the order in which they would be executed by the computer, and recording their effects.

Activity 3.2

Dry running a program

Dry run the following program, and work out what its output would be.

```java
// Prints greetings from two separate methods
// on the screen
// Note that each method calls the other
import javax.swing.JOptionPane;
public class Hello6
{
    public static void splong()
    {
        JOptionPane.showMessageDialog(null,
            "Hello from method splong!");
        spling();
    }
    public static void spling()
    {
        JOptionPane.showMessageDialog(null,
            "Hello from method spling!");
        splong();
    }
    public static void main(String[] args)
    {
        spling();
        System.exit(0);
    }
}
```

When you can, run the program on a computer to check whether your dry run produced the correct results.

When you use the technique of stepwise refinement to break down a complex problem into sub-problems, you often find that each sub-problem can be solved with an algorithm implemented as a separate Java method. This means that the *main()* method can consist essentially of statements to invoke each of the sub-problem methods. When trying to understand such a program, you can ascertain the basic structure by looking at *main()*, then look at the details in each of the sub-problem methods. If a sub-problem is too complex to be implemented as one method, you can break it down further so that the sub-problem method ends up comprising statements which invoke yet more methods. Thus complex programs may comprise a hierarchy of such methods.

Program design in Java is usually rather different from this. Java is an object-oriented language; object-oriented analysis and design includes such tasks as identifying the classes needed to solve the problem, the objects of those classes which must be created, and how those objects should interact by sending messages to each other (actually calling each other's methods). You will return to this in Chapters 11 and 12.

A program to write MOOOO

Write a program with a method called *bigM()*, which uses *println* statements to write a big letter **M**, and another method called *bigO()* which writes a big letter **O**, each letter being made up from its own character, like this:

```
M               M
MM             MM
M  M         M  M
M    M  M    M
M       M       M

OOOOOOOOO
O               O
O               O
O               O
OOOOOOOOO
```

Now write a *main()* method to invoke these methods to write MOOOO in big letters down the screen. Notice how the use of the method *bigO()* means your program requires fewer statements than placing all instructions in *main()*.

When you can, run the program on a computer to check whether your program produced the correct result.

3.4 Variables

To do useful work, programs must be able to operate on data such as numbers, characters etc, and these data items must be stored in the computer's memory. You do this using *variables*, which are named 'pigeon holes' in memory. Associated with each variable is a *type*, which restricts the sort of data that can be stored in the variable. To use variables in a program, you must first *declare* them like this:

    int age;

This declares a variable called *age*, of type *int*. This is a box into which you are allowed to place integers (whole numbers – i.e. no decimal point or fractions).

    char letter;

This declares a variable called *letter*, of type *char*. This is a box into which you are allowed to place characters.

    double distance;

This declares a variable called *distance*, of type *double*. This is a box into which you are allowed to place double precision floating point numbers (i.e. numbers with decimal points) with up to 15 significant digits. If less precision is required, the type *float* can be used, variables of which store floating point numbers in 7 significant digits.

Remember that all Java statements end with a semicolon and declarations are examples of statements. A variable declaration tells the compiler to allocate space in the computer's memory for the variable.

Declarations of more than one variable of the same type can be combined as follows

```
int age, weight, height;
```

Each variable name is separated by a comma, with a final semicolon.

Naming variables

You should always give variables meaningful names, from which a reader might be able to make a reasonable guess at their purpose. For example, the name *age* suggests that the age of someone or something is going to be stored in the box, while *letter* suggests that the char variable will be used to store a letter of the alphabet (although you could store any character represented on the computer keyboard in the box). Use a comment if further clarification is needed. For example

```
int temperature; // in celsius
```

The name of a variable is known as its *identifier*. There are rules about what constitutes a legal identifier:

- It must start with a **letter**, '_' (underscore) or a '**$**' (dollar sign)
- This may be followed by letters, digits, underscores and the dollar sign
- You may not use Java keywords as identifiers (e.g. public, static)
- Note that upper-case and lower-case characters are treated as different letters.

3.5 The assignment statement

How do you place data items into variables? You can:

- Read in values typed at the keyboard by the user
- Use an assignment statement.

Reading in values will be covered in Chapter 4. The assignment statement is illustrated by the following examples:

```
age = 21;
// Note a character value is indicated by single quotes
letter = 'A';
distance = 6.4;
```

The left-hand side (LHS) of the '=' sign is always the **name** of a variable. On the right-hand side (RHS) of the '=' sign is an **expression** of the same type as the variable on the left. The order of events when the computer executes an assignment statement is:

- First, evaluate the expression on the RHS of the '=' sign
- Next, store the resultant value of the expression in the variable on the LHS of the = sign.

Here are some more examples:

```
int timePassed;

timePassed = 5;

age = 16 + 8;
// 16 + 8 = 24 stored in age

age = 16 + timePassed;
// 16 + 5 = 21 stored in age; previous value in
// age overwritten

age = age + 6;
// 21 + 6 = 27 stored in age

age = age + timePassed;
// 27 + 5 = 32 stored in age
```

Note the following points about how assignment works:

- Each time a new value is stored in a variable, the old one is overwritten – a variable can only hold one value at a time.
- Remember that the '=' sign does not mean 'equals'. It is a command to the computer telling it to store the value of the expression on the right in the variable on the left. You could read the '=' sign as 'becomes equal to' or 'takes the value of'.
- When a variable's value is used in an expression, as with timePassed on the right-hand side of two of the above assignment statements, this does not change its value.
- When a variable name appears on the left of the '=' sign, and in the expression on the right of the '=' sign, the variable's current value is used in evaluating the expression on the right, then the resultant value of the expression is stored in the variable, as with the variable *age* in the last two examples above.

You can also *initialise* a variable with a value by combining an assignment with the declaration of the variable.

For example:

```
int age = 21;

char letter = 'z';

double distance = 12.75;
```

This is important because the nature of computer storage does not allow for a variable to exist without a value. In Java if you do not assign a value to a variable declared in *main()* (i.e. between the { and } associated with *main()*; also known as the body of the method) before it is used in output then the variable will not compile. If the variable is declared in the class (i.e. between the { and } associated with the class) but not within a method body, then Java will automatically assign the variable a default value of zero.

It is important to appreciate the difference between the statements:

letter = 'a';

and

letter = a;

In the first statement, the character value 'a' is being stored in variable *letter* by the assignment.

In the second statement, the contents of a variable called *a* will be copied into variable *letter* by the assignment.

3.6 Output of non-string data

You now know how to declare variables and put values in them; we will now look at how to write out the value of a variable on the screen. The methods *print()* and *println()* can be used to output values of basic types directly, but the method *showMessageDialog()* can only output strings of characters:

```
JOptionPane.showMessageDialog(null,
    "I only output strings!");
```

So how can you display the ints, chars and doubles with *showMessageDialog()*?

You must convert them to strings!

For example, you may wish to convert the number 42 into the string "42". How can you do this? Well, Java allows us to join (concatenate) two strings together to make a bigger string, using the + operator.

For example, the statement:

```
JOptionPane.showMessageDialog(null,
    "I only output strings! " + "Really I do!");
```

will display the string on the screen in a dialog box:

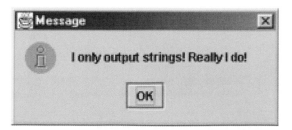

However, if you use the concatenation operator with a string and a number, as in

```
JOptionPane.showMessageDialog(null,
    "The answer is " + 42);
```

then Java will convert the number into the string "42", concatenate this with the string "The answer is", and write the resultant string on the screen in a dialog box:

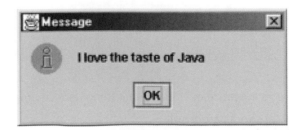

This also works with variables, as shown in the following program.

```java
// Prints a string incorporating a number

import javax.swing.JOptionPane;

public class intOutput
{
    public static void main( String[] args )
    {
        int answer = 42;

        JOptionPane.showMessageDialog(null,
            "The answer is " + answer );

        System.exit(0);
    }
}
```

Here we have declared a variable of type *int*, called *answer*, and initialised it by assigning it the value 42. The output is the same as the previous example. The same method can be used for char and *double* type variables.

As a simple example, consider the following code fragment:

```java
char ch = 't';

JOptionPane.showMessageDialog(null,
    "I love the "  + ch + "aste of Java");
```

Can you work out what it would print – and why?

It would display a dialog box with the string *I love the taste of Java* as shown here:

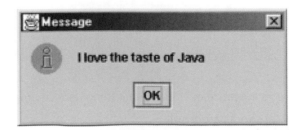

Swapping the values of two variables

What is wrong with the following program, which is supposed to exchange the values stored in variables *first* and *second*?

Do a dry run of the code to see what happens to the variables.

```
// Swaps the values of two variables
import javax.swing.JOptionPane;

public class Swap
{
    public static void main(String[] args)
    {
        // declare and initialise variables
        int first = 3;
        int second = 4;

        // Write out initial values
        JOptionPane.showMessageDialog(null,
            "First variable: " + first +
            "\nsecond variable: " + second);

        // swap values
        first = second;
        second = first;

        // Write out new values
        JOptionPane.showMessageDialog(null,
            "First variable: " + first +
            "\nsecond variable: " + second);

        System.exit(0);
    }
}
```

Now write a version of the program that does work!

When you can, run the program on a computer to check whether your dry run produced the correct results.

3.7 Doing calculations

Java supports all the usual arithmetic operators:

- Addition   +
- Subtraction   –
- Multiplication   *
- Division   /
- Modulus   % (remainder after integer division)

The division operator '/' does *ordinary division* when applied to floating point numbers (doubles), but does *integer division* when applied to integers. Integer division returns the 'whole number' part of the result, discarding the remainder. For example:

- 14 / 3 evaluates to 4
- 27 / 4 evaluates to 6

The modulus operator '%' returns the remainder after integer division. For example:

- 14 % 3 evaluates to 2, since 14 divided by 3 is 4, with remainder of 2
- 27 % 4 evaluates to 3, since 27 divided by 4 is 6, with a remainder of 3

Before you move on, take a moment to determine how the computer would evaluate each of the following expressions:

1	68 / 3
2	35 % 5
3	18 % 17
4	(49 / 6) % 2
5	((17 / 2) / 10) % 16

In the first case, the answer would be 22 (3 goes 22 times into 68); the second question would have a result of 0, as (there is no remainder after dividing 35 by 5). Question 3 should have an answer of 1 (17 goes once into 18, with a remainder of 1). The last two questions both have the answer of 0; (the integer 6 goes into the integer 49 eight times with the remainder of 1 discarded, 8 divided by 2 with remainder 0; and 17 divided (integer division) by 2 is 8, 8 divided (integer division) by 10 is 0, 0 divided by 16 is 0 with remainder 0).

What does this program fragment do?

```
int a = 2;
int b = 3;

JOptionPane.showMessageDialog(null, "a + b");

JOptionPane.showMessageDialog(null,
   "The question is " + a + " + " + b);

JOptionPane.showMessageDialog(null,
   "The answer is " + (a + b));
```

Because the a + b in the *first* statement above is in double quotation marks, the statement simply prints the string

```
a + b
```

The *second* statement prints the concatenation of four strings:

1 "The question is "

2 The result of converting the value of variable a into a String i.e. "2"

3 "+"

4 The result of converting the value of variable b into a String i.e. "3"

In other words, it prints:

The question is 2 + 3

The *third* statement prints the concatenation of two strings:

1 "The answer is"

2 The result of converting the value of expression a + b, in other words 2 + 3 into a String i.e. "5"

In other words, it prints:

> The answer is 5

However, what would have happened if you did not put brackets around (a + b) in the third statement?

If you forgot the brackets around (a+b), Java would evaluate the + operators from left to right. It would see that the first + has a string and the variable *a* as operands, and concatenate them to give the string:

> The answer is 2

Java would then see that the second + has this string and the variable *b* as operands, and concatenate them to give the String:

> The answer is 23

The + operator must therefore be used carefully, as it is *overloaded*, which means that it represents different things in different contexts – string concatenation or addition of numbers.

Priority and precedence in expressions

Consider the following expressions:

- 2 + 4 + 6 / 2
- (2 + 4 + 6) / 2
- 2 + (4 + 6) / 2

They each evaluate differently, as the *order* of evaluation matters (whether you add before dividing etc).

The order in which the operators are evaluated in an expression follows a fixed set of rules:

1 Evaluate things in parentheses ( )

If they are nested (that is, if there is a set of brackets inside *another* set of brackets), then start at the innermost.

Evaluate non-nested parentheses left to right.

> (2 + 4) / 2 evaluates to 3 (2 + 4 = 6, /2 = 3)
> (2 + (4 / 2)) evaluates to 4   (4 / 2 = 2, added to 2, = 4)
> (2 + 4) * (3 + 5) evaluates to 48

2 Evaluate the following operators next: * / %

If there are several, evaluate left to right.

> 1 + 2 * 3 evaluates to 7
> 1 % 2 * 3 evaluates to 3

3 Evaluate the following operators next: + -

If there are several, evaluate left to right.

> 1 + 2 + 3 – 4 evaluates to 2
> 9 + (3 - 2) * 5 / 6 – 4 evaluates to 5

(Explanation of the second statement: 3-2=1; multiplied by 5 = 5; integer division by 6 results in 0; add to 9 = 9; minus 4 = 5)

3.8 Calculating VAT

We will now look at how you can write a program to perform a calculation and print the result on the screen.

Suppose you wish to know the value-added tax (VAT) to be paid on a purchase price of £67. The current rate of VAT is 17.5%. The calculation required is therefore:

> (17.5 * 67) / 100

Here is the program

```
// Computes the VAT to be paid on a purchase price of £67
// Assumes VAT rate of 17.5%
import javax.swing.JOptionPane;

public class calcVAT
{
    public static void main(String[] args)
    {
        final double VATRATE = 17.5;
        // percentage VAT rate

        double price = 67;  // purchase price
        double vat;  // VAT to be paid

        // do the calculation
        vat = price * VATRATE / 100;

        // output the answer
        JOptionPane.showMessageDialog(null,
          "VAT to pay is " + vat);

        System.exit(0);
    }
}
```

Note that in the statement

> vat = price * VATRATE / 100;

the '/' operator will do floating point division because its first operand is a floating point number. In general, it would be safer to make both operands into floating point numbers, to make it clear to the reader what is intended:

vat = price * VATRATE / 100.0;
Constants

In the declaration:

final double VATRATE = 17.5;

the keyword *final* prevents the variable *VATRATE* from being changed during the running of the program. *VATRATE* is therefore made into a *named constant*; whenever you use the name *VATRATE*, it stands for the number 17.5. Such named constants are conventionally written in capitals.

There are a number of good reasons why you do not simply use the number 17.5 in each program calculation instead of associating it with a name:

- The name *VATRATE* is generally more meaningful to a reader than a number, as one might not know what the current rate of VAT happens to be
- Suppose this was a commercial program, doing VAT calculations, comprising half a million lines of code, and not using a named constant as above. Now suppose the government changes the rate of VAT to 12.5%. Someone must now edit those half-million lines, looking for every instance of the number 17.5 and changing them to 12.5. Some of the 17.5s might not refer to the VAT rate at all, but to something else, by coincidence. These numbers must not be changed. There is a lot of potential for error! If the program used a named constant, one simply needs to change the number associated with the constant declaration from 17.5 to 12.5.

Note that this program is rather limited, as it only computes the VAT to pay on one price, namely £67. The program would be much more useful if the user could type in *any* price at the keyboard, and have the program compute the VAT on that price. You will return to this in Chapter 4.

Activity 3.5

A temperature conversion program

Write a program to compute the Fahrenheit equivalent of the temperature 20° Celsius, and write the answer on the screen in the form

The Fahrenheit equivalent of 20 Celsius is XXX

Note that the conversion may be done using the formula:

$F = (9 / 5) * C + 32$

where F is the required Fahrenheit temperature, and C is the Celsius temperature.

If working correctly, the program should display:

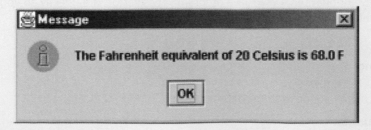

Use constants as much as possible in your program.

There is a subtle, but important, issue raised by the answer to this program, shown at the end of the chapter. As before, named constants (*FACTOR* and *SHIFT*) have been used to improve clarity, in the example solution.

But what would happen if *FACTOR* had been defined as follows:

```
// ratio of F degree to C degree
final double FACTOR = 9 / 5;
```

FACTOR has now been defined using integer division. 9 / 5 evaluates to 1 in integer division, and not 1.8 as required. The program will now give the answer as 52F instead of the correct answer of 68F.

In other words, the program would have a logic error. The only way to detect this sort of error is by running (or dry running) the program, and comparing the result with the correct answer, computed by hand.

This is a very easy error to make. *FACTOR* is defined as a double, and one might suppose that floating point division would take place, but remember how assignment works:

1 Evaluate the expression on the right

2 Store the result in the variable on the left.

You are allowed to store an integer expression in a *double*, but not vice versa.

3.9 Programming errors

When you learn to program, you will make mistakes. Some of these will be small mistakes (typing errors, spelling things wrong) whereas others will be *logical* errors in the initial design of your program and so on. This section describes some of the common errors you are likely to encounter – and make!

Each time you make an error you have the challenge of finding the problem and fixing it. This is a learning experience, and once you have made a mistake two or three times you will be much less likely to make such a mistake again. To learn programming you have to put in many hours at the computer – but once you have got over the first 20 or 30 common errors, you will find you are beginning to be able to sit down and design a program, then implement that program, with fewer and fewer problems.

Syntax errors

A syntax error is an error in the spelling, punctuation or grammar of the program – in other words, you have not written a valid Java program. These errors are directly analogous with their equivalent in the English language.

For example:

Spelling
English: 'The mewn ys maid of blew cheeze'
Java: ' publec statec vood mayn(Streng[] args)'

Punctuation
English: 'John said why study Java he then tore up the textbook'
Java: 'System exit 0)'

Grammar
English: 'Would to like dance me you with?'
Java: ' 42 = ; answer'

You do not need to know the *meaning* of the sentences to see these are mistakes, just the rules for constructing them. The rules for formal languages such as Java are rigid and unambiguous.

Common Java syntax errors include:

- Missing semicolons from the end of lines
- Using capital letters inappropriately: for example using INT or Int instead of int.

Syntax errors in your program are detected by the compiler, which attempts to tell you where they have occurred. Sometimes the compiler messages can be misleading, so if you can't see an error on the line it tells you to look on, take a look at the previous few lines. Sometimes the compiler will tell you that there are lots of errors, but do not be disheartened; try fixing the first few, then recompile – often, apparent errors later in the program are generated because of earlier ones!

Semantic errors

A semantic error is an error in the *meaning* of the statements in the program. In other words, the program is a valid Java program which can be executed, but it does not do what it is supposed to. Such errors are also called *logic errors*.

For example:

- English: 'Windsurf up the stairs'
- Java: age = -20; // negative age!
- A semantic error in a flight simulator program might be if it allowed you to fly your plane through a mountain
- The Year 2000 Bug was a semantic error where programs calculated the wrong dates from 1 Jan 2000 onwards.
- area = width – height; // wrong operator – instead of *

Some logic errors are detected only after running (or dry running) the program with appropriate test data (values for which you know what the program should compute), and comparing the results obtained with the correct results. Others, sometimes called *run-time errors*, manifest themselves by the running program failing to terminate correctly.

For example:

- num = 42 / 0; // division by zero; illegal operation; the program will crash
- The '*spling()* calls *splong()*, and *splong()* calls *spling()*' example of Activity 3. 2 – the program will run forever.

If Java program statements are syntactically correct, the compiler *cannot* detect logic errors such as those above.

Semantic errors indicate mistakes in the algorithm. The program does *something* – it is just that it does the wrong thing. A large, complex program with an obscure logic error may run correctly for years before hitting the problem. Sometimes it proves impossible to cure the error (commonly called a bug). The error is simply documented, and the users try to avoid running the program with the data that caused the error to occur. This is a little disconcerting if the program happens to control a missile defence system, a nuclear power station, a fly-by-wire aircraft or a life-support machine!

Finding errors

What are the syntax errors in the following program?

```
// Computes the area and circumference of a
// circle of radius 4
important javax.swing.JOptionPane;
public glass Circle
{
    public static void main(String[] args)

        double radius = 4;
        double area; // To hold area
        Double circumf; // To hold circumference

        // do the calculations
        JOptionPane.showMessageDialog(null,
            "Area: " + area + \nCircumference: " + circumf);

        circum = 4 * Math.PI * radius;
        // Class Math is from
        // Java.lang package
        area = Math.PI * raduis * radius * radius

        // output the answers

        system.exit(0);
    }
}
```

The program is supposed to compute the area and circumference of a circle. Do a dry run to find the semantic error(s) in the program.

When you have the opportunity, type in and correct the errors you have found when dry running. See if you can make the program give the correct answers.

3.10 Summary

In this chapter you have looked at the following:

- Comments
- Importing pre-written code (such as *JOptionPane*)
- Defining a class and *main()* method for a Java program
- Defining other methods in addition to *main()*
- How to produce output using dialog boxes and using the console (commmand line) window
- Subprograms
- Variables and assignment
- Calculations and operator precedence
- Different kinds of error (syntax and semantic errors).

3.11 Review questions

 Question 3.1   Fill in the blanks in the following:

1 Every Java program begins execution at the method _____.

2 The ____ symbol begins the body of every method.

3 The ____ symbol ends the body of every method.

4 Every Java statement ends with a _____ symbol.

5 Comments are started with either the _____ or _____ characters.

6 The API class imported at the start of all programs in this chapter to draw dialogs is called _____.

7 The _____ symbols define the <newline> character, which moves the output cursor to a new line.

8 Strings start and end with a _____.

9 An error which is caught by the compiler is a _____ error.

10 _____ are often used to document a program and improve its readability – they do not affect the behaviour of a program.

 Question 3.2   What, if anything, is wrong (there may be more than one mistake) with each of the following statements?

In each case give a correct version if there are errors:

1 JoptionPane.showMessageDialog(null, Hello!);

2 spling;

3 4 + x = x

 Question 3.3   Write single Java statements or comments you would enter inside the main() method to do the following:

1 Display the following dialog:

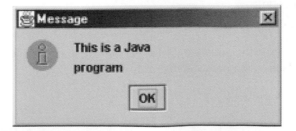

2 Display the following dialog (so the message is on 2 lines):

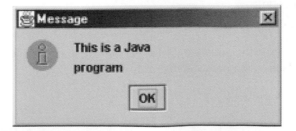

3 Display the dialog showing the message *This is a Java program* with each word on a different line (and no spurious spaces) as follows:

4 A comment that states that a program will calculate the product of three integers.

Question 3.4 What does the following statement do?

JOptionPane.showMessageDialog(null,

"*\n**\n***\n****\n*****");

Question 3.5 Fill in the blanks.

1 Data values are stored in _____ in a Java program.

2 Integer variables are declared using the keyword _____.

3 The % operator calculates and returns the _____ of two integers.

4 The _____ operator does addition when applied to two numbers, and string concatenation when applied to two Strings, or a String and a numeric value.

Question 3.6 Write single Java statements to do the following:

1 Declare the variable *count* to be an integer.

2 Output the difference between the values of variables *a* and *b* with an appropriate message.

3 Display *The product is* followed by the value in the variable *result*.

Question 3.7 Identify and correct the errors in the following statements:

1 integer a;

2 INT value;

3 1nt count;

4 a := 5;

Question 3.8 Given the equation $y = ax^3 + 7$, which, if any, of the following are correct and equivalent Java assignment statements for it?

1 y = a * x * x * x + 7

2 $y = a * x * x * (x + 7)$

3 $y = (a * x) * x * (x + 7)$

4 $y = (a * x) * x * x + 7$

5 $y = a * (x * x * x) + 7$

6 $y = a * x * (x * x + 7)$

 Question 3.9 Write a program that stores three numbers into variables, *a1*, *a2* and *a3*. It should then swap them round so that *a1* holds the value originally in *a3*, *a2* holds the value originally in *a1* and *a3* holds the value originally in *a2*. It should print the contents of the variables before and after swapping them, to demonstrate that it works. An example run is given below.

> Original value of a1: 7
> Original value of a2: 9
> Original value of a3: 13

Output from program:

> *Before the swap...*
>
> > a1 has value 7
> > a2 has value 9
> > a3 has value 13
>
> *After the swap...*
>
> > a1 has value 13
> > a2 has value 7
> > a3 has value 9

 Question 3.10 Answer *true* or *false* to each of the following:

1 *JOptionPane* is a class which allows us to display a message dialog box.

2 Comments are printed on the screen when the program is executed.

3 The statement *JOptionPane.showMessageDialog(null, "Spoke\n");* causes the following dialog to be displayed:

> **Message** ☒
>
> ⓘ **Spoken**
>
> OK

4 A variable can be declared after it is used.

5 All variables that are used must be declared.

6 All variables must be given a type when they are declared.

7 The quotient "/" and modulus "%" operators both do the same operation: divide a number.

8 The "+" and "-" operators have the same precedence.

9 The "+" operator has greater precedence than the "*" operator.

10 Logic errors are reported by the compiler.

3.12 Answers to review questions

Question 3.1

1 *main()*

2 open brace "{"

3 close brace "}"

4 semicolon ";"

5 "//" (or "/*" for multi-line comments – which are terminated with "*/")

6 javax.swing.JOptionPane

7 \n

8 double quote "

9 *Syntax*, or *compile-time*, or *static*

10 Comments

Question 3.2

1 No double quotes around the string "*Hello!*". Also a capital 'O' is needed in *JOptionPane* – remember, Java is a case-sensitive language.

2 No parentheses (round brackets) in the method call; should be
spling();

3 Only a single variable name can appear on the LHS of an assignment statement – i.e. the left-hand side (LHS) of the assignment operator "=" is the name of the variable in which the result of the calculation is to be placed – if you want the result of *4 + x* to be placed into variable *x*, you should write:

x = 4 + x

A semicolon is required to terminate each statement, so you should actually write:

x = x + 4;

Question 3.3

  1 JOptionPane.showMessageDialog(null,
      "This is a Java program");

  2 JOptionPane.showMessageDialog(null,
      "This is a Java\nprogram");

  3 JOptionPane.showMessageDialog(null,
      "This\nis\na\nJava\nprogram");

  4 // program calculates the product of 3 integers

Question 3.4

Draws a right-angled triangle

Question 3.5

  1 variables

  2 int

  3 modulus (remainder after integer division).

  4 +

Question 3.6

  1 int count;

  2 JOptionPane.showMessageDialog(null,
      "The difference between a and b is: " + (a - b));

  3 JOptionPane.showMessageDialog(null,
      "The product is: " + result);

Question 3.7

  1 Wrong keyword used: int a;

  2 Keywords are case sensitive: int value;

  3 Digit 1 used instead of letter i: int count;

  4 Assignment operator is =, not := therefore statement should be a = 5;

Question 3.8

Examples 1, 4 and 5 are correct.

Question 3.9

```java
// Swaps the values of three variables

public class Swap
{
  public static void main(String[] args)
  {
    // declare and initialise variables

    int a1 = 7;
    int a2 = 9;
    int a3 = 13;

    // Write out initial values

    System.out.println("Before the swap...");
    System.out.println("a1 has value " + a1);
    System.out.println("a2 has value " + a2);
    System.out.println("a3 has value " + a3);

    // swap values

    int temp;
    // temporary variable to facilitate the swap

    temp = a3;
    a3 = a2;
    a2 = a1;
    a1 = temp;

    // Write out new values

    System.out.println("After the swap...");
    System.out.println("a1 has value " + a1);
    System.out.println("a2 has value " + a2");
    System.out.println("a3 has value " + a3);
  }
}
```

Question 3.10 Answer *true* or *false* to each of the following:

1 **True** This is a correct description of the predefined class *JOptionPane*.

2 **False** No, comments are ignored by the compiler, and so do not effect the behaviour of the program when it is executed.

3 **False** The String "Spoke\n" is not the same as "Spoken" – the '\n' is the special 'newline' character which causes the output cursor to move to the next line, so only "Spoke" will be displayed in the dialog.

4 **False** Variables *must* be declared before they are used in a program.

5 **True** Although a variable may be declared and not used (although this is wasteful of the computer's memory resources).

6 True You must tell the compiler what type of value a variable is to store, so the computer knows how much memory to reserve for storing values for the variable.

7 False The quotient operator "/" performs division. The modulus operator "%" returns the remainder after integer division.

8 True This makes sense since the order you add or subtract does not matter. For example (3 + 2 − 4) is the same whether you perform the subtraction before or after the addition.

9 False The multiplication operator "*" has greater precedence than addition.

10 False Logic errors have nothing to do with the grammar of a language. Therefore it is possible for a program to compile (to be syntactically correct) but to contain a logic error such as computing the wrong answer.

3.13 Feedback on activities

Activity 3.1: Controlling output

You require output on four lines, which you can achieve by including **\n** (newline) characters in the output string, as in the following program:

```
// Draws a triangle
// in a single dialog box
import javax.swing.JOptionPane;

public class Triangle
{
    public static void main(String[] args)
    {
        JOptionPane.showMessageDialog(null,
            "@\n@@\n@@@\n@@@@");

        System.exit(0);
    }
}
```

Your program is entered into Notepad (or your chosen editor) and saved with the filename 'Triangle.java' – remember the filename must be the same as the class name (case sensitive) with '.java' added:

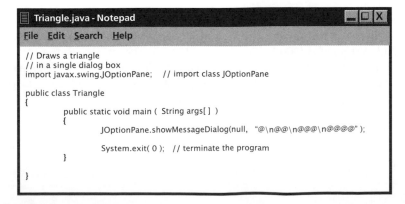

You then compile the program by executing the compiler 'javac' on the file 'Triangle.java', and after successful compilation execute the 'java' interpreter to execute the 'Triangle.class' file.

In the example below we have saved the 'Triangle.java' file into the folder:

D:\jdk1.3\cmt1000\unit03\triangle

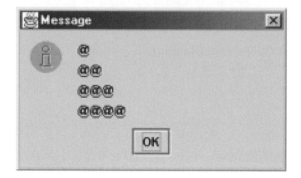

When the program runs, a dialog displaying the triangle of '@' signs is displayed:

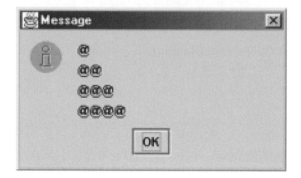

Activity 3.2: Dry running a program

Methods *spling()* and *splong()* each contain a statement invoking the other. Therefore, this program will run forever, with each of the two methods writing its message and calling the other over and over again. You can stop the program by clicking back to the command prompt window, and typing <CTRL> + C at the command prompt. Note that *main()* contains only a call to *spling()*; after this, all the work is done by *spling()* and *splong()*.

Activity 3.3: A program to write MOOOO

```
// Prints MOOOO on the screen using two separate methods

public class Moo
{
  public static void bigM()
  {
     System.out.println("M      M");
     System.out.println("MM    MM");
     System.out.println("M M  M M");
     System.out.println("M  M M  M");
     System.out.println("M   M   M");
  }

  public static void bigO()
  {
     System.out.println(" OOOOOOO ");
     System.out.println("O     O");
     System.out.println("O      O");
     System.out.println("O      O");
     System.out.println(" OOOOOOO ");
  }

  public static void main(String[] args)
  {
     bigM();
     bigO();
     bigO();
     bigO();
     bigO();
  }
}
```

Activity 3.4: Swapping the values of two variables

This type of error is called a *logic error* – the program runs, but doesn't do what it is supposed to! The only ways to detect this type of error are to dry run the program, or to execute it on a computer and see what happens. The problem in this program occurs because when the computer executes the statement

first = second;

the value of *second* is copied into *first*, but this means that the original value of *first* is overwritten and lost. Both variables will end up with the original value of *second*! Therefore, you must temporarily store a copy of the value of *first* in a *third* variable before copying the value of *second* into *first*. You can then copy the value of this third variable into *second*, to achieve the necessary swap.

The following is a correct version of the program.

```java
// Swaps the values of two variables
import javax.swing.JOptionPane;

public class Swap
{
    public static void main(String[] args)
    {
        // declare and initialise variables
        int first = 3;
        int second = 4;

        // Write out initial values
        JOptionPane.showMessageDialog(null,
            "First variable: " + first
            + "\nsecond variable: " + second);

        // swap values
        int temp;
        // temporary variable to facilitate the swap

        temp = first;
        first = second;
        second = temp;

        // Write out new values
        JOptionPane.showMessageDialog(null,
            "First variable: " + first
            + "\nsecond variable: " + second);

        System.exit(0);
    }
}
```

When run, the program should first display:

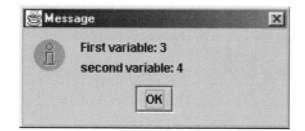

then:

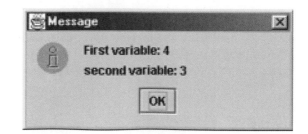

Activity 3.5: A temperature conversion program

The following program is a solution to the problem:

```
// Computes the Fahrenheit equivalent of 20 Celsius
import javax.swing.JOptionPane;

public class ConvTemp
{
   public static void main(String[] args)
   {
      // ratio of F degree to C degree
      final double FACTOR = 9.0 / 5.0;
      final double SHIFT = 32;  // 0 C = 32 F

      double cel = 20;  // temp for conversion
      double fah;  // Fahrenheit equivalent

      // do the calculation
      fah = cel * FACTOR + SHIFT;

      // output the answer
      JOptionPane.showMessageDialog(null,
         "The Fahrenheit equivalent of 20 Celsius is "
         + fah + " F");

      System.exit(0);
   }
}
```

Activity 3.6: Finding errors

You should have found ten syntax errors. Try to find them all by reading the program. Then cut and paste the program into a file, compile it and let the compiler tell you what the syntax errors are – you will get the following:

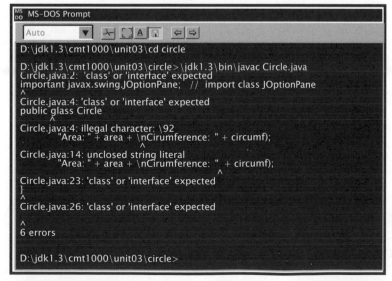

Not *all* errors are displayed when you first compile, since some grammatical errors confuse the compiler – so it does not know whether other parts of the program are correct, or will not, until the earlier ones have been corrected.

The syntax errors are listed below.

Syntax error :: 'import' not 'important'

> important javax.swing.JOptionPane;

should be:

> import javax.swing.JOptionPane;

Syntax error :: 'class' not 'glass'

> public glass Circle

should be:

> public class Circle

Syntax error :: body of main() must start with an open brace (curly bracket)

> public static void main(String[] args)

should be:

> public static void main(String[] args)
> {

Syntax error :: variable declared as 'Double' instead of 'double'

Remember Java is case sensitive (and types like Double when spelt with a capital letter have special meaning in Java, different from the simple numeric type double that you have looked at in this chapter):

> Double circumf; // To hold circumference

should be:

> double circumf; // To hold circumference

Syntax error :: missing quotation before '\n'

> JOptionPane.showMessageDialog(null,
>   "Area: " + area + \nCircumference: " + circumf);

should be:

> JOptionPane.showMessageDialog(null,
>   "Area: " + area + "\nCircumference: " + circumf);

Syntax error :: wrong spelling of variable 'circumf' not 'circum'

> circum = 4 * Math.PI * radius;

should be

> circumf = 4 * Math.PI * radius;

Syntax error :: wrong spelling of variable 'radius' not 'raduis'

area = Math.PI * raduis * radius * radius

should be:

area = Math.PI * radius * radius * radius;

Syntax error :: missing semicolon at end of statement

area = Math.PI * radius * radius * radius

should be:

area = Math.PI * radius * radius * radius;

Syntax error :: 'System' not 'system'

Remember Java is case sensitive:

system.exit(0);

should be:

System.exit(0);

Syntax error ::

The JOptionPane output should appear just before the program terminates, *after* the calculations have been performed. Java displays this as an error, since it will not let you try to display a variable which might not have yet been given its first (initial) value.

Semantic errors

There are semantic (logic) errors in the formulae used to compute area and circumference.

The calculation for AREA should be changed from

area = Math.PI * radius * radius * radius;

to

area = Math.PI * radius * radius;

The calculation for CIRCUMFERENCE should be changed from:

circumf = 4 * Math.PI * radius;

to

circumf = 2 * Math.PI * radius;

The correct program should look like this:

```java
// Computes the area and circumference of a
// circle of radius 4
import javax.swing.JOptionPane;

public class Circle
{
    public static void main(String[] args)
    {
        double radius = 4;
        double area; // To hold area
        double circumf; // To hold circumference

        // do the calculations

        circumf = 2 * Math.PI * radius;
        // Class Math is from
        // Java.lang package

        area = Math.PI * radius * radius;

        // output the answers
        JOptionPane.showMessageDialog(null,
        "Area: " + area + "\nCircumference: " +      circumf);

        System.exit(0);
    }
}
```

When compiled and run the results should be:

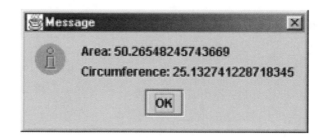

CHAPTER 4

Inputs and strings

OVERVIEW

So far, your programs have been limited in the sense that all the data on which they have operated has had to be defined within the program text. In other words, the data was fixed before the program was compiled.

In this chapter, you will learn how to write programs which enable data to be entered via the keyboard by the user of the program, while the program is running. The advantage of this is that, without changing the program source code, the program can be made to operate upon different data every time it runs, making the program much more flexible and useful. You will also learn more about objects; in particular about *Strings*.

Learning outcomes	On completion of this chapter you should be able to.

- Write programs that obtain data in the form of Strings from the keyboard

- Write the code necessary to obtain numerical data from Strings

- Dry run simple Java programs

- Explain the value of having a comprehensive library of pre-written classes such as the Java API.

4.1 Adding two numbers

Suppose you wish to write a program which adds together two numbers entered at the keyboard by the user.

As with any problem-solving effort, you should first ensure that you fully understand the specification of the problem. If you do not do this, you risk wasting lots of time writing a program which doesn't solve the problem. Even for an apparently simple problem such as this one, there are some initial questions which you should ask in order to clarify what is required. For example:

- What do you mean by 'numbers'?

  Remember, there is more than one type of number in Java – are you talking about *integers* or *floating point* (*decimal*) numbers? (Remember, these are stored differently in Java.) You can use the '+' operator to add either, but you cannot store floating point numbers in integer-type variables

- Can the numbers be negative, or will they always be positive?
- What do you do with the answer?
  - write it into a file on the hard disk?
  - write it on the screen in a dialog box?
  - write it on the screen in the command window?
  - use it in a further calculation?
- Will you use a graphical user interface (GUI) or command line input and output?

Let us suppose that you are going to read in two integers, and write their sum on the screen using methods from *JOptionPane* for input and output.

The plan

- Ask the user to enter an integer
- Read the number in and store it in a variable
- Ask the user for a second integer
- Read it in and store it in a variable
- Add together the two numbers and store the result in a variable
- Display the result on the screen.

You already know how to do the last two steps; you must now learn how to read in data entered at the keyboard by the user of the program.

Getting input

Class *JOptionPane* has a method called show*InputDialog()*.

As with the method *showMessageDialog()*, this method takes a String as a parameter (but only one parameter this time – no need for *null*), and displays it on the screen in a box.

The difference is that this box contains a text field, into which the user may type a String. The parameter String is used as a *prompt* to the user, telling them what kind of thing the program would like them to type.

When the user clicks the box's OK button, the String of text they typed is captured by the *showInputDialog()* method.

To use this String value in the program, you can assign it to a *String variable*.

Example
To read in the first number for the addition problem.

```
String numString1;
numString1 = JOptionPane.showInputDialog("Enter your first integer");
```

In fact, the declaration of the String variable and the call to *showInputDialog()* can be combined like this.

```
String numString1 = JOptionPane.showInputDialog("Enter your first integer");
```

The call to the *showInputDialog()* method will cause the following box to appear on the screen:

Suppose the user then types 42 into the text field:

When the user clicks the OK button, the *showInputDialog()* method *returns* the String "42" .

The term *returns* means that the method call, when executed effectively *becomes* a particular value – in this case the String "42".

Now, what can you do with the String "42"?

- You can write it on the screen in a box using the method *showMessageDialog()*
- You can write it on the screen using *System.out.println()*
- You can assign it to a String variable as above.

You could assign the String "42" to *numString1* as follows:

```
numString1 = "42";
```

but you want to assign the String returned by the *showInputDialog()* method call.

Remember, when an assignment statement is executed, the expression on the right-hand side of the = is evaluated, then the result is stored in the variable on the left-hand side.

If the method call

```
JOptionPane.showInputDialog("Enter your first integer");
```

evaluates to "42" then the assignment

```
numString1 = JOptionPane.showInputDialog("Enter your first integer");
```

stores this value in *numString1*.

Before you go any further, you should learn a little more about Strings.

String variables

So far, you have met variables of type *int*, *char* and *double*. These are effectively 'pigeon holes' in the computer's memory into which you can place literal values which are integers (e.g. 4), characters (e.g. 'A') and floating point numbers (e.g. 3.142) respectively.

These are called *primitive type* variables.

You have also met the idea of Strings of characters such as 'Hello world', which you can print on the screen by passing them as parameters to the JOptionPane.showMessageDialog method. These were *String values*, just as 4 is an integer value and 'A' is a character value.

You have now seen that you can also define String variables; for example:

```
String s;
```

declares a variable s of type String.

You can assign a String to this variable in the usual way, for example:

```
s = "Hello world";
```

So must *s* be a named pigeon hole in memory in which you can store Strings? Unfortunately, this is not quite the case!

Reference variables

String variables are an example of so-called *reference variables*. A reference variable does not actually contain its associated data, but contains a *reference* to the data (effectively the address of the location where the data is stored in the computer's memory). You can represent the reference as an arrow, pointing to the data.

Primitive type variable

```
int x;
x = 5;

x     5
```

String reference variable:

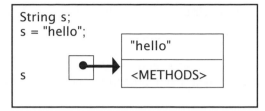

For our current purposes, this distinction is not important, but later it will be very important. The things pointed at by reference variables are called *objects*. Thus, a String in Java is an example of an *object*, and the type String is a *class*. Classes and objects are the fundamental elements of object-oriented programming, about which more later.

Objects are different from ordinary data items in many ways. For example, an object can contain more than one piece of data, so you could have an object to represent a football score, containing two integers: one for the home team's score, and one for the away team's score.

Additionally, objects can have a set of *methods* associated with them which allow us to do things to the object. For example, the football score object could have a method to work out the total number of goals scored in the game by adding the two scores. You will learn how to define and use your own objects later.

Coming back to Strings, this means that, in addition to its value (a sequence of characters), a String object also has *methods* associated with it – as shown in the example on the previous page. These methods are defined in the class String, which is in package java.lang, (remember, a package is a collection of classes) and every String object has access to these methods. This makes Strings a very flexible and useful part of Java programming.

The type of an object

Note that the type of an object reference variable will always be the name of a class, and will therefore, by convention, always begin with a capital letter (i.e. String, not string).

Our programs can create and destroy objects at any time, and access them using reference variables. This is an extremely important feature of the Java language, to which we will return.

Back to our addition program; *numString1* is a String reference variable; the assignment makes it refer to the String typed by the user.

So now surely all you need to do is repeat the above steps for another variable, say *numString2*, and simply add *numString1* and *numString2* together?

```
String numString1 = JOptionPane.showInputDialog( "Enter your first integer");

String numString2 = JOptionPane.showInputDialog( "Enter your second integer");

int result = numString1 + numString2;
```

Well, as before, it isn't quite that simple!

Before you move on, pause to consider the value of the expression

```
numString1 + numString2
```

assuming the user types *42* and *24* when prompted by the program. What do you think it would be?

In fact

numString1 + numString2

would have the value of the String "4224".

Remember, *numString1* and *numString2* are *Strings*; the strings of characters they contain might consist of digit characters, but a sequence of digit characters is not the same thing as a Java int.

The binary bits which make up an int represent a 2's complement binary number (2's complement is a system which stores the sign and magnitude of integers in a convenient way for the computer to do arithmetic on the integers). The binary bits which make up a String value comprise a series of binary Unicodes, one for each character in the String.

Therefore the expression:

42 + 24

represents the addition of two ints. This evaluates, as we might expect, to the int:

66

However, the expression:

"42" + "24"

represents the *concatenation* (joining together) of two Strings, and evaluates to the String:

"4224"

Our problem is that input of data with *showInputDialog()* is via Strings. Before you can do your addition, you must first compute the int representation of each of your input Strings.

You could write code to do this conversion, but luckily someone has already done it for you! It's time to learn a little more about objects.

4.2 The Integer class

Remember, the types int, char and double are called *primitive types*. Variables of these types may be thought of as named boxes in memory into which you may place integer, character and floating point values respectively. But you now know that there is another sort of variable, the reference variable, which can contain a reference to an object of a specified class.

You have already met the class *String*; another class in the package java.lang is *Integer*.

Remember that a String object is a piece of data such as

"hello"

bundled up with some methods which enable us to operate on the String object itself. These methods are defined in the class *String*.

Well, in the same sort of way, an Integer object is a piece of data such as:

4

bundled up with some methods which enable us to operate on the Integer object itself. These methods are defined in the class *Integer*.

Now, you can use some of these methods from the *Integer* class without ever creating any *Integer* objects. They are associated with the *Integer* class itself, and you can use them by giving the class name, followed by a dot, followed by the method name.

You have already done this sort of thing with the class:

JOptionPane

when, for example, you use method *showMessageDialog()*:

JOptionPane.showMessageDialog(null, "Hello world");

or when you use method *showInputDialog()*:

numString1 = JOptionPane.showInputDialog("Enter your first integer");

These methods, accessible using the class name, are called *class methods*, or *static methods*.

You have already used class methods in your own program classes, for example:

public static void main(String[] args)

and

public static void spling()

You can tell that these are class methods from the key word *static* in their headings.

In this context, you may view a class as a collection of useful methods, which you can utilise in your programs.

This is an oversimplified notion of what a class is, but it will suffice for our current purpose. Of course, the Java programs you have written so far are also classes. One of the things that distinguishes our program classes from classes such as *String* and *Integer* is that our programs contain a *main()* method, which is the first method to be executed when you run the program.

The *main()* method can then call other methods, which may also be in our program class, or in other classes such as *String* and *Integer*. If the method called is in the same class as the calling method, then you do not need the class name and the dot in the method call.

The Java API

The classes *JOptionPane*, *String* and *Integer* are part of an enormous collection of pre-written, tried-and-tested classes called the Java Applications Programming Interface (API). These contain hundreds of useful methods which can be used in our programs. When writing a program, the Java programmer will search through the API documentation to find classes and methods which they can *reuse*. If a class doesn't quite do the job, then there are ways in which a modified version can be created and used. This speeds up, enormously, the process of constructing reliable, maintainable and easily debugged software. You will learn more about this in chapter 12.

The Java API

1   The documentation of the Java API is very easy to browse through, because it is in hypertext format. Go to **www.java.sun.com** and search for the classes String, Integer and JOptionPane from the main index (e.g: Type 'Integer class API' in the search field and hit 'Search'). Then explore the online documentation to see what methods are available for each of these classes.

2   Note that *Integer* is a so-called *wrapper class*, which enables the creation of the object equivalent of the primitive type int (a bit like an int, but with useful methods bound up with the numerical data). There are similar wrapper classes equivalent to the primitive types char and double. Find these and also take a look at their methods.

So how does all this help us to convert our input number *String* into an *int*?

Well, the class *Integer* has a static method called *parseInt()* which takes a *String* as an argument and returns the equivalent *int* value.

If you define an *int* type variable *firstNum* you can then store the *int* equivalent of the String *numString1* in this variable as follows:

```
int firstNum = Integer.parseInt(numString1);
```

Note that the method *parseInt()* returns its result in the same way as method *showInputDialog();* the result is an *int* value, which you can then assign to the variable *firstNum*.

What do you think would be the effect of the statement:

```
int firstNum = Integer.parseInt(numString1);
```

if the String **numString1** contains the String value "forty-two"?

The program will crash! The *parseInt()* method assumes that the String passed to it represents an integer comprised of digits and possibly a sign, but it isn't clever enough to deal with numbers represented as words.

To read in *chars* and *doubles*, you must input their String equivalents in the same way as with *ints*. For *doubles*, you can then use the method *parseDouble()*, from the *Double* class, to do the conversion in the same way as you did with *parseInt()*.

For *chars*, you can use the method *charAt()*, which is part of every *String* object. This method takes an integer as a parameter, and returns the character at the position in the String given by that integer. Note that positions always start at 0.

For example, given the following

```
String s = "Hello";
```

The value of

```
s.charAt(0);
```

is the character 'H'.

The value of

    s.charAt(1);

is the character 'e' – and so on.

Note, again, that the first character in the String object occupies position 0 not position 1!

Notice that this method is part of the String *object* s, which is called by giving the object name, followed by a dot, followed by the method name. On the other hand, *parseInt()* and *parseDouble()* are part of the *Integer* and *Double classes* respectively (called by giving the class name, followed by a dot, followed by the method name).

Why? Because the method *charAt()* is required to find the character at a specific position in a particular object (String), whereas the methods *parseInt()* and *parseDouble()* are given a String to parse as a *parameter* (i.e. they are not part of any individual object).

Before you read on, try writing a program to try out these methods.

4.3 The program

Are we ready to complete our program?

Almost!

We obtain the int equivalent of the second input number String in the same way.

    int secondNum = Integer.parseInt(numString2);

We can now use assignment to add the two int variables together and store the result in a third int variable.

    int result = firstNum + secondNum;

We then output the result.

    JOptionPane.showMessageDialog(null,
        "The sum of " + firstNum + " and " + secondNum +
        " is " + result);

If the value of *firstNum* was 42 and the value of *secondNum* was 24, then the box would look like this:

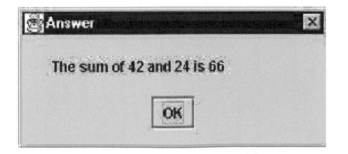

Here is the complete program.

```java
// Program to input two integers from the keyboard and display their sum

import javax.swing.JOptionPane;

public class Add
{

    public static void main(String[] args)
    {
        String numString1 = JOptionPane.showInputDialog( "Enter your first integer");
        String numString2 = JOptionPane.showInputDialog(
            "Enter your second integer");

        int firstNum = Integer.parseInt(numString1);
        int secondNum = Integer.parseInt(numString2);

        int result = firstNum + secondNum;

        JOptionPane.showMessageDialog(null,
            "The sum of " + firstNum + " and " + secondNum +  " is " + result);

        System.exit(0);
    }
}
```

Activity 4.2

Extending the program

Load up and run the Add program. Change the program to make it read in and add three integers. Then modify it to compute the average of the three numbers.

Activity 4.3

Shop transaction

Write a program to read in a sum tendered for a purchase, and the price for the item, and output the change to be given to the customer. What problem is there with this program?

When the opportunity arises, run the program on a computer.

4.4 **More about object references**

In the previous program, you have two Strings, *numString1* and *numString2*, in which to store the two input numbers.

In the statement:

```
String numString1 = JOptionPane.showInputDialog("Enter your first integer");
```

the call to *showInputDialog()* creates a String containing the characters typed by the user in response to the prompt in the input dialog box, and the assignment stores the address of that String object in the String reference variable *numString1*. The presence of the address of the String in variable *numString1* can be represented by an arrow from *numString1* pointing to the String object.

The program does the same thing for a second number:

```
String numString2 = JOptionPane.showInputDialog(
    "Enter your second integer");
```

giving the scenario shown (assume the user types 42 and 24 in response to the prompts).

What are the names of the two Strings in the following diagram?

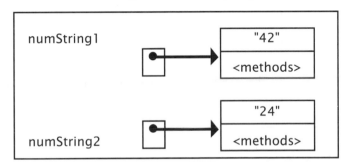

Strictly, they do not have names – they are *de-referenced*. However, you can refer to them using the names of the two reference variables *numString1* and *numString2*.

Yet, you do not actually need *two* String reference variables to do the input of the two numbers.

This can be done by changing the statements of the program as follows.

- Firstly, you obtain the first number from the user, in a String, which you could call *numString*
- Use *parseInt()* to obtain the int equivalent of the first number String
- Now use *numString* again, to obtain the second number String from the user
- Use *parseInt()* to obtain the int equivalent of this second number String.

In Java:

```
String numString = JOptionPane.showInputDialog("Enter your first integer");

int firstNum = Integer.parseInt(numString);

numString = JOptionPane.showInputDialog("Enter your second integer");

int secondNum = Integer.parseInt(numString);
```

What happens to the first input number String when you read in the second number String and assign it to *numString*?

Your first reaction would probably be to say, 'the first String is overwritten by the second' – and this is indeed what happens when you assign a new value to a primitive type variable (int, char or double); the existing value stored in the variable is overwritten by the new value, and is therefore lost.

However, with Strings (and indeed, with any objects), the mechanism is different. Remember, the String reference variable does not contain the actual String, but a *reference* to the String (usually shown as an arrow). The sequence of events is as follows.

Initial state:

```
┌─────────────────────────────────────────────────┐
│                                                 │
│   numString1        □                           │
│                                                 │
│                                                 │
│   firstNum          □                           │
│                                                 │
│                                                 │
│   secondNum         □                           │
│                                                 │
└─────────────────────────────────────────────────┘
```

State after execution of the statement:

```
numString = JOptionPane.showInputDialog("Enter your first integer");
```

assuming user types *42* in response to the prompt.

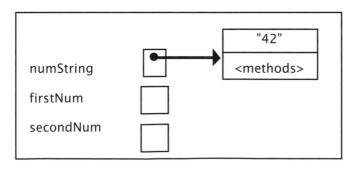

State after execution of the statement:

  int firstNum = Integer.parseInt(numString);

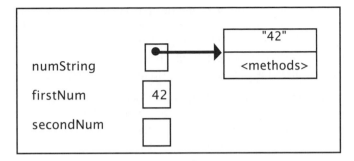

State after execution of the statement:

  numString = JOptionPane.showInputDialog("Enter your second integer");

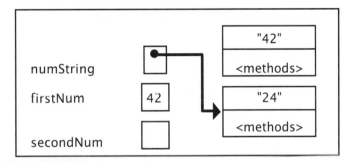

State after execution of the statement:

  int secondNum = Integer.parseInt(numString);

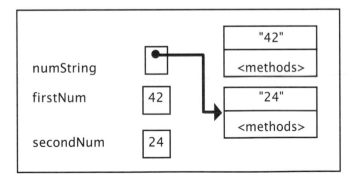

So there are now two further questions which you might ask yourself: firstly, what is the name of the first String object created (the one with "42" in it), after you create the second String object?

It does not have one! Remember, you can only refer to an object using a reference variable in which a reference to that object is stored. The reference to the first String object is overwritten by the reference to the second String object. This means that the first String object has been de-referenced and you cannot get at it.

The second question that arises is what happens to the first String object after you remove the reference to it.

This is a good question because, in some other languages such as C++, *nothing* would happen to this discarded object; it would remain in memory, taking up space which therefore could not be used to create new objects, until the program terminates. In the previous program, this would not be a problem, as you are only dealing with one small object. However, it is possible to write programs that create thousands of large objects which take up lots of space in memory, and if these are discarded, then the memory can fill up and crash the program.

However, in Java this is not a problem, because any object which becomes anonymous in this way is effectively destroyed automatically by the Java run-time system, and the space occupied by the object is freed up to be used for creating new objects. This process is called *garbage collection*, and is another useful 'automatic' feature of the Java language. In the C++ language, the responsibility for carrying out this garbage collection falls upon the programmer!

4.5 Dry running

As discussed in the previous chapter, you can test your program without using a computer by *dry running* it on paper.

You act as the computer, following the instructions of the program, recording the values of the variables at each stage.

You can do this using a table with columns headed with the names of the variables in the program. Each row in the table will be labelled with a line number from the program, and the entries in each row of the table will be the values of the variables after the execution of the statement on that line. You do not need to have a row for *every* line in the program, just those lines where some significant change to the state of the program occurs; for example, a variable gets a new value.

In this table, you can record all relevant changes to the variables as the program progresses, and thereby test whether the logic of the program is correct for various test data.

This is usually easier than getting the program to run on a computer, because you do not need to worry whether the details of the syntax are correct – you do not have to make the program *compile*. This means that you can just concentrate on the *logic* of the algorithm.

When you are happy with the dry run tests, you can then try it on a computer. If errors in the program logic come to light during the dry running, you can easily correct them, as your program is merely written on a piece of paper. If, on the other hand, you did not dry run the program but went straight into typing it into the computer, compiling it and then testing it on the machine, then you risk doing a lot of abortive work if the program subsequently turns out to contain logic errors.

Activity 4.4

Dry running the Add program

Draw up a dry run table for the Add program, assuming that the user types the integers 17 and 24 in response to the prompts. Here is a version of the program again, with relevant lines numbered. Note that you are only interested in lines where the values of variables can change. The contents of the table for a given row should be the values of variables *after* the statement with the line number for that row has been executed.

```java
// Program to input two integers from the keyboard and display their sum

import javax.swing.JOptionPane;

public class Add
{

    public static void main(String[] args)
    {
        String numString1;
        String numString2;
        //LINE 1
        numString1 = JOptionPane.showInputDialog(
            "Enter your first integer");

        //LINE2
        numString2 = JOptionPane.showInputDialog(
            "Enter your second integer");

        //LINE 3
        int firstNum = Integer.parseInt(numString1);

        //LINE 4
        int secondNum = Integer.parseInt(numString2);

        //LINE 5
        int result = firstNum + secondNum;

        //LINE 6
        JOptionPane.showMessageDialog(null,
            "The sum of " + firstNum + " and " + secondNum +
            " is " + result);

        System.exit(0);
    }
}
```

4.6 **Summary**

In this chapter you have looked at the following:

- Input of Strings
- Conversion of String representations into other data types
- Browsing the Java API documentation
- Objects and object reference variables
- Class and object methods
- Dry running programs using a table.

4.7 **Review questions**

 Question 4.1   What is the difference between a primitive type variable and a reference variable?

 Question 4.2   What does it mean when you say a method returns a value?

 Question 4.3   What are the characteristics of objects?

 Question 4.4   What is the difference between the String "42" and the int 42?

 Question 4.5   What is the difference between the method call

      s.charAt(3)   where s is a String variable,

   and the method call

      Integer.parseInt(t)   where t is a String variable?

 Question 4.6   What is the Java API?

 Question 4.7   What happens to an object when it is no longer referenced by any reference variables?

 Question 4.8   Show how the following picture would change when the statement below executes.

    numString1 = numString2;

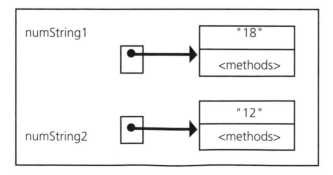

Question 4.9 How should one dry run a program, and what are the advantages of dry running?

Question 4.10 Answer *true* or *false* to each of the following:

1 *JOptionPane* is a class which has methods for doing input and output operations.

2 The method which you use for input is called *showMessageDialog()*.

3 The statement

   String s = JOptionPane.showInputDialog("Enter your first integer");

   causes the following dialog to be displayed:

4 A variable of type String is like a box in memory into which you can place Strings.

5 The value of the expression "12" + "14" is "26".

6 The declaration Integer x; creates a primitive type variable in which you can store integers.

7 The Java API is a useful collection of classes that you may use in your programs.

8 Assigning one String reference variable to another causes both to contain the address of the same String object.

9 Dry running a program means running it without any input data.

10 Dry running is best carried out using a table.

4.8 Answers to review questions

Question 4.1 The primitive type variable is a named 'box' in memory in which a data value can be stored. The reference variable is a box in which the *address of an object* can be stored, after which the object can be referenced by using the name of the reference variable.

Question 4.2 Some methods simply act as little programs, doing calculations, input and output. Other methods compute a value and 'return' it. The difference is apparent in the way in which you use (call) the methods. A call to a method which does not return a value is simply a program *statement*. For example:

   JOptionPane.showMessageDialog(null, "Hello");

However, a call to a method which returns a value *becomes* that value after the method executes. The value is then treated as any other value of that type would be. For example, you can assign it to a variable:

```
String str = JOptionPane.showInputDialog(
    "Tell me how you feel");
```

Question 4.3 Objects comprise some data 'bound up' with some methods which can operate on that data. You can call a method by using the object name, followed by a dot, followed by the method name.

Question 4.4 The String is an object, and the int is a primitive type. Also, the int is stored in a format which allows integer arithmetic operations to be performed on it, whereas the data in the String is simply a sequence of character codes.

Question 4.5 The first method, *charAt()*, is attached to the specific String object *s*, whereas the second method, *parseInt()*, is associated with the class *Integer*. They both return a value.

Question 4.6 This stands for Applications Programming Interface, and is a large collection of pre-written classes which you can use in your programs.

Question 4.7 The Java run-time system effectively destroys it, freeing up the memory it was occupying for use by the program. This is called *garbage collection*.

Question 4.8

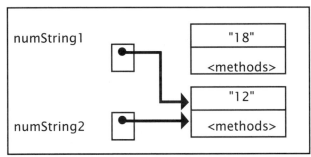

Note that one String object now effectively has two names, while the other has become anonymous! The latter object will be destroyed by the Java garbage collection system.

Question 4.9 You can produce a table, with variable names across the top, and significant line numbers down the side, to keep track of the changing values of variables as you mentally 'execute' the program.

The advantages are that you gain a deeper understanding of the logic of your algorithm, and may identify and correct errors before you have developed the program to the stage where it can be executed on a computer.

Question 4.10

1 **True** This is a correct description of the predefined class *JOptionPane*

2 **False** *showMessageDialog()* is used for output; *showInputDialog()* is the method used for input.

3 True The parameter String is used as a prompt to the user.

4 False It is a reference variable, which can store the *address* of a String *object*.

5 False When + is applied to two Strings, it does String concatenation (joining together). The value of the expression is the String "1214".

6 False It declares an object reference variable that can contain the address of an Integer object. Note the difference between this and an int.

7 True The API may be browsed using its hypertext-based documentation. It contains many useful classes which can save you a lot of development time, as you do not have to write them yourself.

8 True If both variables were originally referencing different String objects, then one object will now have two references to it, and the other will have none.

9 False Dry running means executing the program on paper rather than on the computer.

10 True A good format is to have variable names along the top and significant line numbers down the side.

4.9 Feedback on activities

Activity 4.1: The Java API   You will have noticed the enormous volume of classes and methods available to you   Many of the tasks you might want your program to do have already been considered by other programmers, and classes and methods written to achieve them. You shouldn't try to 'reinvent the wheel' when programming, so you should always check the API documentation before writing code to see if there is anything you can reuse. At the present time in particular, you should be aware of the methods available in the String, Integer, Character and Double classes, and that some methods are accessed using the class name, whereas others may be accessed using the names of individual objects.

Activity 4.2: Extending the program   You should have noted that the average of three integers is, in general, a floating point number. Therefore, the variable in which the average is to be stored must be declared as a double.

Furthermore, the expression which computes the average will involve dividing the sum of the three numbers by 3. You might have done something like this:

```
double average = (num1 + num2 + num3) / 3;
```

where num1, num2 and num3 are the three numbers obtained from the user.

However, if the three numbers were declared as ints, then the output would not be correct. Both operands of the '/' operator are integers, so '/' will carry out integer division. What do you think the expression would evaluate to, if num1, num2 and num3 have the values 3, 5 and 6 respectively?

The answer to that is simply: 4.

To force the '/' operator to do floating point division, you must make at least one of the operands into a double. You can do this by making the second operand into a double as follows:

double average = (num1 + num2 + num3) / 3.0;

In mixed type expressions like this, the 'lower' type integer operand will be *promoted* to the status of the 'higher' double type for the purpose of evaluating this expression only (num1, num2 and num3 are not themselves changed by the promotion).

You could achieve the same result by *casting* the first operand into being treated as a double for the purposes of the calculation, as follows

double average = (double) (num1 + num2 + num3) / 3;

Activity 4.3: Shop transaction   The program is required to obtain the sum tendered and the price as Strings from the user, convert each into an int, subtract the price from the sum tendered, and output the value of the change required. If you struggled with this problem, you should take the Add program and modify it to do the task. This reduces the likely number of syntax errors, because the code you are reusing and modifying has already been tried and tested.

The problem with this program is that it cannot handle the situation where insufficient money is tendered for the purchase – the program will simply output a negative amount of change! A better version of the program would need to be able choose between two actions; if sufficient money is tendered, then compute the change required, otherwise output a message asking for more money. This problem will be solved in the next chapter.

Activity 4.4: Dry running the Add program   You should have come up with a table something like this:

After execution of line	numString1	numString2	firstNum	secondNum	result
LINE 1	U	U			
LINE 2	"17"	U			
LINE 3	"17"	"24"			
LINE 4	"17"	"24"	17		
LINE 5	"17"	"24"	17	24	
LINE 6	"17"	"24"	17	24	41

This dry running technique is very useful when our programs get a little more complicated. The dry run enables us to locate logical errors in our algorithms before even writing compilable Java code, and this can save time in the process of developing our programs. Note that U is used to indicate that a variable exists, but its value is undefined. Where there is no value shown for a variable, this indicates that the variable has not yet been declared, so it does not yet exist.

CHAPTER 5

The 'if-else' statement

OVERVIEW

You now know how to write programs which enable data to be entered via the keyboard by the user of the program, while the program is running. However, your programs still consist of sequences of statements which are executed one after the other in the order in which they appear in the program text. To write more sophisticated and useful programs you need to be able to introduce ways of altering the 'flow' of statements within your programs. This chapter shows you how to write programs within which alternative sequences run depending upon specific choices. These choices will be based on truth-valued (boolean) expressions.

Learning outcomes	On completion of this chapter you should be able to:

- Write programs that make decisions about what instruction(s) to execute next, rather than just executing them one by one, in the order given

- Identify and correct errors in branching programs

- Analyse what a branching program does step by step, by dry running it

- Explain the constructs used in Java programs to implement branching.

5.1 An exam-mark recording problem

Suppose that some students have been given their marks for an exam (out of 100) and need to know whether they have passed (scored 40 or more). You are asked to write a method that asks a student for their mark and then tells them whether or not they have passed.

A plan (pseudocode)
1 Get the mark from the student

2 IF it is greater than the pass mark
     tell them they have passed
ELSE
     tell them they have failed

3 Thank them for using the system.

To implement the plan in Java, you must convert each of the above instructions into the equivalent Java instructions. This mapping is not necessarily one to one. For instance, instruction number 1 requires two Java statements; one to get the mark as a String, and one to get the int equivalent of the String.

Here is the Java method:

```java
public static void passOrFail()
{
   int mark;
   String numStr;

   numStr = JOptionPane.showInputDialog("What is the mark?: ");

   // convert from String to int
   mark = Integer.parseInt(numStr);

   if (mark > 40)
      JOptionPane.showMessageDialog(null, "Passed");
   else
      JOptionPane.showMessageDialog(null, "Failed");

   JOptionPane.showMessageDialog(null, "Bye");
}
```

You will notice that the syntax of the Java selection (*if-else*) statement is very similar to the pseudocode example above, and to the 'chillies on the pizza' example from Chapter 2.

We will look at the Java *if-else* statement in detail shortly although, hopefully, the logical structure should be apparent even before you learn the details. The above method is syntactically correct Java, but can you see a problem with the semantics (the logical meaning) of the method?

Put it this way; how would you feel if you were a student who got precisely 40% in the exam, when the method reported your result?

The test

    (mark > 40)

(the value of which determines the choice between reporting a pass and reporting a fail) will have the value *false* if *mark* is 40; that is, the value of

    (40 > 40)

has the value *false*. Therefore, the program will tell the student they have failed! The correct test should be

(mark >= 40)

which is only false if *mark* is less than 40.

You will now learn a bit more about truth-valued expressions.

5.2 Boolean expressions

You are already familiar with *integer expressions*, for example:

    (a + 5) * 7;

They evaluate to an integer value, such as -5, 0, 1, 42 …

Clearly there are many possible values for integer expressions.

A *boolean expression* is one which evaluates to a *boolean* value.

Boolean values

There are only two possible values for boolean expressions: *true* and *false***.**

Relational operators

You can construct simple boolean expressions from the *relational operators,* which are as follows

<	less than	5 < 6
>	greater than	m > n
<=	less than or equal	5 <= (a+1)
>=	greater than or equal	a >= 7
==	equals	(a+1) == (b+1)
!=	not equals	5 != 6

As you can see, the operands for the relational operators are numerical expressions. Character values may also be used, as these are represented as 16-bit ISO Unicode numbers. For example ('a' < 'b') is true and ('4' > '3') is false.

Consider the following expression:

    (((2 * 5) / (18 − 15)) * 2) >= ((120 / 25) − (63 % 2))

What is the boolean value?

The answer is: *true*: however complex the operands, the only possible values that a boolean expression can take are *true* and *false*. Here, the expression evaluates to 6 >= 3, which is true.

Operator precedence

As you saw earlier, precedence determines the order in which operations are evaluated.

For example, in the expression

2 + 3 * 4

you evaluate 3 * 4 first, then add the result to 2. This gives a final value of 14. You do this because '*' has a higher *precedence* than '+'.

If you want to override the default precedence, you must use brackets; for example:

(2 + 3) * 4

This gives a final value of 20 as you now evaluate 2 + 3, then multiply the result by 4.

Here is the order of precedence (from highest to lowest) of the operators you have been using:

Operator precedence

1	( )				
2	*	/	%		
3	+	−			
4	<	<=	=	>=	>	!=

If two operators are at the same level of precedence, then they are evaluated from left to right, for example the expression:

3 * 2 / 4

evaluates to 1, not to 0.

To make explicit the implicit evaluation order, we could add brackets to:

count + 6 < 8 * b

to give:

(count + 6) < (8 * b)

5.3 The if-else statement – the details

The syntax of the Java *if-else* statement is as follows:

```
if (<TEST>)
    <STATEMENT S1>
else
    <STATEMENT S2>
```

if and **else** are Java *reserved words*, which give the *if-else* statement its structure and tell the compiler that this is an *if-else* statement.

- <TEST> is a boolean expression. Note that this must be enclosed in parentheses **(** and **)**.
- <STATEMENT S1> is any Java statement
- <STATEMENT S2> is any Java statement

Semantics of the if-else statement

When the Java Virtual Machine comes to an if-else statement, the first thing that happens is that <TEST> is evaluated.

If <TEST> has the value *true*, then <STATEMENT S1> is executed;

if <TEST> has the value *false*, then <STATEMENT S2> is executed.

Take a look at the following if-else statement; can you think of alternative Java code to this?

```
if (x > y)
        x = 5;
else
        x = 5;
```

We can see that whatever the value of the boolean expression (x > y) (i.e. *true* or *false*), the same statement is carried out; therefore, there is no need for the if-else statement at all – a simple assignment does the same job. So: x = 5; is equivalent to the above if-else statement.

Comparing numbers

Write a program that inputs two values from the user and prints out the larger.

> **Plan (pseudocode)**
> **Input 2 values from the user**
>
> **IF   the first is largest**
>   **Print the first.**
> **ELSE**
>   **Print the second.**

Purchase program, revisited

Modify the 'purchase' program from Chapter 4 so that, if the sum tendered is less than the purchase price, it prints a message saying 'More money needed: purchase price is X; you must tender at least Y pence more'.

5.4 Compound statements

By default, each branch of an if-else statement contains just one statement to be executed. But suppose you wish to use a char variable to record whether or not a student has passed an exam and also to output a consolation message if the student has failed. This means you will need to develop a branch containing more than one statement. To do this, curly brackets are needed around the group of statements in such a branch. The curly brackets cause the system to treat the group of statements as if they were one statement in the logical structure of the if-else statement. Such a group of statements is often called a *compound statement*.

The relevant code for the student pass/fail and message program might look like this:

```
char result;

if (mark >= 40)
    result = 'P';
else
{
    result = 'F';
    System.out.println("Try again!");
}
```

In the above fragment, if the test

```
(mark >= 40)
```

is *true*, then the single statement

```
result = 'P';
```

is executed. If the test is *false*, then the next two statements are executed:

```
result = 'F';
```

```
System.out.println("Try again!");
```

Consider the following code fragment: what are the values of the variables a, b and c after the code has executed?

```
int mark = 25;
int a = 6;
int b = 4;
int c = 5;

if (mark < 40)
    a = b;
else
    a = c;
    b = c;
```

At first sight, you might imagine the answer to be:

> a has the value 4
> b has the value 4
> c has the value 5.

But this is not the case...

The layout suggests that the statements

    a = c;
    b = c;

are associated with the *else* part, but closer inspection reveals that there are no brackets around these two statements, which means that only the statement

    a = c;

is in the *else* part, and the statement

    b = c;

is simply the next statement in the sequence, and will therefore be executed every time.

The correct answer is therefore:

    a has the value 4
    b has the value 5
    c has the value 5

5.5 Nested *if-else* statements

It is important to realise that the statement or statements in each branch of an *if-else* statement can be any valid Java statements, including other *if-else* statements.

For example, assume that you want to write a program which accepts an exam mark (percentage) from the user, and writes out the grade corresponding to that mark. Say that the grades to be apportioned are as follows:

    A: Greater than 69%
    B: Greater than 59% and less than 70%
    C: Greater than 49% and less than 60%
    D: Greater than 39% and less than 50%
    E: Greater than 34% and less than 40%
    F: less than 35%

The Plan
Get a mark from the user.

    IF the mark is greater than 69
         The grade is A.
    ELSE
         IF the mark is greater than 59
              The grade is B.
         ELSE
              IF the mark is greater than 49
                   The grade is C.
              ELSE
                   IF the mark is greater than 39
                        The grade is D.
                   ELSE
                        IF the mark is greater than 34
                             The grade is E.
                        ELSE
                             The grade is F.

The plan can be translated into Java as follows:

```
int mark;
char grade;

<CODE TO READ IN A MARK>

if (mark > 69)
   grade = 'A';
else
   if (mark > 59)
      grade = 'B';
   else
      if (mark > 49)
         grade = 'C';
      else
         if (mark > 39)
            grade = 'D';
         else
            if (mark > 34)
               grade = 'E';
            else
               grade = 'F';
```

The structure of the above is an if-else statement, whose 'else' part is itself an if-else statement, whose 'else' part is an if-else statement, and so on. There is no else-if statement in Java – although you may have come across such statements in other programming languages.

Nesting layout

Note how the above layout 'creeps' across the page! An alternative way of laying out nested if-else statements, which is sometimes clearer, is as follows:

```
if (mark > 69)
      grade = 'A';
else if (mark > 59)
      grade = 'B';
else if (mark > 49)
      grade = 'C';
else if (mark > 39)
      grade = 'D';
else if (mark > 34)
      grade = 'E';
else
      grade = 'F';
```

With programs that contain control structures such as if-else statements, it is important to employ consistent rules of layout, to make the logical structure of the program clear to the human reader. This is particularly important where control structures are nested *within* other control structures, as in the above example.

Pause for a moment to consider which of the two programs – shown above and on the next page – is the easier to read, and why this is so.

```
if (mark > 69
)  grade = 'A'; else if (mark > 59) grade = 'B';
else
if
(mark > 49)
grade = 'C';
else if (
mark > 39)  grade = 'D';    else if (mark
> 34)
grade = 'E';
else grade
= 'F';
```

To the compiler, either version is perfectly acceptable – but to a person who has to understand and/or modify the program, the former is obviously preferable!

Layout of if-else statements

- Line up the reserved words *if* and *else* one above the other
- Indent the statements in each branch by the same amount
- With nested ifs, use a consistent indentation style, shown earlier
- Put a blank line before and after each if-else statement to make it clear where it begins and ends.

Activity 5.3

Purchase program, revisited revisited!

Modify the program from Activity 5.2 so that, if the exact price is tendered, a message is printed saying 'Thank you! Exact amount tendered.'

5.6 Scope of variables

You have been asked to write a program which inputs two integer values, then stores the larger in variable 'largerValue' and the smaller in variable 'smallerValue'.

Plan (pseudocode)
1.   Input value 1 into a
2.   Input value 2 into b

3.   IF a is the larger
          leave them alone
       ELSE
          swap them round

Here is the Java solution

```java
public static void largeSmall ()
{
    int largerValue, smallerValue;
    String numStr;

    // Get the numbers

    numStr = JOptionPane.showInputDialog("First Integer?: ");
    largerValue = Integer.parseInt(numStr);

    numStr = JOptionPane.showInputDialog("Second Integer?: ");
    smallerValue = Integer.parseInt(numStr);

    if (largerValue > smallerValue)
        JOptionPane.showMessageDialog(null,
            "Values were already in correct variables");
    else  //swap them round
    {
        int temp;
        temp = largerValue;
        largerValue = smallerValue;
        smallerValue = temp;
        JOptionPane.showMessageDialog(null,
            "Values have been moved into correct variables");
    }
}
```

The idea of swapping the values of two variables using a third variable for temporary storage should be familiar from Chapter 3.

The new thing about the above code is the *declaration* of the variable *temp*. This variable can be accessed (i.e. assigned to, printed, used in expressions or be referred to in any way by name) only within the enclosing brackets **{** and **}** in the else part of the if-else statement.

Local declarations

- You can make local declarations within any pair of curly brackets **{** and **}**
- Such variables only exist within the brackets. This area of the program code within which a variable exists is called its *scope*
- A variable cannot be accessed outside its scope.

Declaring variables locally is a *good thing*. It prevents the value of the variable being changed by mistake elsewhere in the program. One does not have to read through lots of code to check where the variable might be changed, which makes debugging the program much easier. You can even use the same name for more than one variable, as long as they are not in the same method, although this is not necessarily a good idea, as it could confuse the human reader.

Scope of variables

Try dry running the following program and then, when possible, run it on a computer. Try to establish the rules of scope by experimenting with the program.

```java
// Experiment with variable scope

import javax.swing.JOptionPane;

public class Scope
{
   public static int b = 25;
   // This is a class variable.
   // It is not declared in the body of any methods.
   // What do you think its scope will be?

   public static void doStuff()
   {
      int a = 3;

      if (a > b)
         JOptionPane.showMessageDialog(
            null, a + " is larger than " + b);
      else
         JOptionPane.showMessageDialog(
            null,  a + " is smaller than " + b);
   }


   public static void main(String[] args)
   {
      int a = 15;
      int b = 2;

      doStuff();

      System.exit(0);
   }

}
```

Comparing numbers, revisited

Modify the program of Activity 5.1 to produce a program which reads in three numbers, and prints out the value of the biggest and the smallest.

5.7 The logical connectives

Problem

A student must pass both the coursework and the examination to pass a module. The pass mark for each is 40%. Write a program to input the two marks and say whether or not the student passed.

A plan
Input the 2 marks

```
IF (mark1 > 40)
    IF (mark2 > 40)
        Pass
    ELSE
        Fail
ELSE
    Fail
```

A different plan
Input the 2 marks

```
IF (mark1 > 40) AND (mark2 > 40)
    Pass
ELSE
    Fail
```

Note that the first plan utilises two simple tests and a more complex (nested) control structure, whereas the second plan utilises a more complex test with a simple (non-nested) control structure.

Here is a Java version of the second plan.

```
if ((mark1 > 40) && (mark2 > 40))
    System.out.println("Passed");
else
    System.out.println("Failed");
```

The symbol && is an example of a *logical connective*.

Logical connectives are used to combine boolean expressions to make larger boolean expressions.

Java logical connectives

Let p and q be any boolean expressions.

&&   **AND**   p&&q is true if and only if p is true and q is true.
|| **OR**   p||q is true if p or q or both are true.

(In other words, p || q is only false if both p *and* q are false.)

!   **NOT**   !p is true if p is false, and vice versa.

Here is the table of operator precedences again, with the logical connectives included:

Operator precedence

1	()				
2	!				
3	*	/	%		
4	+	-			
5	<	<=	>	>=	==
6	++	!=			
7	&&				
8	||				

Consider the following declarations:

```
int a = 3;
int b = 4;
int c = 5;
```

Without looking at the answer shown at the top of the next page, work out what the values of the following expressions would be, using the above declarations.

1   (a <= l) && (b > 3)

2   (a == l) || (b >= 5)

3   !(a == l) && (b > a)

4   !((a < c) && ((b >= c) || !(a == b)))

You should have come up with answers of false, false, true and false, in that order.

Activity 5.6

Dry run exercises with if-else statements

Part 1: Dry run the following method when:

a the user types 6, then 3

b the user types 5, then 7

```java
public static void main(String[] args)
{
    String first, second;
    int a;                                              // L1
    int b;                                              // L2
    int t;                                              // L3

    first =  JOptionPane.showInputDialog("First number?");       // L4
    second =  JOptionPane.showInputDialog("Second number?");// L5
    a = Integer.parseInt(first);                        // L6
    b = Integer.parseInt(second);                       // L7

    if (a > b)                                          // L8
        JOptionPane.showMessageDialog(null,"No swap");
    else
    {
        JOptionPane.showMessageDialog(null, "Swap");
        t = a;                                          // L9
        a = b;                                          // L10
        b = t;                                          // L11
    }

    JOptionPane.showMessageDialog(null,"Larger is " + a);    // L12

    JOptionPane.showMessageDialog(null, "Smaller is " + b);

    System.exit(0);

}
```

... continued

Part 2: With nested *if* statements it is sometimes hard to tell which 'else' is related to which 'if'.

The golden rule is:

> An 'else' is linked to the closest preceding 'if' *that does not already have an 'else' associated with it*.

Dry run the following method. Then try running the program and playing with it. The changes in output are dependent upon the values held in x and y.

```java
public static void main(String[] args)
{
    int x = 2;                                          //L1
    int y = 3;                                          //L2

    if (x == 2)                                         //L3
        if (y == 1)                                     //L4
            JOptionPane.showMessageDialog(null, "FIRST");
        else
            JOptionPane.showMessageDialog(null, "FINAL");
    else
        JOptionPane.showMessageDialog(null, "SING");

    JOptionPane.showMessageDialog(null, "SONG");

    x = 2;                                              //L5
    y = 1;                                              //L6

    if (x == 2)                                         //L7
        if (y == 1)                                     //L8
            JOptionPane.showMessageDialog(null, "FIRST");
        else
            JOptionPane.showMessageDialog(null, "FINAL");
    else
        JOptionPane.showMessageDialog(null, "SING");

    JOptionPane.showMessageDialog(null, "SONG");

    x = 1;                                              //L9
    y = 3;                                              //L10

    if (x == 2)                                         //L11
        if (y == 1)                                     //L12
            JOptionPane.showMessageDialog(null, "FIRST");
        else
            JOptionPane.showMessageDialog(null, "FINAL");
    else
        JOptionPane.showMessageDialog(null, "SING");

    JOptionPane.showMessageDialog(null, "SONG");
}
```

5.8 Summary

- An if-else statement is used where a program must decide between two groups of statements
- Either the true branch or the false branch is executed depending on the value of a test
- The test is a boolean expression
- Simple boolean expressions are made from relational operators
- More complex boolean expressions may be constructed by using the boolean connectives &&, || and !. The logical connectives often remove the need for the nesting of if-else statements
- If a branch of an if-else statement contains more than one statement, then the statements in that branch must be surrounded by curly brackets {}
- If-else statements may be nested; layout is then very important
- Local declarations can be made within compound statements.

5.9 Review questions

Question 5.1   Explain what is meant by:

1   An identifier

2   A boolean expression

3   An if-else statement.

Question 5.2   Explain what the following fragment of code does, assuming the variables concerned have been previously declared and initialised.

```
max = x;
if (y > x)
{
  max = y;
}
```

Question 5.3   'All comments are useful.' Discuss the truth or otherwise of this statement.

Question 5.4   Explain the terms:

1   semantic error

2   syntax error

3   type error

Question 5.5   Which of these errors can the compiler detect: *semantic*, *syntax* or *type*?

Question 5.6 Write out what is printed to screen when the code fragment below is executed:

1 if score has a value of 30?

2 if score has a value of 87?

```
if (score >= 60)
    JOptionPane.showMessageDialog(null,
        "You go through to the next round");
else
    JOptionPane.showMessageDialog(null, "Tough luck");

    JOptionPane.showMessageDialog(null, "You're out of the game");
```

Question 5.7 'Indentation improves programs.' Discuss the truth or otherwise of this statement.

Question 5.8 What does the following fragment do if x is 1 and y is 3?

```
if (x == 1)
    if (y == 2)
        System.out.println("CAMPUS ");
    else
        System.out.println("WORLD ");
else
    System.out.println("SHOOT ");
    System.out.println("WIDE");
```

Question 5.9 Modify the fragment of Question 5.8 so that WIDE is printed only when SHOOT is printed.

Question 5.10 Answer *true* or *false* to each of the following questions:

1 The value of the expression (x = x) is true.

2 The expression:

$$((x >= 5) \text{ \&\& } (y < 8)) \text{ || } ((z == 6)$$

has the same value as the expression:

$$x >= 5 \text{ \&\& } y < 8 \text{ || } z == 6$$

3 If x and y are ints, the expression below is a valid boolean expression which states that x and y are both greater than 6.

$$x \text{ \&\& } y > 6$$

4 Local variables may be declared within any pair of matching curly braces { and }.

5 In the if-else statement

```java
if (x == 1)
{
    if (y == 2)
        System.out.println("CAMPUS ");
    else
        System.out.println("WORLD ");
}
else
{
    System.out.println("SHOOT ");
    System.out.println("WIDE");
}
```

the *first set* of curly brackets is essential to preserve the semantics (meaning) of the code.

6 In the if-else statement

```java
if (x == 1)
{
    if (y == 2)
        System.out.println("CAMPUS ");
    else
        System.out.println("WORLD ");
}
else
{
    System.out.println("SHOOT ");
    System.out.println("WIDE");
}
```

the *second set* of curly brackets is essential to preserve the semantics (meaning) of the code.

7 The following program fragment contains no errors.

```java
if (x == 1)
{
    int z = 4;
    System.out.println("Hello ");
}
else
{
    z = 3;
    System.out.println("Goodbye");
{
```

8 The following program fragment contains no errors.

```
public class test
{
    public static int z = 8;      // Note class variable

    public static void main(String[] args)
    {
      if (z == 8)
      {
        int z = 4;
        System.out.println("z has the value " + z);
      }
      else
      {
        z = 3;
        System.out.println("z has the value " + z);
      }
    }
}
```

5.10 **Answers to review questions**

Question 5.1

1 An identifier – the name of a variable, class or method. Note rules of construction (must not start with a digit, etc).

2 A boolean expression – a truth-valued expression, often using relational operators (>, <, >= etc) and boolean connectives.

3 An if-else statement – control structure implementing the concept of choice between groups of statements to execute based upon the value of a boolean expression.

Question 5.2   The fragment of code will copy the contents of the larger of variables x and y into the variable max.

Question 5.3   'All comments are useful' – well, no. Comments are used to supplement the source code with appropriate explanation. They can tell the reader when the program was written and modified, and by whom. They can explain particularly complex pieces of code. They should be used to state the purpose of each method. But if there are too many comments, they can obscure the code, and they should not be used to state the obvious.

Question 5.4

1 Semantic error – an error in the logic of the algorithm.

2 Syntax error – an error in the spelling/grammar/punctuation of the program.

3 Type error – an error in the type of an expression; incompatible types.

Question 5.5 The compiler can detect syntax errors and some type errors. It cannot detect semantic errors.

Question 5.6

1 If score has a value of 30?

Dialog box with 'Tough luck'
Followed by dialog box with 'You're out of the game'.

2 If score has a value of 87?

Dialog box with 'You go through to the next round'
Followed by dialog box with 'You're out of the game'.

Note: this is probably not what the programmer intended!

Question 5.7 'Indentation improves programs' – sure does! Good layout of programs is the single most important aid to the readability of the code. It becomes more and more important as the complexity of the code increases.

Question 5.8 Prints

```
WORLD
WIDE
```

Question 5.9

```
if (x == 1)
   if (y == 2)
      System.out.println("CAMPUS ");
   else
      System.out.println("WORLD ");
else
{
   System.out.println("SHOOT ");
   System.out.println("WIDE");
}
```

Question 5.10

1 False – This is not a boolean expression, but an assignment statement, assigning the value of x to x. The expression $(x == x)$ is a boolean expression with the value *true*.

2 True – The brackets are not needed due to the precedence of the operators involved.

3 False – This is not a correctly formed boolean expression. The operands to && must themselves be boolean expressions. The first operand, x, is simply an int, which is not a boolean expression. The correct expression is: (x>6) && (y>6).

4 True – such variables only exist within the innermost **{** and **}** which enclose them.

5 **False** – The 'true' branch of the enclosing if-else statement only contains one statement (albeit this is, itself, an if-else statement). Therefore, the first set of curly brackets can be removed without changing the meaning of the code fragment.

6 **True** – The 'false' branch of the enclosing if-else statement contains two statements. If the second set of curly brackets were removed, then the statement

   System.out.println("WIDE");

would no longer be associated with the 'false' branch.

7 **False** – The variable z is declared within the first set of curly brackets, and only exists within those brackets. Therefore, you cannot make an assignment to z within the second set of curly brackets (or anywhere else in the program).

8 **True** – The z referred to in the if-else test, and in the second set of curly brackets, is the z globally declared in line 1. However, the z referred to in the first set of curly brackets is the z declared within those brackets. The local declaration overrides the more global declaration. This means that the global z cannot be accessed within the first set of brackets after the declaration of the local z. The program prints 'z has the value 4'.

5.11 Feedback on activities

Activity 5.1: Comparing numbers. Here is a solution.

```java
// Inputs two integers and prints out the larger

import javax.swing.JOptionPane;

public class CompareNums
{

    public static void findBigger()
    {
        int num1, num2;   String numStr;

        numStr = JOptionPane.showInputDialog("Enter first number: ");
        num1 = Integer.parseInt(numStr);

        numStr = JOptionPane.showInputDialog(
            "Enter second number: ");
        num2 = Integer.parseInt(numStr);

        if (num1 > num2)
            JOptionPane.showMessageDialog(null,
                "Largest number is " + num1);
        else
            JOptionPane.showMessageDialog(null,
                "Largest number is " + num2);

    }
```

```
        public static void main(String[] args)
        {
          findBigger();

          System.exit(0);
        }
      }
```

Note that if the two numbers are the same, then the value printed will be that stored in the second variable. Of course, in this example, either variable would do.

Activity 5.2: Purchase program revisited   The core of your program should have been an if-else statement something like this:

```
    if (tendered < price)
      JOptionPane.showMessageDialog(null,
        "More money needed: Price is " + price +
        " ; You must tender at least " +
        (price – tendered) + " pence more.");
    else
      JOptionPane.showMessageDialog(null,
        "Your change is " + (tendered – price) );
```

Note that if the buyer tenders the exact amount required, the program outputs

Your change is 0

which is not really satisfactory. See the next activity.

Activity 5.3: Purchase program revisited revisited!   To deal with the extra case of the exact amount being tendered, the core of your program could be something like this:

```
    if (tendered < price)
      JOptionPane.showMessageDialog(null,
        "More money needed: Price is " + price +
        " ; You must tender at least " +
        (price – tendered) + " pence more.");
    else if (tendered == price)
      JOptionPane.showMessageDialog(null,
        "Thank you! Exact amount tendered! ");
    else
      JOptionPane.showMessageDialog(null,
        "Your change is " + (tendered – price) );
```

Here you have an if-else statement nested within the else part of an if-else statement. The best way to lay out such structures is as above.

Activity 5.4 : Scope of variables   The output from the program is:

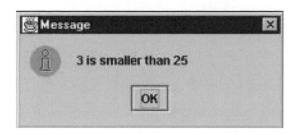

Note that the variables *a* and *b* declared in *main()* only exist in *main()*.

Therefore the value of *b* used in method *doStuff()* is that of the class variable *b*, which is declared in the class but not within any method and therefore has *global* scope within the class. In other words, its scope is the whole of the class including all the methods. (Note the words *public static* prefixing this declaration. These will be discussed further in Chapter 11.)

The value of *a* used within *doStuff()* is that of the variable *a* declared in *doStuff()*.

Activity 5.5 : Comparing numbers revisited   Here is a method to do the task.

```
public static void findBiggestAndSmallest()
{
   int num1, num2, num3;
   String numStr;

   numStr = JOptionPane.showInputDialog("Enter first number: " );
   num1 = Integer.parseInt(numStr);

   numStr = JOptionPane.showInputDialog("Enter second number: " );
   num2 = Integer.parseInt(numStr);

   numStr = JOptionPane.showInputDialog("Enter third number: " );
   num3 = Integer.parseInt(numStr);

   if ((num1 > num2) && (num1 > num3))
   // i.e.  num1 is the largest
   {
      JOptionPane.showMessageDialog(null,"Largest is " + num1);

      if (num2 < num3)
        JOptionPane.showMessageDialog(null,"Smallest is " + num2);
      else
        JOptionPane.showMessageDialog(null,"Smallest is " + num3);
   }
```

```
        else if (num2 > num3)
        // num2 is the largest
        {
           JOptionPane.showMessageDialog(null,"Largest is " + num2);

           if (num1 < num3)
             JOptionPane.showMessageDialog(null,"Smallest is " + num1);
           else
             JOptionPane.showMessageDialog(null,"Smallest is " + num3);
        }
        else // num3 must be the largest
        {
           JOptionPane.showMessageDialog(null,"Largest is " + num3);

           if (num1 < num2)
             JOptionPane.showMessageDialog(null,"Smallest is " + num1);
           else
             JOptionPane.showMessageDialog(null,"Smallest is " + num2);
        }
     }
```

Activity 5.6: Dry run exercises with if-else statements

Part 1   The user types the number **6,** then **3**. You should have come up with a table something like this:

After	first	second	a	b	t	(a > b)
LINE 1	U	U	U			
LINE 2	U	U	U	U		
LINE 3	U	U	U	U	U	
LINE 4	"6"	U	U	U	U	
LINE 5	"6"	"3"	U	U	U	
LINE 6	"6"	"3"	6	U	U	
LINE 7	"6"	"3"	6	3	U	
LINE 8	"6"	"3"	6	3	U	true
…						
LINE12	"6"	"3"	6	3	U	

Note that you now have a column for the value of the test on line 8, which determines which branch of the if-else statement is to be executed.

As before, note that U is used to indicate that a variable exists, but its value is undefined. Where there is no value shown for a variable, this indicates that the variable has not yet been declared, so it doesn't yet exist.

You can do a similar table for the second run, and the results are as follows:

First run:

Program outputs
No swap
Largest is 6
Smallest is 3

Second run:

Program outputs:
Swap
Largest is 7
Smallest is 5

Part 2:   Prints successive dialog boxes with content as follows:

FINAL
SONG
FIRST
SONG
SING
SONG

CHAPTER 6

Repetition using loops

OVERVIEW

Now you know how to write programs in which choices can be made between executing alternative sequences of statements. Such programs are useful, but limited. What makes computers powerful is the ability to execute many instructions in a very short time. In this chapter, you will learn about control structures called *loops*, which allow your programs to exploit this ability. This will let you write more sophisticated and useful programs, which fully utilise the power of the underlying hardware.

Learning outcomes On completion of this chapter you should be able to:

- Explain how repetition can be implemented in programming languages

- Recognise when repetition constructs are needed to solve programming problems

- Write programs using the *while* repetition construct of Java

- Analyse what a program containing loops does, by dry running it

- Identify and correct errors (both compile-time and run-time) in programs containing loops

- Explain what is meant by a structured program.

6.1 A problem

Write a method to output the following statement to the screen 100 times: 'I must practise my programming':

Plan (pseudocode)
Set a counter to 1

WHILE the counter is <= 100
    Print the important information
    Add 1 to the counter

To implement the plan in Java, you need to convert the above instructions into the equivalent Java instructions. As with the if-else statement example in the last chapter, this is not necessarily a one-to-one mapping. For instance, you need to be specific about what you mean by a *counter.* In Java, this will be an int type variable, which must be declared before it can be used.

Here is the Java method:

```
public static void lines()
{
    int counter;
    counter = 1;

    while (count <= 10)
    {
        System.out.println("I must practise my programming");
        counter = counter + 1;
    }
}
```

The above method contains an example of a Java *while loop*. You will notice that the syntax of the Java while loop is very similar to the pseudocode example above, and to the 'heating up the oil' example from Chapter 2.

Can you, however, notice anything wrong with the while loop in this example? Consider it for a moment, and then read on.

The while loop statement – the details

The syntax of the Java *while loop* statement is as follows:

while (<TEST>)

    <STATEMENT>

- **while** is a Java *reserved word*, which tells the compiler that this is a *while loop* statement
- <TEST> is a boolean expression. Note that this must be enclosed in parentheses **(** and **)**.
- <STATEMENT> is any Java statement. This is known as the *body* of the loop
- Note that <STATEMENT> can be, and indeed usually is, a compound statement; in other words, several Java statements surrounded by **{** and **}**.

Semantics of the while loop statement

When the Java Virtual Machine comes to a while loop statement, the first thing that happens is that <TEST> is evaluated. If <TEST> has the value *false*, then <STATEMENT> is not executed, and control passes to the next statement in the program following the while loop. If <TEST> has the value *true*, then <STATEMENT> is executed. <TEST> is then evaluated again, and if it is still *true*, then <STATEMENT> is executed again. This cycle of evaluating <TEST> and executing <STATEMENT> continues until <TEST> evaluates to *false*.

In the above program we have two errors. There is a syntax error; the variable *counter* is called *count* in the loop test. There is also a semantic error; the test becomes false when the value of *counter* is greater than 10. The loop is supposed to iterate 100 times.

6.2 Counter-controlled loops

As in the above example, loops often use some form of counter variable (also called a *control variable*) to determine how many times the loop should be executed.

This counter must be *initialised* (given a starting value) before the loop is entered; for example:

```
int counter;
counter = 1;
```

A counter declaration and initialisation assignment can be combined; for example:

```
int counter = 1;
```

Counter-control is one of several common patterns of usage for loops.

The counter-control pattern

```
counter = <start value>;

while (counter <= <finish value>)
{
   <instructions to be repeated>
   counter = counter + <increment>;
}
```
... where <start value>, <finish value> and <increment> are numbers chosen to suit the particular application.

The loop is executed a fixed number of times, controlled by the counter variable.

Often, we simply want the counter to count the iterations of the loop, in which case:

- <start value> can be 1
- <finish value> can be the number of times we want the loop to iterate
- <increment> can be 1.

```
while (counter <= <number of repetitions>)
{
   <instructions to be repeated>
   counter = counter + 1;
}
```

Example

Write Java statements to print the sum of the numbers from 0 up to n, where n is input by the user.

Plan
Initialise total and counter to 0
Get n from the user

WHILE the counter is <= n
   update the total
   add 1 to counter

Print total

This is a good time to introduce the *increment operator* **++**. The variable *counter* is to be increased by 1 on each iteration of the loop. We can do this with the assignment

```
counter = counter + 1;
```

but it is neater and clearer to use the operator + + like this

```
counter++;
```

This has the same effect (i.e. adds 1 to *counter*). There is also a *decrement operator*, **–**, to subtract 1 from a variable; it looks like this.

```
counter - -;
```

Here is the completed Java implementation of the plan:

```
int counter = 0;
int total = 0;

String numString;

numStr = JOptionPane.showInputDialog("Enter a value for n:" );
int n = Integer.parseInt(numStr);

while (counter <= n)
{
   total += counter;
   counter++;
}
JOptionPane.showMessageDialog(null,"Sum to " + n + " is " + total);
```

Note the use of **+ =** in the above program. This operator is another convenient shorthand for a common pattern of assignment.

```
total += counter;
```

is equivalent to

```
total = total + counter;
```

Similar shorthand assignment operators can be used for the other arithmetic operators as follows:

```
-=
*=
/=
%=
```

Pause for a moment and consider what would happen if the user typed the number –1 in response to the prompt in the above program segment.

Remember how the while loop works: the test is done first, and the loop body statement(s) are only executed if the test has the value *true*.

The first time the test is done in the above example, the boolean expression is

$(0 <= -1)$

This clearly has the value *false*, which means that the loop body is not executed, and total remains at 0.

Now pause to consider how many times, in general, the loop body will be executed.

Clearly, if n is less than 0, the loop body will not execute at all. Otherwise we can establish a pattern:

If n = 0, the loop executes once

If n = 1, the loop executes twice

etc.

Therefore, in general, the loop executes n + 1 times for all values of n >= 0.

Finally, ask yourself if the code would work properly if *counter* was initialised to 1 instead of 0.

You probably realised that the loop body would not execute at all if n was 0 (leaving total at 0, as it should be), and would execute n times if n was greater than 0, so it would, therefore, work correctly.

Example

Write Java statements to print a line of *n* stars in the command window.

Plan
Initialise counter to 1

WHILE the counter is <= n
    print a star
    add 1 to counter

The Java implementation of the plan is shown here.

```
String numStr;

numStr = JOptionPane.showInputDialog("How many stars?");
int n = Integer.parseInt(numStr);

int counter = 1;
```

```
while (counter <= n)
{
  System.out.print("*");
  counter++;
}
```

Factorial

Write a program to calculate n! (n factorial) which is defined as follows:

$$0! = 1$$
$$n > 0: n! = 1 \times 2 \times 3 \times \ldots \times (n - 1) \times n$$

where n is any non-negative whole number.

The Fibonnaci series

The Fibonnaci series is as follows:

1, 1, 2, 3, 5, 8, 13, 21, 34, . . .

Can you see how each successive number is generated? After the first two numbers, each number is the sum of the two previous numbers.

This series is unusual in that it can be used to describe natural phenomena, such as predicting the growth of rabbit populations, and the optimal angular displacement of plant leaves for maximising incident light.

Write a program to compute the *n*th term in the series.

Temperature conversion table

Remember the temperature conversion program from Chapter 3? Extend it to print a table of Celsius temperatures and their equivalent Fahrenheit temperatures from –10 Celsius to +10 Celsius inclusive.

6.3 Sentinel-controlled loops

Counter-control is one common form of loop usage. Another is the *sentinel-controlled* loop. This form is used when we want the program to input a series of data items, but the number of items is not known in advance. On each repetition of the loop, a value is input. The repetition stops when a particular value is input, which we must test for in the loop test. Clearly this data item cannot be a valid part of the input data; it is used only to indicate the end of the input. For this reason, this special-purpose data item is often called the *sentinel* value.

The sentinel-control pattern

```
<get valueInput>

while (valueInput != sentinelValue)
{
  <manipulate valueInput>
  <get next valueInput>
}
```

The program should prompt the user to let him/her know what sentinel value must be entered to indicate the end of the input.

The sentinel value may be declared as a constant using keyword *final*.

Problem

Write a method that adds a series of numbers input by the user. It is not known in advance how many values will be input, but it is known that zero cannot be one of the numbers. Therefore zero can be used as the sentinel to indicate the end of input.

Plan

```
Initialise total to 0
Input a number

WHILE the number is not zero
    update the total
    input a new number

Print out the total.
```

Implementation in Java

```java
public static void addSeries()
{
    final int SENTINEL = 0;
    int latestNum;
    int total = 0;
    String numStr;

    JOptionPane.showMessageDialog(null,
      "Enter positive numbers, -1 to end: " );

    numStr = JOptionPane.showInputDialog("First number?  " );
    // convert from String to int
    latestNum = Integer.parseInt(numStr);

    while (latestNum != SENTINEL)
    {
        total = total + latestNum;
        numStr = JOptionPane.showInputDialog("Next number?");
        latestNum = Integer.parseInt(numStr);
    }

    JOptionPane.showMessageDialog(null,"Total is "  + total);
}
```

6.4 Dry running programs containing loops

The technique of dry running can be particularly useful for understanding and/or debugging programs containing loops.

Look at the technique using the following Java method, which is a cut-down version of the above method with line numbers added.

```
public static void addseries2()
{
    final int SENTINEL = 0;                                      // LINE L1
    int latestNum;                                               // LINE L2
    int total = 0;                                               // LINE L3
    String str;                                                  // LINE L4
    str = JOptionPane.showInputDialog("First number?");          // LINE L5
    latestNum = Integer.parseInt(str);                           // LINE L6

    while (latestNum != SENTINEL)                                // LINE L7
    {
        total = total + latestNum;                               // LINE L8
        str = JOptionPane.showInputDialog("Next number?");       // LINE L9
        latestNum = Integer.parseInt(str);                       // LINE L10
    }

    JOptionPane.showMessageDialog(null,"Total is: " + total);    // LINE L11
}
```

Suppose that the user types the sequence 3, 5, 2, 0 when asked for numbers by the program; construct the table in the usual way, with line numbers down the side and variable names/ tests across the top. The difference is that when a loop is executed, the lines containing the loop test and the loop body statements may be executed more than once.

Here is a table for the above data set.

After execution of line	SENTINEL	latestNum	total	(latestNum != SENTINEL) ?
L1	0	Not declared	Not declared	
L2	0	unknown	Not declared	
L3	0	unknown	0	
L6	0	3	0	
L7 (first time)	0	3	0	3 != 0 ? true
L8 (first time)	0	3	3	
L10 (first time)	0	5	3	
L7 (second time)	0	5	3	5 != 0 ? true
L8 (second time)	0	5	8	
L10 (second time)	0	2	8	
L7 (third time)	0	2	8	2 != 0 ? true
L8 (third time)	0	2	10	
L10 (third time)	0	0	10	
L7 (fourth time)	0	0	10	0 != 0 ? false
L11	0	0	10	

When the program runs, input dialog boxes with the following contents appear:

First number: 3
Next number: 5
Next number: 2
Next number: 0

Followed by the message dialog box:

Total is 10

Activity 6.4

Dry running programs with loops

Dry run the *addSeries2()* method when the user types just the number 0.

6.5 More complex loop tests

Sometimes you may want to include more than one condition in your loop tests. In such cases, you can use boolean connectives (&& and ||) to construct more complex loop tests.

As an example, let us consider the *Syracuse sequence*, which is generated as follows:

1 Think of a positive whole number.

2 If the number is even, halve it, otherwise triple it and add 1.

3 Repeat step 2 until the number is 1.

Depending upon the starting value, the sequence might be very long or very short, but it always ends up at 1 eventually.

Let us now look at a program to accept a number from the user, and generate the Syracuse sequence for that number – but remember your user gets bored if s/he sees a sequence of more than 10 numbers, so the program should stop if:

- The sequence finishes (reaches 1) *or*
- The sequence reaches 10 numbers.

```
public static void syracuse()
{
    int length = 0;  // Initially no numbers generated

    String str = JOptionPane.showInputDialog("Enter starting number?");

    int num = Integer.parseInt(str);

    while ((num != 1) && (length < 10))
    {
        if (num % 2 == 0) // num is even
            num = num / 2;
        else // num is odd
            num = 3 * num + 1;
```

```
            System.out.println("Next number is " + num);

            length++;
        }
    }
```

In this example the sign && (logical AND) is used to conjoin the two tests which determine whether or not the loop continues. In other words, the loop will stop if either or both of the tests are false.

This example also demonstrates the nesting of one control structure (the if-else statement) within another (the while loop). On each iteration of the loop, the if statement is executed to make the decision as to how to generate the next number in the sequence.

Activity 6.5

Guessing game

Write a method that asks the user to play a 'guess the number' game. The program accepts guesses from the user, and for each guess, reports whether the guess was too high, too low, or correct and stops when the guess is correct.

6.6 Control structures and structured programming

In our programs so far, assignment, input and output statements do the actual work.

Control structures determine the order in which those statements are executed (i.e. they govern the flow of control through the program).

It can be shown that all programs can be written using just three control structures:

- **Sequence:** statements executed one after the other, in order
- **Selection:** choosing between alternative groups of statements, such as using if-else
- **Repetition:** executing statements over and over, such as when using while.

In the next chapter, you will meet more Java control structures, but these are really variations of what you have already seen, and are used because they are sometimes more convenient, rather than because they are essential.

Note that in Java programs, of course, flow of program control is also determined by *method calls*.

Structured programming is a methodology for writing programs just using structure statements (i.e. variants of the three control structure types: sequence, selection and repetition).

In the early days of programming, languages did not contain these control structures. The only way of altering the flow of control was via arbitrary jump (goto) statements. A test was made, and depending on the truth value, control could be 'jumped' to a statement on another numbered line.

With this system, programmers were effectively making up their own control structures. While this was very flexible for the programmer, it meant that programs were difficult for other programmers to understand, debug and modify.

Even the programmer who wrote the program might not understand it a few weeks later! This so-called 'spaghetti programming' was clearly not a good way of doing things, but standard patterns of usage of the goto statements were emerging by consensus, and in the early 1960s these were encapsulated in the control structures we find in modern programming languages.

Object-oriented development

Structured programming is a good technique for writing single algorithms (methods).

Object-oriented software development builds on this by providing a way of modelling solutions to problems in a natural and intuitive way. The focus is on the 'objects' in the real-world system being modelled, and the ways in which they interact with each other. For example, a traffic simulation program might have car, lorry, motorbike, traffic light and roundabout objects. Object-oriented programming languages such as Java enable these models to be realised as final implementations. Such models enable us to put algorithms and data together to construct robust, easily maintainable software systems. You will learn more about this in Chapters 11 and 12.

6.7 Summary

- If you need to do something over and over again – use a while loop
- If you know in advance the number of times the loop is to be executed, use a counter-controlled loop
- Remember to initialise any counter variable you use
- If the number of repetitions is not known in advance, use a sentinel-controlled loop
- The sentinel value is used to indicate the end of the input data
- Structured programming involves using only variations of sequence, selection and repetition for program control (i.e. single-entry, single-exit control structures rather than simply jumps with goto)
- Object orientation is a means of analysing, designing and coding software systems which builds upon the fundamental structured programming concepts.

6.8 Review questions

Question 6.1   Fill in the blanks in the following:

1 In counter-controlled repetition a _____ is used to count the number of times a group of instructions should be repeated.

2 All programs can be written in terms of three control structures: _____, _____ and _____.

3 The _____ repetition structure specifies that a statement or group of statements is to be executed repeatedly while some condition remains true.

4 When it is not known in advance how many times a set of statements will be repeated, a _____ value can be used to terminate the repetition.

5 Specifying the execution order of statements executed by the computer is called _____ _____.

6 The _____ acts as a counter to determine when a loop terminates.

7 _____ is an informal language that combines English and structuring constructs.

Question 6.2   What, if anything, is wrong (note that there may be more than one mistake) with the following code fragments? Give a correct version.

1

```
while (c <= 5)
{
  product = product * 5;
  c = c + 1;
```

2

```
While (a != b)
{
  sum = sum + a;
  b = b + 2;
}
```

3

```
int x = 1;
int total;
while (x <= 10)
{
  total = total + x;
  x = x + 1;
}
```

4

```
while (x < 10)
{
  int x = 0;
  JOptionPane.showMessageDialog(null,"x " + x);
  x = x + 1;
}
```

5

```
while (x > 0)
{
  x = x - 1;
  JOptionPane.showMessageDialog(null,"x " + x)
}
```

Question 6.3   What type of loop control is demonstrated by the 'guess the number' program of Activity 6.5?

Question 6.4   Here is another version of the 'guess the number' program. What can you say about the statement commented XXX?

```
public static void guessyguessy()
{
    final int SECRETNUMBER = 75;

    String str = JOptionPane.showInputDialog("Guess the number?");
    int guess = Integer.parseInt(str);

    while (guess != SECRETNUMBER)
    {
        if (guess > SECRETNUMBER)
            JOptionPane.showMessageDialog(null,"Too high!");
        else if (guess < SECRETNUMBER)
            JOptionPane.showMessageDialog(null,"Too low!");
        else // The user guessed correctly!
            JOptionPane.showMessageDialog(null,"Correct!!!");     //XXX

        str = JOptionPane.showInputDialog("Try again");
        guess = Integer.parseInt(str);
    }
}
```

Question 6.5   How could the version of the 'guess' program in review question 6.4 be modified so that the user is informed of a correct guess within the loop body?

Question 6.6   Answer *true or false* to each of the following:

1 Executing a *while* loop is the same as executing its body a fixed number of times.

2 The most difficult part of solving a problem by computer is developing a correct algorithm. The process of producing a correct Java program is then normally straightforward.

3 The *while* statement executes its body at least once.

4 You can write any program using sequence, selection and repetition.

5 Dry running is a useful technique for understanding/ debugging programs containing loops.

6 The *while* statement is the only loop we need.

7 A *while* loop body is always executed before the *while* loop test is done.

8 The *while* loop test has the same type as the *if-else* statement test.

9 The *while* loop is introduced by the reserved word *WHILE*.

10 Sentinel loop control is appropriate where it is known in advance how many times the loop should iterate.

6.9 Answers to review questions

Question 6.1

1 control variable

2 sequence, selection and repetition.

3 while

4 sentinel

5 program control

6 control variable

7 pseudocode

Question 6.2

1 Missing end brace.

```
while (c <= 5)
{
  product = product * 5;
  c = c + 1;
}
```

2 *While* should be all lower case.

```
while (a != b)
{
  sum = sum + a;
  b = b + 2;
}
```

3 *total* must be initialised.

```
int x = 1;
int total = 0;
while (x <= 10)
{
  total = total + x;
  x = x + 1;
}
```

4 *x* should be declared and initialized outside the loop not in it.

```
int x = 0;
while (x < 10)
{
  JOptionPane.showMessageDialog(null,"x " + x);
  x = x + 1;
}
```

5 Missing semicolon:

```
while (x > 0)
{
  x = x - 1;
  JOptionPane.showMessageDialog(null,"x " + x);
}
```

Question 6.3   Sentinel control. The loop iterates until the correct number is guessed, which acts as sentinel to stop the loop.

Question 6.4   This statement will never be executed! There is a logic error in this version:

- If the user guesses correctly first time, the loop body will not be executed, and the user will not be told of their success before the program terminates

- If the user guesses correctly on any subsequent attempt, the statements accepting the guess are the last ones in the loop body. Therefore, the next thing to happen is the loop test. The test will be false, and again the loop body will not be executed and the only indication to the user of their success will be the termination of the program!

Question 6.5   You could initialise the guess to any incorrect value before entering the loop, which will ensure that the loop test is true first time and, therefore, the loop body executes. You could then change the order of the statements in the loop body, placing the input statements before the if-else statement, so that each 'real' guess (including the first one) is evaluated by the if-else structure and an appropriate response given.

When the user does guess correctly, the correct response is given, and the next loop test is false, ensuring that the loop is not re-entered. You do not need a further statement after the loop to tell the user of their success.

Here is this new version:

```
public static void guessyguessy()
{
    final int SECRETNUMBER = 75;
    int guess = SECRETNUMBER + 1; // incorrect guess

    String str;

    while (guess != SECRETNUMBER)
    {
        str = JOptionPane.showInputDialog("Have a guess");
        guess = Integer.parseInt(str);

        if (guess > SECRETNUMBER)
          JOptionPane.showMessageDialog(null,"Too high!");
        else if (guess < SECRETNUMBER)
          JOptionPane.showMessageDialog(null,"Too low!");
        else // The user guessed correctly!
          JOptionPane.showMessageDialog(null,"Correct!!!");
    }
}
```

Which version is best; this one or the answer to Activity 6.5? This is largely a question of personal preference; both programs work, and are straightforward to understand. However, this one is probably more elegant, and uses fewer statements. The point is that there are usually several different approaches to solving a problem, and therefore there is not usually only one 'correct' answer!

Question 6.6

1 False It terminates when a condition goes false – that doesn't have to be a fixed number of times (though for some programs it could be).

2 True However, writing a correct program may seem harder at first when you are unfamiliar with the language and are only looking at simple examples.

3 False It may not execute the body at all.

4 True Although to write any large program, you would certainly want to use methods to break our problem solution down into smaller chunks, and use the concepts of object orientation to express the more abstract levels of the solution.

5 True It is also useful when developing a program, because it enables one to test the logic of an algorithm before having to make it work on a computer.

6 True Although there are other types of loop in Java, which you will learn about in the next chapter, these simply make certain types of loop pattern more straightforward to implement.

7 False The test is always done first; the body is only executed if the test is true.

8 True Each test is a boolean (truth-valued) expression.

9 False The reserved word is while (in lower-case letters).

10 False A sentinel data value is used to indicate the end of a non-deterministic sequence of data; that is, at the time when the program is written, it is not known how many times the loop processing the data should iterate.

6.10 Feedback on activities

Activity 6.1: Factorial

Plan
1. Get the value of n from the user.
2. Multiply together all the whole numbers from 1 to n inclusive.

For step 2, you can use the same idea that you used in the 'sum to n' program, of generating each number in turn, and adding it to an accumulating running total. This time, however, on each iteration you will *multiply* the accumulating answer by the current number.

What should be the initial value of the accumulating answer?

It should be 1 (if it was 0, the final answer would always be zero!).

Refined plan

> Get the value of n from the user
> initialise accumulating variable to 1.
>
> WHILE n is greater than 0
>   multiply accumulating variable by n
>   subtract 1 from n

Here is the Java implementation of the plan:

```java
int fact = 1;

String numString;

numStr = JOptionPane.showInputDialog("Enter a value for n: " );
int n = Integer.parseInt(numStr);

while (n > 0)
{
    fact *= n;
    n--;
}

JOptionPane.showMessageDialog(null, numStr + "! = " + fact);
```

Activity 6.2: The Fibonnaci series

Plan

1. Get the value of *n* from the user.

2. Generate each term in succession until you get the *n*th one.

For step 2, you will require a loop, on each iteration of which you must generate the next number by adding together the current number and the previous number. You will therefore require three variables, the values of which will be shuffled on each iteration of the loop.

Here is the Java implementation of the plan:

```java
int lastTerm = 1;
int thisTerm = 1;
int nextTerm;
int termNumber = 2;
```

```
String numStr;

numStr = JOptionPane.showInputDialog(
   "Which term would you like? " );
int n = Integer.parseInt(numStr);
while (termNumber < n)
{
   nextTerm = lastTerm + thisTerm;
   lastTerm = thisTerm;
   thisTerm = nextTerm;
   termNumber++;
}

JOptionPane.showMessageDialog(null, "term " + n + " is " + thisTerm);
```

Note that *termNumber* is initialised to 2. If the user requests a term less than 3, the loop test will be initially false, the loop will not be entered, and the variable *thisTerm* will contain the correct answer.

Activity 6.3: Temperature conversion table   This is an example of counter control where the counting range does not start at 1. We need to count from −10 to +10, generating each row of the table as we go.

Note that sometimes a counter variable is used simply to count repetitions, as in the first example in this chapter, while at other times the value of the counter plays a part in the computations within the loop.

Here is a possible Java solution:

```
public class TempTable
{
   public static void main(String[] args)
   {
      final double FACTOR = 9.0/5.0;
      // ratio of F degree to C degree
      final double SHIFT = 32;  // 0 C = 32 F
      final int START = -10;
      final int FINISH = 10;

      int thisTemp = START;
      double thisInFahrenheit;

      // print table headings

      System.out.println("Celsius Fahrenheit");

      while (thisTemp <= FINISH)
      {
         thisInFahrenheit = thisTemp * FACTOR + SHIFT;
         System.out.println(thisTemp + "       " + thisInFahrenheit);
         thisTemp++;
      }
   }
}
```

Activity 6.4: Dry running programs with loops   Here is the table where the user enters 0.

After execution of line	SENTINEL	latestNum	total	(latestNum != SENTINEL) ?
L1	0	Not declared	Not declared	
L2	0	unknown	Not declared	
L3	0	unknown	0	
L6	0	0	0	
L7	0	0	0	0 != 0 ? false
L11	0	0	0	

The loop test on line 7 is false the first time, which means that the loop body is not executed, and control passes directly to line 11.

Activity 6.5: Guessing game   A solution is given below. Note that the if-else statement in the loop does not have to test whether the guess is correct, because this is done by the loop test.

```
public static void guessyguessy()
{
    final int SECRETNUMBER = 75;

    String str = JOptionPane.showInputDialog("Guess the number?");
    int guess = Integer.parseInt(str);

    while (guess != SECRETNUMBER)
    {
        if (guess > SECRETNUMBER)
            JOptionPane.showMessageDialog(null,"Too high!");
        else // guess must be too low
            JOptionPane.showMessageDialog(null,"Too low!");

        str = JOptionPane.showInputDialog(null,"Try again");
        guess = Integer.parseInt(str);
    }

    JOptionpane.showMessageDialog(null, "Correct!");
}
```

CHAPTER 7

More control structures

OVERVIEW

The Java *if-else* and *while* statements are useful basic control structures for programs but it is convenient to have alternative control structures for different applications. This chapter will extend your knowledge of Java loop constructs to include the *for loop* and *do-while loop*. You will also learn about Java's additional selection constructs, *single branch if* and *switch*. We will use these constructs in various forms of nesting in order to solve more interesting problems. This will necessarily include learning more about debugging and testing programs.

Learning outcomes

On completion of this chapter you should be able to:

- Explain the different types of repetition used in programming languages

- Select appropriate repetition constructs for a given programming problem

- Explain the different types of selection used in programming languages

- Choose appropriate selection constructs for a given programming problem

- Write programs using nested loops and selection statements

- Analyse what a program containing nested loops and selection statements does, by dry running it.

7.1 **Non-termination**

Look at the following method, and see if you can work out what it actually does.

```java
public static void rabbits()
{
    int count = 2;

    while (count > 0)
    {
    JOptionPane.showMessageDialog(null,
        "Rabbits have a lot of fun.\n" +
        "Why do they have a lot of fun?\n" +
        "Because there are lots of them.\n" +
        "Why are there a lot of them?\n" +
        "Because...\n");
    }
}
```

The loop test (count > 0) will always be true, because the variable *count* is initialised to 2 before the loop begins, and is not changed by the code in the loop body. Therefore, the loop will execute forever!

This is an example of a non-terminating loop (also called an *infinite loop*). It occurs when there is *either*:

- No provision in the loop body for changing the variable(s) used in the loop test (as above) *or*
- The variable(s) are changed, but not in such a way that the test can eventually take the value *false*.

The following program fragment is supposed to output the positive numbers counting down from 20 in steps of 2 – but can you see what is the problem with the program?

```java
int count = 20;

while (count != 1)
{
    System.out.println(
        "Boo bee doo count down by 2 " + count);
    count = count - 2;
}
```

The loop body reduces the value of *count* on each iteration of the loop, but because the program is counting down in twos from an initially even number, all values of *count* will be even. Therefore, *count* cannot ever reach the value 1. Instead, *count* will continue to be decremented, taking the values of the increasingly negative even numbers. In other words, we have another infinite loop.

If we wanted to use the number 1 in the loop test, we could make it work by changing the relational operator

   (count >= 1)

The test now does not require count to be precisely 1 in order to take the value false.

Activity 7.1

Counting, counting

Here is the earlier program fragment, with the improved loop test included.

```
int count = 20;

while (count >= 1)
{
    System.out.println(
        "Boo bee doo count down by 2 " + count);
    count = count - 2;
}
```

1 Modify the program so that it prints a descending sequence of all the numbers from n down to 0 in steps of s, where the values of n and s are entered by the user. You may assume that n and s will be positive numbers.

2 Think about how the program could be modified to deal with the possibility of negative values of n.

An unintentionally non-terminating loop is an example of a *run-time* error. The program runs forever, and has to be stopped by the user (this can be done by typing <CTRL> + C in the command window).

However, non-termination is not always an error; some control programs are not supposed to stop – for example, software to control a hospital life-support machine, or the cooling system of a nuclear power station!

7.2 Nesting of if-else and while statements

In Activity 7.1 you saw an example of nesting *while* statements in an *if-else* statement, where you needed the program to choose which of two *while* statements to execute. Now you will look at examples of nesting *if-else* statements within loop bodies; in other words, programs where each iteration of a loop requires a choice to be made.

Using counter-controlled repetition, can you write some code to write out the following potato-counting rhyme familiar to many children in Britain?

```
1 potato
2 potato
3 potato
4
5 potato
6 potato
7 potato
more
```

Plan

Set a counter to 1

WHILE the counter is <=7
    print the value of the counter followed
    by the word "potato"

Add 1 to the counter

Here is an attempt at a Java solution:

```java
int counter = 1;

while (counter <= 7)
{
    System.out.println(counter + " potato\n");
    counter = counter + 1;
}

System.out.println("more");
```

Do you think the code does the job? Well, almost, but not quite! Can you see what would happen with the code as shown?

The above code will write the following:

```
1 potato
2 potato
3 potato
4 potato
5 potato
6 potato
7 potato
more
```

The problem is that you do not want the loop to do the same thing (print the counter and the word 'potato') on *every* iteration. On the fourth iteration, you do not want the word 'potato'; just the value of *counter*.

This means that the program must, within the loop body, test whether this is the fourth iteration and if so, do something different. In other words, it must make a choice; we need an *if-else* statement nested within the loop.

Here is a solution.

```java
int counter = 1;

while (counter <= 7)
{
    if (counter == 4)
        System.out.println("4\n");
    else
        System.out.println(counter + "potato\n");
    counter = counter + 1;
}

System.out.println("more\n");
```

Here is an alternative version, in which the output String is built up by the loop iterations, and then sent to the screen all in one go after the loop has finished. This is a very common way of doing output in Java. The String is initialised to be the empty string (that is, a String with no characters in it), and then each successive loop iteration is used to append a line of the song to this String so that eventually the String contains the entire song.

```java
int counter = 1;

// initialise String to the empty String
String str = "";

while (counter <= 7)
{
   if (counter == 4)
      str = str + "4\n";
   else
      str = str + counter + "potato\n";
   counter = counter + 1;
}

str = str + "more\n";

// Output the whole rhyme
System.out.println(str);
```

Indentation

When writing programs with nested control structures, it becomes even more important to use consistent indentation. This makes the program much easier to understand, and thus facilitates debugging and/ or modification.

7.3 The single-branch if statement

Sometimes you want your programs to choose, not between two alternative actions, but between one action and doing nothing. In these cases you may use a single-branch if statement.

Problem

Write Java code which, for each number from 1 to 10, prints a message if that number is odd. It should print nothing for even numbers.

Plan

```
Set count to 1

WHILE count <= 10
   IF count is odd
        Print a message saying so
   ELSE
        Do nothing

Add 1 to count
```

In Java

```
int count = 1;

while (count <= 10)
{
   if (count % 2 == 1)
   {
      System.out.println(count + " is odd\n");
   }

   count++;
}
```

Single-branch if statement
Syntax

```
if (<TEST>)
   <STATEMENT>
```

- <TEST> is a boolean expression. Note that this must be enclosed in parentheses (and)
- <STATEMENT> is any Java statement, and can be a compound statement.

Semantics

- If <TEST> is *true* <STATEMENT> is executed, then the rest of the program continues
- If <TEST> is *false* <STATEMENT> is not executed and the rest of the program continues.

Guess again!

Here is the 'guess the number' method from review question 6.5 (Chapter 6).

Modify this program to help guide the user towards the correct answer, by telling them whether they are 'getting warmer'. In other words, give them an indication of whether their current guess is closer to the correct answer than their previous guess.

```java
public static void guessyguessy()
{
    final int SECRETNUMBER = 75;

    int guess = SECRETNUMBER + 1;          // incorrect guess
    String str = "";

    while (guess != SECRETNUMBER)
    {
        str = JOptionPane.showInputDialog("Have a guess");
        guess = Integer.parseInt(str);

        if (guess > SECRETNUMBER)
            JOptionPane.showMessageDialog(null, "Too high!");
        else if (guess < SECRETNUMBER)
            JOptionPane.showMessageDialog(null, "Too low!");
        else     // The user guessed correctly!
            JOptionPane.showMessageDialog(null, "Correct!!!");
    }
}
```

7.4 Dry running programs containing nested while and if-else statements

The more complicated the program structure becomes, the more useful dry running can be as a means of understanding and/or debugging the program. The principles are exactly the same as you have used in previous examples (i.e. you create a table with significant line numbers down the side and the names of all variables and tests across the top).

A *significant line number* is one on which a test takes place or the value of a variable might change.

The contents of each row of the table will be the values of the variables/tests after the execution of the statement on that line.

The best way to learn this is to try it, so have a go at the following activities.

Dry running programs containing ifs and whiles

The following method is intended to input a series of student's exam marks, each of which should be in the range 0-100, and tell each student whether they have passed or failed. To pass, a student must score 40 or more.

Investigate whether or not it always works, by choosing an appropriate series of input values that give convincing evidence that the method either always does the correct thing, or should reveal any possible errors which might exist. Dry run the method with this test data, correct any problems found and dry run your new method with the same input values to ensure that it now works.

```java
public static void main(String[] args)
{
  int mark;
  String str;                                          // LINE1

  str = JOptionPane.showInputDialog(
    "First mark?(101 terminates): ");                  // LINE2

  mark = Integer.parseInt(str);                        // LINE3

  while (mark != 101)                                  // LINE4
  {
    if (mark > 40)                                     // LINE5
      JOptionPane.showMessageDialog(null,"Passed");    // LINE6
    else
      JOptionPane.showMessageDialog(null, "Failed");   // LINE7

    str = JOptionPane.showInputDialog(
      "Next mark?(101 terminates): ");                 // LINE8

    mark = Integer.parseInt(str);                      // LINE9
  }

  System.exit(0);                                      // LINE10

}
```

More dry runs

Dry run the following program with the given values, then answer the questions which follow.

First run: User enters 3, then 6, then 5

```
public static void main(String[] args)
{
    int a = 4;                                                    //L1
    int b;                                                        //L2
    String str;

    str = JOptionPane.showInputDialog("Enter an integer:");
    b = Integer.parseInt(str);

    while (a <= 10)                                               //L3
    {
        if (a > b)
            b = b * 2;
        else
            b = a * 3;

        a = b + 2;

        JOptionPane.showMessageDialog(null, "a, b: " + a + " " + b);  //L4

        str = JOptionPane.showInputDialog("Enter another integer:");
        b = Integer.parseInt(str);
    }

    JOptionPane.showMessageDialog(null, "a, b: " + a + " " + b);      //L5

    System.exit(0);
}
```

If the value of a variable cannot be known, write *UNKNOWN* as the answer.

1 What is the value in variable *a* immediately after the line commented L1 is executed?

2 What is the value in variable *b* immediately after the line commented L2 is executed?

3 What expression is evaluated on the line commented L3 to test for the first iteration of the body of the loop?

4 What is printed to the screen when the line commented L4 is executed the first time?

5 What expression is evaluated on the line commented L3 to test for the second iteration of the body of the loop?

6 What is printed to the screen when the line commented L4 is executed for the second time?

7 What expression is evaluated on the line commented L3 to test for the third iteration of the body of the loop?

8 What is printed to the screen when the line commented L5 is executed?

Second run: User enters **4,** then **3**

Dry run the program again with this data. How does the program's execution differ from the first run?

7.5 The do-while loop statement

Problem

Write a method to print the numbers from 1 to n, where n is provided by the user. If n is 0 or a negative number, then print just 1.

Plan

In this problem, the method must *always* print something – if the data is inappropriate, the method should print the number 1.

You could solve this by using an *if-else* statement to test whether or not the data is valid, printing 1 if it is not valid, and employing a *while* loop to print the numbers from 1 to n if the data is valid.

However, a neater way would be to place the while loop test after the loop body, as follows:

```
Initialise counter to 1
Get n from the user

DO
    print the counter
    add 1 to the counter
WHILE   the counter <= n
```

This construction is implemented in Java as a *do-while* loop. Here is the method:

```java
public static void printToN()

{
    int count = 1;
    String input, output = "";
    input = JOptionPane.showInputDialog("Give me a value for n");
    n = Integer.parseInt(input);

    do
    {
        output += count + " ";
        count++;
    } while (count <= n);

    JOptionPane.showMessageDialog(null, output);
}
```

do-while loop statement

Syntax

> **do**
>> <STATEMENT>
>
> **while** (<TEST>);

- <STATEMENT> is any Java statement or compound statement
- <TEST> is a boolean expression. Note that this must be enclosed in parentheses (and).

Semantics

- Similar to the while loop, but the body is executed first, then the condition is evaluated
- This means that the body is always executed at least once.

7.6 The *for* loop statement

The *for* loop is very versatile, but is usually used as a neater alternative to the while loop, when counter control is required.

for loop statement

Syntax

> **for** (<STATEMENT A>; <EXPRESSION>; <STATEMENT B>)
>
>> <STATEMENT>

Semantics

The following is the order of events when the for loop is executed.

1 Execute <STATEMENT A> (this is usually the declaration and initialisation of a counter variable).

2 Evaluate <EXPRESSION> (this is a boolean expression used to determine whether the loop continues)

3 If <EXPRESSION> is *true*, <STATEMENT> is executed (the loop body); otherwise the loop terminates

4 If <STATEMENT> has been executed, then <STATEMENT B> is executed – this is usually the increment of the counter variable. The cycle then returns to step 2 and continues.

The **while** *loop equivalent of the* **for** *loop*

The above structure is equivalent (in most cases) to:

```
<STATEMENT A>

while (<EXPRESSION>)
{
  <STATEMENT>
  <STATEMENT B>
}
```

Example plan

```
FOR counter stepping from 1 to 10
   Print a message
```

The Java code

```
for (int counter = 1; counter <= 10; counter++)
{
   System.out.println(counter + " potato\n");
}
```

Another example – a celebration

```
String output = "";

for (int counter = 1; counter <= 3; counter++)
{
   output += "For he's a jolly good fellow\n";
}

output += "and so say all of us!";
JOptionPane.showMessageDialog(null, output);
```

Important

- The control variable must be declared. If it is declared in the *for* loop header as in the above examples, its scope is only within the *for* loop itself
- The control variable must be given an initial value
- Be careful with the choice of relational operator: the above example uses <= instead of <, otherwise the loop would iterate 1 fewer times than required.

Note the use of the **+=** symbol in the assignment statement. Here this is shorthand for 'variable *output* becomes equal to its existing variable with the following String appended to it'. The variable *output* builds itself from an empty String (as declared in the first line) into a single variable containing all the lines of the song.

The for loop

Modify the following method to use a for loop instead of the while loop:

```
public static void sumTo()
{
    int n;
    int total = 0;
    int count = 0;
    String output = "";
    String str;
    str = JOptionPane.showInputDialog("Give me a number to sum to ");
    n = Integer.parseInt(str);
    while (count <= n)
    {
        total = total + count;
        output += count + ":\t" + total + "\n";
        count = count + 1;
    }
    JOptionPane.showMessageDialog(null, output);
}
```

7.7 Nesting of loops within loops

In many programs it is necessary to use loops nested within other loops. This can be done with any combination of the three types of loop you have seen, but in this section we will look at examples based on the *for* loop.

Programs which draw things on the screen are good for illustrating these ideas, so here are some programs to draw simple shapes in the command window.

Do you remember the example from the last chapter of a *while* loop to draw a line of n stars?

Here it is again, translated into a *for* loop.

```
String numStr;

numStr = JOptionPane.showInputDialog( "How many stars?");
int n = Integer.parseInt(numStr);

for (int count = 1; count <= n; count++)
    System.out.print("*");
```

If the user enters 6, this code draws

```
******
```

Let us modify the above code to draw a square block of stars of side n, where n is a number entered by the user.

For example, if the user enters 6, the program should draw:

```
******
******
******
******
******
******
```

Plan

> FOR counter stepping from 1 to n
> > Draw a line of n stars
> > Place the cursor at the start of the next line

We already have the code to draw one line of stars using a *for* loop, so we need to place this *for* loop inside another *for* loop, which causes the line of stars to be drawn n times.

Here is the code:

```java
String numStr;

numStr = JOptionPane.showInputDialog( "Size of square?");
int n = Integer.parseInt(numStr);

for (int rows = 1; rows <= n; rows++)
{
   // Draw a line of stars
   for (int count = 1; count <= n; count++)
      System.out.print("*");

   System.out.println();  // Go to new line
}
```

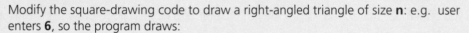

Activity 7.6

Drawing a triangle

Modify the square-drawing code to draw a right-angled triangle of size **n**: e.g. user enters **6**, so the program draws:

```
*
**
***
****
*****
******
```

Activity 7.7

Drawing another triangle

Modify the program of Activity 7.6 to draw the 'mirror image' right-angled triangle of size **n** – for example, if the user enters **6**, the program should draw:

```
     *
    **
   ***
  ****
 *****
******
```

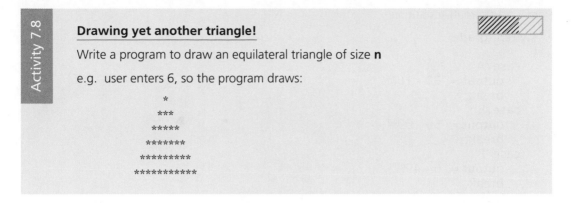

Activity 7.8

Drawing yet another triangle!

Write a program to draw an equilateral triangle of size **n**

e.g. user enters 6, so the program draws:

```
      *
     ***
    *****
   *******
  *********
 ***********
```

If you have tried each of these drawing program activities, you should be getting a feel for using loops in the solution of more complex problems. Activities 7.7 and 7.8 demonstrate that it is often possible to solve a new problem by making (sometimes minor) changes to an existing solution. This is an important principle: in programming, never re-invent the wheel!

If you are still hungry to do more drawing, you could make up your own shapes and try to write programs to draw them. For example, how about a hollow square of side **n**?

e.g. user enters 6, program draws:

```
* * * * * *
*         *
*         *
*         *
*         *
* * * * * *
```

7.8 The *switch* statement

Problem

Write a program which, given a student's grade stored as a char variable, prints out the corresponding mark range.

One possible solution is to use an if-else 'ladder' structure.

```
String output;

if (grade == 'A')
   output = "70 - 100%";
else if (grade == 'B')
   output = "50 - 69%";
else if (grade =='F')
   output = "0 - 49%";
else
   output = "Invalid grade";

JOptionPane.showMessageDialog(null, output);
```

Here is an alternative solution:

```
switch (grade)
{
   case 'A':
      output = "70 - 100%";
      break;
   case 'B':
      output = "50 - 69%";
      break;
   case 'F':
      output = "0 - 49%";
      break;
   default:
      output = "Invalid grade";
      break;
}
```

Syntax

```
switch <EXPRESSION>
{
   case <CONSTANT-EXP1>
         <STATEMENT 1>
      break;

   case <CONSTANT-EXP2>
         <STATEMENT 2>
      break;

      .
      .
      .

   default:
         <STATEMENT>
      break;
}
```

switch is used instead of an *if-else* ladder and is appropriate when testing a variable (or expression) against a constant value. This can be either an integer constant or a character constant.

break is needed for each case – causes control to pass out of the *switch* statement. Without this, control would drop through to the next case's statement(s).

default is an optional 'catch-all', but it is good practice to always add a default case, which should be placed at the end.

Multiple similar cases

You can have more than one case associated with each action in the *switch* statement. For example, suppose you want the program to accept both upper- and lower-case characters:

```
case 'A':
case 'a':
output = "70-100%";
break;
```

Activity 7.9

Coin values

Write a program to input an integer value and, if it is equivalent to the value of a British coin, to print it out in words. Otherwise, it should print out an error message.

Input	Print
1	One penny
2	Two pence
5	Five pence
10	Ten pence
50	Fifty pence
100	One pound
200	Two pounds

7.9 Test plans

Compilers can reveal syntax errors but not semantic errors. In the computing industry, software development teams often assign specific people to test software for semantic errors. Often, whole teams do nothing but testing. They do not just run the program a few times, and approve it, if it seems to work. If they did that, they would have many angry clients! Instead, *test plans* are devised. These are a large series of tests designed to catch as many errors as possible. In each case, the correct answer is calculated separately and compared with the one given by the program.

For example, if a program has a branch in it, at least one test must be run to check that each branch works. Extreme values (like 0 or negative numbers) are tested in addition to 'normal' values. Testing the *bounds* is a most effective way of detecting run-time errors. So, how would you do this?

The following method (intended to print the larger of the two numbers input) contains a run-time error. Devise a test plan for it (in this case a series of values to be input in variables *first* and *second* on different runs of the method).

```
public static void main (String[] args)
{
    int first;
    int second;
    int max;
    String str;

    str = JOptionPane.showInputDialog("Enter an integer:");
    first = Integer.parseInt(str);

    str = JOptionPane.showInputDialog("Another integer:");
    second = Integer.parseInt(str);

    if (second > max)
        max = first;

    JOptionPane.showMessageDialog(null,"Maximum is " + max);

    System.exit(0);
}
```

A possible plan is as follows:

first	second	Reason
18	12	first bigger than second, both positive
10	15	second bigger than first, both positive
17	17	both the same and positive
0	0	both the same and zero
-10	-10	both the same and negative
-30	-25	first bigger than second, both negative
-12	-6	second bigger than first, both negative
20	-5	first bigger than second, first positive, second negative
-17	40	second bigger than first, first negative, second positive

You should now dry run the program based on the values from the test plan, and see if the test plan shows up the errors. This is left as an exercise for you! Of course, if the plan is not good enough, there might still be undetected errors. For example, you have not tested for the entry of non-numerical data, floating point numbers, or combinations of floats with integers – all of which would crash the program.

The conclusion you can draw from this is that even for a simple program, a lot of work is required to test it thoroughly; testing a large program is, therefore, a major exercise.

The program we have just looked at is not a good program! The programmer's idea was to store one of the numbers in a variable called *max*, then compare this with the other number, storing the latter in *max* if it is bigger than the current value of *max*. This is an over-complicated way of doing things, made worse by the fact that it is done incorrectly. The variable *max* is never initialised so the program will not compile, and the assignment in the if statement uses the value of the wrong variable!

Here is a corrected version of the program (although it would have been easier to simply compare the two input numbers with an if-else, printing an appropriate message in each branch).

```java
public static void main(String[] args)
{
    int first;
    int second;
    int max;
    String str;

    str = JOptionPane.showInputDialog("Enter an integer:");
    first = Integer.parseInt(str);

    str = JOptionPane.showInputDialog("Another integer:");
    second = Integer.parseInt(str);

    max = first;

    if (second > max)
        max = second;

    JOptionPane.showMessageDialog(null,"Maximum is " + max);

    System.exit(0);
}
```

Activity 7.10

Test plans

Doctors use something called a person's 'body mass index' to decide if their weight is a medical problem that needs treating (if they are seriously overweight or underweight for their height). This is done by calculating:

(10 x *weight*) / (*height* x *height*)

where *weight* is the person's weight in grams and *height* is their height in centimetres. If the result of this calculation is less than 20, then the person is medically underweight. If the result is greater than 30 then the person is medically overweight. The incomplete program below is required to calculate whether a given person is *underweight*.

1 Finish the program by adding code in the place indicated. The method *test()* implements a test plan by calling the method *weightIllness()* with different values. If there is a mistake in your program, the different calls to *weightIllness()* may show this. Your program does not need to cope with a person entering a height of 0.

```
public static void weightIllness(double weight, double height)
{
  //add code here
{

// This method contains a test plan to test the weightIllness method.
// If it is correct it should print the commented answers

public static void test()
{
    weightIllness (40500, 150);              // underweight
    weightIllness (51200, 160);              // underweight
    weightIllness (64000, 160);              // not underweight
    weightIllness (100440, 180);             // not underweight
    weightIllness (97200, 180);              // not underweight
}

public static void main(String[] args)
{
    int choice;
    String str;

    str = JOptionPane.showInputDialog(
        "Type 1 to run the test plan, 0 to enter your details ");
    choice = Integer.parseInt(str);

    if (choice == 1)
        test();                              // run test plan
    else
    {                                        // or enter your own details
        int h;                               // height in cm
        int w;                               // weight in g
        str = JOptionPane.showInputDialog(
            "Type in your weight (grams)");
        w = Integer.parseInt(str);
```

... continued

```
        str = JOptionPane.showInputDialog("Type in your height (cm)");
        h = Integer.parseInt(str);

        weightIllness(w, h);
    }

    System.exit(0);
}
```

2 Modify your above code to deal sensibly with heights of 0 (adding an appropriate entry to the test plan).

3 Further modify it to also indicate if a person is overweight. Justify whether or not the given test plan is sufficient for the new program, adding extra entries if it is not.

7.10 Summary

- Non-termination: If a loop condition never becomes false, the loop will not terminate
- When a choice is to be made between an action and doing nothing, use a single-branch *if* statement
- The *do-while* loop executes the body first and only then checks the exit condition; thus it always iterates at least once. In a *while* loop the body can be executed zero times
- The *for* loop makes counter-controlled repetition easier
- Nesting of *if-else* statements within loops, and loops within loops, allows us to write programs to solve more complex problems
- The *switch* statement is used to compare the value of an expression with an integer or character constant, doing something different on each case. It is often clearer than an *if-else* ladder
- Carefully designed test plans are important to ensure that a program works properly.

7.11 Review questions

Question 7.1 Fill in the blanks in the following:

1 A program which never stops is said to be _____.

2 The _____ statement handles all the details of counter-controlled repetition.

3 The _____ statement can be used in place of an if-else ladder.

4 If none of the other cases are true in a *switch* statement, the _____ case is executed.

5 A single-branch *if* executes its body if the test condition evaluates to _____.

Question 7.2   State whether the following are true or false.

1 Some programs never halt.

2 A non-terminating program is always a mistake.

3 The control variable in a *for* loop does not need to be declared.

4 The control variable in a *for* loop must be initialised.

5 The *while* statement executes its body at least once.

6 The *do-while* statement terminates when its condition is *true*.

7 The *switch* statement can test against a constant character or integer.

8 The *switch* statement can only test against the value in a variable.

Question 7.3   What, if anything, is wrong (there may be more than one mistake) with the following code fragments? Give a correct version.

1
```
while (x < 10)
{
  int x = 0;
  JOptionPane.showMessageDialog(null,"x " + x);
  x = x + 1;
}
```

2
```
while (z >= 0)
  sum = sum + z;
```

3
```
switch (n)
{
  case 1:
    JOptionPane.showMessageDialog(null, "The number is 1");
  case 2:
    JOptionPane.showMessageDialog(null, "The number is 2");
    break;
  default:
    JOptionPane.showMessageDialog(
        null, "The number is not 1 or 2");
    break;
}
```

4
```
switch (n)
{
  case 1:
    JOptionPane.showMessageDialog(null, "A");
    break;
```

```
      case2:
        JOptionPane.showMessageDialog(null, "B");
        break;
      default:
        JOptionPane.showMessageDialog(null, "C");
        break;
  }
```

 Question 7.4 Dry run the following method, assuming the user enters **2** then **3** when prompted, then answer the questions that follow.

```
      public static void main(String[] args)
      {
        int E = 30;
        int x; int y; int t;                                    // L1

        String str = JOptionPane.showInputDialog("Input first number ");
        x = Integer.parseInt(str);
        str = JOptionPane.showInputDialog("Input second number ");
        y = Integer.parseInt(str);                              // L2

        while (y <= E)
        {
          System.out.println(y);                                // L3

          if (y < 8)
          {
            t = y;
            y = y + x;
            x = t;
          }
          else
            y = y + 12;
        }

        System.out.println(x);                                  // L4
        System.out.println(y);                                  // L5
      }
```

If the value of the variable cannot be known, write *UNKNOWN* as the answer to the question.

1 What is the value in variable *y* immediately after the line commented L1 is executed?

2 What is the value in variable *y* immediately after the line commented L2 is executed?

3 What is printed to the screen when the line commented L3 is executed the 1st time?

4 What is printed to the screen when the line commented L3 is executed the 2nd time?

5 What is printed to the screen when the line commented L3 is executed the 3rd time?

6 What is printed to the screen when the line commented L3 is executed the 4th time?

7 What is printed to the screen when the line commented L4 is executed?

8 What is printed to the screen when the line commented L5 is executed?

Question 7.5   Answer *true* or *false* to each of the following:

1 A *while* loop always terminates.

2 The keyword *if* must always be accompanied by the keyword *else*.

3 The *do-while* statement executes its body at least once.

4 The *for* loop is convenient for programs where counter control is required.

5 The counter variable in a *for* loop need not be declared.

6 The *switch* statement is a convenient alternative to an *if-else* ladder.

7 You should always include *break* in the branches of a *switch* statement.

8 Testing is one of the most time-consuming aspects of the programming process.

9 When writing programs using nested control structures, consistent indentation is very important.

10 Dry running is not useful when dealing with nested control structures.

7.12 Answers to review questions

Question 7.1

1 non-terminating

2 for

3 switch

4 default

5 true

Question 7.2

1 **True** For example, a *while* loop with a condition that is always *true*.

2 **False** Many computer programs are intended to continuously collect data. They will only stop if the power is cut off (for example, in a video recorder).

3 **False**

4 **True**

5 False It may not execute the body.

6 False It terminates when the condition is false like a normal while.

7 True

8 False Any expression that evaluates to an integer or character can be used.

Question 7.3

1 *x* should be declared and initialised outside the loop, not in it.

```
int x = 0;
while (x < 10)
{
  JOptionPane.showMessageDialog(null,"x " + x);
  x = x + 1;
}
```

2 Will never terminate – the counter has not been decremented. Also not initialised.

```
int z = 10;
while (z >= 0)
{
  sum = sum + z;
  z = z - 1;
}
```

3 *break* missing on first branch.

```
switch (n)
{
   case 1:
     JOptionPane.showMessageDialog(null, "The number is 1");
     break;
   case 2:
     JOptionPane.showMessageDialog(null, "The number is 2");
     break;
   default:
     JOptionPane.showMessageDialog(null,
        "The number is not 1 or 2");
     break;
}
```

4 Space missing between *case* and 2

```
switch (n)
{
   case 1:
     JOptionPane.showMessageDialog(null, "A");
     break;
   case 2:
     JOptionPane.showMessageDialog(null, "B");
     break;
```

```
            default:
                JOptionPane.showMessageDialog(null, "C");
                break;
        }
```

Question 7.4

1 U

2 3

3 3

4 5

5 8

6 20

7 5

8 32

Question 7.5

1 **False** It terminates only when the loop condition becomes *false* – if this doesn't happen the loop continues forever.

2 **False** The word *else* (and the associated statements) may be omitted, in which case the test decides between executing the 'true' branch of the *if* statement, and doing nothing.

3 **True** Because the test follows the loop body.

4 **True** Although you can solve any iteration problem using only *while* loops.

5 **False** It is necessary to declare the counter; this is usually done in the loop heading.

6 **True** You do not need *switch*, but it is neater than a long series of *if-else*.

7 **True** Without this, control would simply drop through to the next limb of the *switch* statement.

8 **True** Even testing a small program thoroughly can take a long time; testing a large program may require a team of people.

9 **True** Without careful indentation, the program will become very difficult to understand, debug or modify.

10 **False** Dry running is particularly useful with more complex programs, to gain a deeper understanding of the program logic.

7.13 Feedback on activities

Activity 7.1: Counting, counting

1 The problem here is that you do not know in advance what the values of n and s will be, so the test must be designed to work with any possible values. Here is a solution:

```
String str = JOptionPane.showInputDialog("Enter the start value");
int n = Integer.parseInt(str);

str = JOptionPane.showInputDialog("Enter the step value");
int s = Integer.parseInt(str);

while (n >= 0)
{
    System.out.println("Counting " + n);
    n = n - s;
}
```

2 There is no particular problem with *n* being negative. You would want the program to count from *n* to 0, whether *n* is negative or positive. However, if *n* is negative, you need to count *up* in steps of *s*, not *down*. You can check whether *n* is negative by using an *if* statement, and modify your actions as appropriate.

Here is a solution:

```
String str = JOptionPane.showInputDialog("Enter the start value");
int n = Integer.parseInt(str);

str = JOptionPane.showInputDialog("Enter the step value");
int s = Integer.parseInt(str);

if (n >= 0)
    while (n >= 0)
    {
        System.out.println("Counting " + n);
        n = n - s;
    }
else
    while (n <= 0)
    {
        System.out.println("Counting " + n);
        n = n + s;
    }
```

You might also want to think about how you could deal with the possibility of negative values for *s*!

Activity 7.2: Guess again! You now need variables to store the current guess and the previous guess, so that these can be compared. You also need a more complex *if-else* structure to tell the user not only whether the guess is too high or too low, but also whether it is closer than last time.

To compare the 'nearness' of this guess with that of the previous guess, you need to compare how far each guess is from the answer (i.e. the difference between the answer and the guess). However, the guess can be too high or too low, so it is the *magnitude* of the difference that is important (i.e. you need to be able to ignore the *sign* of each difference). You could write your own code to do this, but Java provides a method called *abs()*, which returns the absolute value of its numerical argument.

For example:

> abs(42) is 42
> abs(-42) is 42

This method is part of a class called *Math*, a part of the package *java.lang*, which defines a number of useful static methods. To call static methods, you must give the name of the class, followed by a dot, followed by the method name.

For example:

> Math.abs(-25);

However, for the first guess, there is no previous guess, so you test within the loop for whether this is the first iteration, and if so, initialise the previous guess to be a long way off, so that the program doesn't tell the user they are getting colder. The test uses a *boolean* variable, which is a primitive type variable in which a truth value can be stored; on the first iteration of the loop this variable will be set to *false* so that subsequent iterations will know that they are not the first!

This part of the program also uses a single-branch *if* statement, because if this is not the first iteration of the loop, then no action is required.

Can you spot any errors in this aspect of the logic of the program?

The program will tell the user, on their first guess, that they are getting warmer (unless their guess is actually worse than the initial value of *prevGuess*).

Whether or not the current guess is closer than the previous guess is also stored in a *boolean* variable, which is then used to tell the user whether they are getting warmer.

Here is the program.

```java
import javax.swing.JOptionPane;

public class Guess
{
    public static void guessyguessy()
    {
        final int SECRETNUMBER = 75;
        final int WAYOUT = 1000000;

        int guess = SECRETNUMBER + 1;  // incorrect guess

        boolean firstTime = true;

        while (guess != SECRETNUMBER)
        {
            int prevGuess = guess;
            if (firstTime)
            {
                prevGuess = WAYOUT;
                firstTime = false;
            }

            String str = JOptionPane.showInputDialog("Have a guess");
            guess = Integer.parseInt(str);

            if (guess == SECRETNUMBER)
                str = "Correct!!! ";
            else
            {
                int newDiff = SECRETNUMBER - guess;
                int oldDiff = SECRETNUMBER - prevGuess;
                boolean warmer =
                (Math.abs(newDiff) < Math.abs(oldDiff));

                if (warmer)
                  str = "Getting warmer";
                else
                  str = "Not getting warmer";

                if (guess > SECRETNUMBER)
                  str = str + "Too high! ";
                else if (guess < SECRETNUMBER)
                  str = str + "Too low! ";
            }

            JOptionPane.showMessageDialog(null, str);
        }
    }

    public static void main(String[] args)
    {
        guessyguessy();
        System.exit(0);
    }
}
```

Activity 7.3: Dry running programs containing *ifs* and *whiles* You need to consider whether the program works for significant data. The kinds of things you could test for are:

- Numbers greater than 100

- Numbers less than 0

- Marks of precisely 40 (the pass mark)

- Marks of 39 (one less than the pass mark)

- Marks of 41 (one more than the pass mark)

- Marks entered as floating point numbers (e.g. 47.5)

These are the kind of input which you might anticipate giving problems. For thorough testing, you need to think of as many potential problem values as possible, and try them all. The actual amount of effort put into this exercise in the real world depends on the importance of the program. For example, the testing of life-support machine software is more important than a payroll program. However, no matter how thorough you are, it is still not possible to be certain that all possible problems have been discovered by testing alone. The only way to do this is by mathematically proving that a program works, which is not practical for the vast majority of programs.

As an example, here is a dry run table for the case where the user enters **55**, **40** then **101**.

Line	str	mark	(mark!=101)	(mark>40)	Output
1	u	u			
2	"55"	u			
3	"55"	55			
4	"55"	55	true		
5	"55"	55		true	
6	"55"	55			passed
8	"40"	55			
9	"40"	40			
4	"40"	40	true		
5	"40"	40		false	
7	"40"	40			failed
8	"101"	40			
9	"101"	101			
4	"101"	101	false		
10					

Note that on line 7, the program reports a fail for a student who got 40%, which should be a pass. The problem is with the if-else statement test, which should use >= rather than >.

Other problems which further dry runs might have revealed include:

- Negative numbers: program will indicate as fails

- Numbers larger than 101: program will indicate as passes

- Strictly, the program should also validate for and reject any non-integer input, but this would require much more programming effort.

Activity 7.4: More dry runs

First run

1 4

2 Unknown

3 4 <= 10

4 8 6

5 8 <= 10

6 a, b: 14 12

7 14 <= 10

8 a, b: 14 5

Second run:

The test on line 3 fails the second time, so the body of the loop only executes once.

Activity 7.5: The for loop   The following is one possible solution:

```java
public static void sumTo()
{
    int n;
    int total = 0;
    String output = "";
    String str;
    str = JOptionPane.showInputDialog("Give me a number to sum to ");
    n = Integer.parseInt(str);

    for (int count = 0; count <= n; count++)
    {
        total = total + count;
        output += count + ":\t" + total + "\n";
    }

    JOptionPane.showMessageDialog(null, output);
}
```

Activity 7.6: Drawing a triangle This problem is very similar to the square-drawing one, except that on each iteration of the outer loop, you wish to draw an increasing number of stars. In other words, the variable which determines the number of stars drawn on a line must be 1 the first time, 2 the second time, etc up to n on the final iteration of the outer loop. You can use the variable *rows* for this purpose.

Here is the code:

```
String numStr;

numStr = JOptionPane.showInputDialog(
   "Size of triangle?");
int n = Integer.parseInt(numStr);

for (int rows = 1; rows <= n; rows++)
{
  for (int count = 1; count <= rows; count++)
    System.out.print("*");

  System.out.println(); // Go to new line
)
```

Activity 7.7: Drawing another triangle This time, the program must draw a number of spaces and a number of stars on each line. The number of spaces must decrease by 1, and the number of stars must increase by 1 each time. You need one loop for the spaces, and one loop for the stars.

Here is a possible solution:

```
String numStr;

numStr = JOptionPane.showInputDialog("Size of triangle?");
int n = Integer.parseInt(numStr);

int noOfSpaces = n - 1;        // Number required for first row
int noOfStars = 1;             // Number required for the first row

for (int rows = 1; rows <= n; rows++)
{

  // Draw line of spaces
  for (int spCount = 1; spCount <= noOfSpaces; spCount++)
    System.out.print(" ");

  // Draw line of stars
  for (int stCount = 1; stCount <= noOfStars; stCount++)
    System.out.print("*");

  System.out.println();              // Go to new line

  noOfSpaces—; noOfStars++;          // Change ready for next row
}
```

Activity 7.8: Drawing yet another triangle!   This is similar to the program of Activity 7, except that this time the number of stars drawn on each successive line must increase by 2 each time. The program is therefore identical, except that instead of:

noOfStars++;

you must use:

noOfStars = noOfStars + 2;

Activity 7.9: Coin values

Plan

Input the coin value

compare the coin value against
1:       Print "One penny"
2:       Print "Two pence"
5:       Print "Five pence"
10:      Print "Ten pence"
50:      Print "Fifty pence"
100:     Print "One pound"
200:     Print "Two pounds"
default: Print "That is not a coin"

In Java:

```
numStr = JOptionPane.showInputDialog("Enter a coin value");
int value = Integer.parseInt(numStr);

switch (value)
{
   case 1:
      JOptionPane.showMessageDialog(null,"One penny");
      break;
   case 2:
      JOptionPane.showMessageDialog(null,"Two pence");
      break;


   .
   .  // cases for 5, 10, 50, 100
   .

   case 200:
      JOptionPane.showMessageDialog(null,"Two pounds");
      break;

   default:
      JOptionPane.showMessageDialog(null,"That is not a coin");
      break;
}
```

Activity 7.10: Test plans The following method works. Note that / in the assignment statement does integer division, which means no fractional part, but that is fine because fractional parts are not necessary for this problem.

```
public static void weightIllness (double weight, double height)
{
    long index;

    if (height == 0)
        JOptionPane.showMessageDialog(
            null,"Cannot have zero height");
    else
    {
        index = (10 * weight) /(height * height);

        if (index < 20)
            JOptionPane.showMessageDialog(null,"Underweight");
        else if (index > 30)
            JOptionPane.showMessageDialog(null,"Overweight");
        else
            JOptionPane.showMessageDialog(null,"Weight OK");
    }
}
```

CHAPTER 8

Methods and more complex programs

OVERVIEW

The algorithm structuring constructs of Java that we have been exploring are necessary when implementing single algorithms, but most programs consist of many communicating algorithms. You now need to learn how to implement parameterised self-contained subprograms, which will allow you to construct such programs – another important step along the way to creating truly powerful programs.

Learning outcomes On completion of this chapter you should be able to:

- Write larger programs, by breaking them into smaller parts and passing data between the parts

- Explain the concepts associated with *methods* and their implementation in Java

- Identify and correct errors in Java programs which use multiple methods.

8.1 Designing programs

When writing a very small program, it is possible to place all the code in a single *main()* method.

However, for a problem of any reasonable size, this quickly becomes impracticable. Such problems require breaking down into manageable chunks in order to understand them and implement a solution. Each chunk will correspond to a separate problem, which you try to design an algorithm to solve. If a chunk is still too complex for a solution to be found, you break it down further into yet smaller chunks, and design algorithms to implement these. This process is called *top-down design*, and it is a well-established way of tackling difficult programming problems.

However, sometimes it is not clear how to begin this process of breaking down a difficult problem. In such cases it is common to find an aspect of the problem for which one knows a solution, and tackle that first. You then look for other bits that can be tackled, and continue breaking bits off in this piecemeal way in an attempt to move towards a solution.

These techniques have been used for many years, but are nowadays subsumed within the process of *object-oriented design*. Here, you tackle a problem by searching the problem description for *objects*. For example, in a traffic simulation problem, the objects could be cars, lorries and motorbikes. You then think about what properties these objects should have in the context of the problem. For example, in a traffic simulation, you are more likely to be interested in the current speed of a car rather than the colour of the paintwork. The relevant properties or *attributes* of each object may be implemented using *variables*. For example a car's speed could be an integer variable. The other aspect of each object in which you are interested is its *behaviour* (i.e. what it can do and what can be done to it). For example, you might command a *car* object to increase its speed, or it might be caused to crash into another *car* object. Conceptually, you tell objects what to do, or make enquiries of objects, by sending them *messages*. However, in Java, these messages are actually calls to *methods* associated with the object.

Object orientation is a very powerful analysis, design and implementation technique. We will return to this later, but the point is that algorithms implemented as methods are a fundamental part of every program, whatever design technique is used.

8.2 Types of method

You have already used these methods:

- *showMessageDialog()*
- *showInputDialog()*
- *main()*
- *guessyguessy()*   (the guessing game method from Chapter 7)
- Pizza base recipe (from Chapter 2 – not Java!).

Remember that *methods* always belong to *classes* – but to which class does each of the above methods belong?

Methods and classes

- *showMessageDialog()* and *showInputDialog()* belong to class *JOptionPane*. *JOptionPane* is one of the classes of the Java API, which contains lots of pre-written useful methods
- *main()* belongs to whatever class you choose to place it in
- *guessyguessy()* belongs to class *Guess* which you saw in Chapter 7
- The pizza recipe belongs to the recipe book, which is analogous to a Java class.

The next issue to consider is the type of *parameters* that you can give to each of the methods:

- **showMessageDialog():** *null* and a String. For example:
  showMessageDialog(null, "Hello!")

  Action: Writes the String on screen.

- **showInputDialog():** a String. For example:
  showInputDialog("Enter a thingy")

  Action: Writes a prompting String on the screen, and gets an input String from the user.

- **main():** an *array* of Strings. The parameters are optional, and are supplied on the command line when you run the program (the array here is a sequence of Strings; we will discuss arrays in detail in the next chapter).
  Action: Used to implement any algorithm you choose.

- **guessyguessy():** this one takes no parameters.
  Action: Plays the 'guess the number' game with the user.

- **Pizza base recipe (not Java!):** a list of ingredients.
  Action: Makes a pizza!

Calling the methods

- The method *main()* is called automatically when you run the program.
- *showMessageDialog()* and *guessyguessy()* are called by using their name (with parameters, if any) as a *statement*, for example:
  guessyguessy();
  JOptionPane.showMessageDialog(null, "Hello!");

Note

With *static* methods such as these, when the called method is not in the class from which it is being called, you must include its class name in the call:

<classname>.<methodname>   as with   **JOptionPane.showMessageDialog()**

- **showInputDialog()** is called like this.
    ```
    String input = JOptionPane.showInputDialog("Enter a thingy");
    ```

This one is different! You call it by using <classname>.<methodname>, as with the others, but the call is an *expression*, not a statement.

Chacteristics of an expression

An expression has a *value*. For example:

- 2 + 2 is an *integer expression* with value 4
- (5 >= 3) is a *boolean expression* with value *true*
- 4.25 – 0.75 is a *double expression* with value 3.5.

An expression is *not*, in general, a command to the computer. When a program evaluates an expression, it can do two things with the result:

- The result can be passed to a method as a parameter
- The result can be assigned to a variable of the appropriate type.

Consider the following expression; what is its value?

```
JOptionPane.showInputDialog("Enter a thingy");
```

Its value is whatever String the user enters in response to the prompt. To capture the result, you must *either* assign it to a variable:

```
String input = JOptionPane.showInputDialog("Enter a thingy");
```

or pass it to another method as an parameter.

To illustrate the latter, consider the following code fragment; what does it do?

```
JOptionPane.showMessageDialog(null,
    JOptionPane.showInputDialog("Say something") );
```

We have passed the result of the call to

```
showInputDialog()
```

as a parameter to

```
showMessageDialog()
```

so *showInputDialog()* gets a String from the user, and when the input dialog box OK button is clicked, this String is passed to *showMessageDialog()*, which displays it on the screen.

There are two types of method:

- Methods that **carry out an action** (have a side effect):
    - These methods have return type *void*, which indicates that they do not return any value
    - Calls to such methods are *statements*

- Methods that **compute and return a value:**
  - These methods have a non-void return type. For example, if the method returns an integer, the return type is *int*
  - Calls to these methods are *expressions*.

Consider the following method; what is its return type?

    showInputDialog()

The method returns a String, so the return type is:

    String

8.3 Writing your own methods

To illustrate each of the above kinds of method, let us look at two methods that do the job of squaring a number:

- **Version 1**

```
public static void square1(int y)
{
   System.out.println((y * y));
}
```

- **Version 2**

```
public static int square2(int y)
{
   return y * y;
}
```

square1() has the word *void* in its heading. This indicates that the method does not return a value. The last part of the method heading

    (int y)

indicates that when you call this method, it expects a single integer parameter. The method works by computing the square of the parameter and printing it on the screen.

In the heading of *square2()*, the first int is the *return type*; in other words, this method returns a value, which must be an int. As with *square1()*, this method requires a single *int* parameter.

The value is returned via a *return* statement, which is the reserved word

    return

followed by any expression of the type stated in the method heading; in this case, type *int*.

Note

A method with return type *void* must not return a value; it may have a *return* statement without an expression

    return;

but this is simply used to terminate the method.

A method with a return type other than *void must* contain a *return* statement with an expression of the return type.

Activity 8.1

Table of squares

Write a program that uses the method *square1()* to print a table of the squares of the numbers from 1 to 10 as follows.

Number	Square
1	1
2	4
3	9
4	16
5	25
6	36
7	49
8	64
9	81
10	100

Now write another version that does the same thing using the method *square2()*

An obvious question to pose is 'What is best: a method which operates via a side effect such as printing a result to the screen, or a method which operates by returning a result?'

As with everything else in science, the answer is, 'It depends!'

There is a lot to be said for subprogram units like *square2()*, which have no external effect whatsoever.

They do *not*:

- **Change** the value of any variables outside their own code
- **Open** any files
- **Write** anything to the screen
- **Read** anything from the keyboard.

However, they *do:*

- Simply **return** (effectively, 'become') the result which they compute.

Such methods can be separately developed and tested, then plugged into a program in the knowledge that they can have no unwanted effects on the rest of the program. They implement the pure mathematical idea of a *function* – you plug in a value or values via parameters, and out comes a result, and that is *all* that happens.

This type of subprogram unit is actually the basis of an entire programming paradigm called *functional programming*.

Unlike Java, a functional programming language has no variables, no statements and no loops. It may seem very strange to those accustomed to conventional programming, but it provides a very clean, elegant, programming environment. All things being equal, it is a good idea to mimic this functional style, even when programming in non-functional languages such as Java, in order to reap some of the benefits. However, all things are not always equal!

Sometimes it might be appropriate for a method to have a side effect *and* return a result. For example, a method to get a number from the user:

```java
public static int getAge()
{
  String str = JOptionPane.showInputDialog("How old are you?");
  return Integer.parseInt(str);
}
   .
   .
   .
int age = getAge();
```

Activity 8.2

Factorial, revisited

Write a side-effect-free method to compute the factorial of a number supplied as a parameter. You will find it easier to reuse the code developed to compute the factorial of a number in Chapter 6.

Place your method in a program that uses the method to compute the factorial of a succession of numbers entered by the user, stopping when the user enters −1.

Activity 8.3

Temperature conversion, revisited

Write a side-effect-free method to compute the Fahrenheit equivalent of a Celsius temperature supplied as a parameter. You will find it easier to reuse the code developed to do the conversion in Chapter 6.

Place your method in a program to test it out.

8.4 Parameters

You have already seen how you must indicate in the heading of a method declaration that it is to take parameters and/or return results.

Here are some examples:

- A method that takes a single *int* parameter, and does not return a value:
  ```java
  public static void thingy(int x)
  ```

- A method which takes a *char* parameter and an *int* parameter and returns an *int* value:
  ```java
  public static int kingy(char ch, int y)
  ```

- A method which takes an *int* parameter, a *char* parameter and a *double* parameter, and returns a *char* result:

  public static char dinghy(int x, char y, double z)

Before you read on, jot down some possible calls to the above methods.

Possible calls for these methods could include:

```
int a = 15;
char letter = 'A';
double pi = 3.142;

thingy(5);
thingy(a);
a = kingy('z', 42);
a = kingy(letter, a);
letter = dinghy(36, 'k', 21.24);
letter = dinghy(a, letter, pi);
```

Note

- The parameters declared in a method heading are called the method's *formal* parameters
- The parameters supplied when a method is called are called *actual* parameters
- The actual parameters supplied when a method is called must correspond in number, order and type to the formal parameters declared in the method heading
- 'Correspond in type' does not necessarily mean that they must be of the *same* type. For example, an *int* parameter could be passed to a method that expects a *double* (but not vice versa); the types are compatible for this purpose.

Before you read on, pause to consider what is wrong with each of the following calls:

1   thingy(2.4);

2   kingy('A', 4, 7);

3   dinghy('z', 4.2)

4   dinghy(4, '*', 22, 12);

In the first example, this is a *double* parameter instead of *int*; in the second example, a third parameter has been supplied, where only two are allowed; the first *int* parameter is missing in the third example; and in the final example, a fourth parameter has been supplied when the method requires three. Note that 22 is acceptable as the third parameter; an *int* can be used where a *double* is required.

Romance

Write the body of the following method, which is to print the value of *str1* if *likes* is *true*, and print *str1* concatenated with *str2* if *likes* is *false*.

Place the method in a program to test it.

```
public static void romance(String str1, String str2, boolean likes)
```

You can regard the heading of a method as part of a *specification* for that method. If you provide the heading, together with a description of what the method is to do, then someone can write the body of that method, while others write the code that uses the method, confident that if they provide the correct parameters, the method will do the job.

This provides a good way of organising work for a team of programmers; decide what methods are required, what they are to do and what their interfaces (headings) are; then different members of the team can write the different method bodies and test them separately. All that then remains is to plug the methods together in a program and test that they all work correctly together.

So how does the parameter-passing mechanism of Java actually work?

The process is known as *call by value* (or *pass by value*). Look again at the method *square1()* and three calls to it:

```
public static void square1(int y)
{
   System.out.println(y * y);
}

public static void main(String[] args)
{
   int x = 4;

   square1(4);               // Call 1

   square1(x);               // Call 2

   square1((x + 10) % 3);    // Call 3
}
```

What happens when *Call 1* is executed?

- The value of the actual parameter *4* is copied into the formal parameter *y* within *square1()*
- This mechanism is known as *call by value*
- *y* behaves as if it was an initialised local variable within *square1()* that is, a variable declared within, and only existing in *square1()*
- *square1()* writes 16 on the screen.

What happens when *Call 2* is executed?

- The value of the actual parameter variable *x* is copied into the formal parameter *y* within *square1()*
- Again, *y* behaves as if it was an initialised local variable within *square1()*
- Note that any subsequent changes to *y* do NOT affect *x*
- *square1()* writes 16 on the screen.

What happens when *Call 3* is executed?

- The value of the actual parameter expression *(x + 10) % 3* is computed, which is 2. This value is then copied into the formal parameter *y* within *square1()*
- Again, *y* behaves as if it was an initialised local variable within *square1()*
- If the formal parameter is of a primitive type, then any expression of that type may be used as a parameter
- *square1()* writes *4* on the screen.

Method composition

Method *square2()* expects an *int* parameter which, as you have already seen, can be any integer expression. However, that expression could be a call to a method that returns an integer. Therefore, a call to *square2()* could be used as a parameter to a call to *square2()*.

What is the value of the following expressions?

```
square2(square2(3))

square2(square2(square2(2)))
```

- The first expression gives a value of eighty-one: the square of 3 is 9, and the square of 9 is 81
- The second expression gives a value of two hundred and fifty-six: the square of 2 is 4, the square of 4 is 16 and the square of 16 is 256.

This technique of supplying the result of a method call as a parameter to another method call is known as *method composition*. It can be used to write new methods using old ones. For example, if you wanted a method to find the fourth power of a number, you could do it like this:

```
public static int fourthPower(int y)
{
   return square2(square2(y));
}
```

4Activity 8.5

Activity 8.5: Pythagoras

Write a method to return the length of the hypotenuse of a right-angled triangle, given the lengths of the other two sides as parameters.

Note: you may use the static method *sqrt()* from the *Math* class, which returns the square root of a double-type parameter.

For example

```
Math.sqrt(100.0);
evaluates to 10.0
```

Program development – some guidelines

- Each method should perform one simple, well-defined task
- If you find that a method is going to be doing two or more tasks, think about splitting them into separate methods
- Each method should not normally be bigger than one screen full of code
- If a method is getting much bigger than this, think about splitting it into more than one method
- Programs should comprise collections of small methods (but see Chapter 11 on classes and objects for more clarification on this)
- Each method can be written by a different person
- Each method can be separately tested, then 'plugged in' to the program
- Using methods makes programs easier to develop, debug and modify.

Activity 8.6

Line drawing

Write a method *drawLine()*, that draws a line of stars of length n, where n is supplied as a parameter.

You should modify the code written in the last chapter (section 7.7) to do this.

Activity 8.7

More versatile line drawing

Now modify your method so that the symbol to be drawn is also provided as a parameter. This will enable the method to draw a line of any symbol, not just stars.

Drawing a triangle

Write a method *drawTriangle()* to draw an equilateral triangle of size n, where n is supplied as a parameter.

e.g. the call   drawTriangle(6); would draw the following triangle.

```
     *
    ***
   *****
  *******
 *********
***********
```

Again, modify the code you looked at in the last chapter (section 7.8), and use the drawLine method above.

Activity 8.9: A Christmas tree

Now write a method to draw a 'bucket' and trunk:

```
    *
    *
*********
 *******
  *****
```

and finally use this and the *drawTriangle()* method to write a method to draw a Christmas tree like this:

```
      *
     ***
    *****
      *
     ***
    *****
   *******
  *********
      *
     ***
    *****
   *******
  *********
 ***********
*************
      *
      *
  *********
   *******
    *****
```

Note that you will have to modify the *drawTriangle()* method so that it draws a triangle at a given level of indentation (supplied as a parameter), so that the sections of the tree line up neatly one below the other.

Duration and scope of identifiers

- The *duration* of an identifier is the time during which it exists in memory
- The *scope* of an identifier is that part of the program in which it may be referenced.

Parameters and local variables declared in a *method body* have so-called *automatic* duration. They are *created* when their declaration is reached, and *destroyed* on termination of the block they are in, delimited by { and }.

A variable declared in a block (between any pair of { and }) has *block scope* – it can only be used between its declaration and the end of that block.

Later you will learn about variables with other scopes and durations.

Guidelines

- If a variable is only required within a single method (or block), it should be declared within that method (or block)
- The rule is: always declare variables as *locally* as possible. This limits the likelihood of the variable inadvertently being changed by the program, and makes debugging easier.

Method overloading

You can have more than one method with the same name in a class, as long as each differs in the number, type and/or order of its parameters. This can be useful in object-oriented programming, as you will see later, but is also useful where you want a method, conceptually, to do the same kind of operation while operating upon different types of data.

For example, the *square2()* method only works with an *int* parameter. However, you might well also want to apply it to *doubles*.

You can overcome this problem by writing more than one version, as demonstrated by the following code:

```
public static int square(int y)
{
   return y * y;
}

public static double square(double y)
{
   return y * y;
}

public static void square()
{
  System.out.println("Be there or be square");
}

public static void main(String[] args)
{
  System.out.println("Square of 4  is " +  square(4));

  System.out.println("Square of 4.5  is " +  square(4.5));

  square();

  square("fred");
}
```

Each of the method calls in *main()* will invoke a different method called *square()*:

- The first call will invoke the first method, which expects an *int* parameter
- The second call will invoke the second method, which expects a *double* parameter
- The third call will invoke the third method, which expects no parameter
- The fourth call is an error, as there is no version of square which expects a String parameter.

In fact, the final *square()* method is not really good practice. You should use method overloading where the overloaded method does the same kind of operation in each case, for example squaring a number. The final square method does no such thing, and should really be called something else!

8.5 Going for a song

Remember this nursery song?

> Old MacDonald had a farm, E-I-E-I-O
>
> And on this farm he had a pig, E-I-E-I-O
>
> With an oink-oink here and an oink-oink there
>
> Here an oink, there an oink, everywhere an oink-oink
>
> Old MacDonald had a farm, E-I-E-I-O

Think about how you would you write a program to print several verses of the song.

It would be easy to do this with loads of output statements, but this would produce a very long and boring program. You can do better than this by noting that a main feature of the song is its repetitiveness – every verse is the same except for the name of the animal and its sound. You can take advantage of this by writing a method to return a single verse, and call this method for each verse you wish to print. However, each time the method is called, you must tell it which animal and which sound to include (cow, moo; dog, woof; etc). You can do this by passing the animal name and its sound as *parameters* to the method. The parameters here will be Strings of characters.

The method must construct and return a String that comprises all the repetitive parts of the verse, with the animal name and its sound inserted in the correct places, by String concatenation.

Here is the method, and a main method that calls it to build up, then print, the verses of the song.

```
import javax.swing.JOptionPane;

public class OldMac
{

    public static String buildVerse(String creature, String sound)
    {
        return "\nOld MacDonald had a farm, E-I-E-I-O"
            + "\nAnd on this farm he had a " + creature
            + ", E-I-E-I-O"
            + "\nWith a " + sound + "-" + sound
```

```
                + " here and a "
                + sound + "-" + sound + " there"
                + "\nHere a " + sound + " there a " + sound
                + " everywhere a " + sound + "-" + sound
                + "\nOld MacDonald had a farm, E-I-E-I-O\n";
    }

    public static void main(String[] args)
    {
        String lyrics = buildVerse("cow", "moo")
            + buildVerse("sheep", "baa")
            + buildVerse("duck", "quack")
            // plus any other verses;

        JOptionPane.showMessageDialog(null, lyrics);

        System.exit(0);
    }
}
```

8.6 Summary

- Methods are the essential building blocks for constructing larger programs
- There are two kinds: those that operate only by side effects and those that return values
- There are hundreds of methods already available for use in the classes of the Java API. These can save us a lot of development effort
- Java methods use call-by-value semantics in parameter passing
- Methods with appropriate return types can be composed together or even with themselves
- Variables should always be declared as locally as possible
- Methods may be overloaded by creating different versions with different parameter lists.

8.7 Review questions

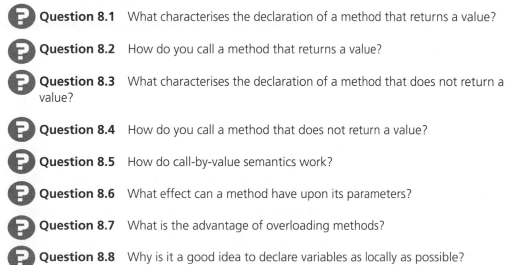

Question 8.1 What characterises the declaration of a method that returns a value?

Question 8.2 How do you call a method that returns a value?

Question 8.3 What characterises the declaration of a method that does not return a value?

Question 8.4 How do you call a method that does not return a value?

Question 8.5 How do call-by-value semantics work?

Question 8.6 What effect can a method have upon its parameters?

Question 8.7 What is the advantage of overloading methods?

Question 8.8 Why is it a good idea to declare variables as locally as possible?

? **Question 8.9**   Answer *true* or *false* to each of the following:

   1 Methods are one of the major structuring mechanisms for Java programs.

   2 Every method must return a value.

   3 A program can only use methods that are declared in its own class.

   4 A method cannot make changes to its actual parameters.

   5 A method cannot make changes to its formal parameters.

   6 A formal parameter behaves as an initialised local variable.

   7 A method should always perform one well-defined task.

   8 One can always compose two methods together.

   9 Variables should always be declared as locally as possible.

   10 It is not possible to have two methods with the same name in the same class.

8.8 Answers to review questions

Question 8.1   There is a return type declared in the method heading, and at least one *return* statement with an expression of the return type in the method body.

Question 8.2   You give the method name, together with any parameters required in brackets. The call is an expression, which may be used in any appropriate context for an expression of that type; for example, included in a larger expression, or passed as a parameter to another method.

Question 8.3   The type *void* is declared in the method heading, which indicates that a value is not returned. The method operates only by side effects such as printing to the screen or changing global variables. A *return* statement may optionally be included, but without an accompanying expression and the effect is simply to terminate the method.

Question 8.4   You call the method by using its name, together with any parameters in brackets, but this time the call is a statement.

Question 8.5   The values of the actual parameters supplied with the method call are copied into the corresponding formal parameters declared in the heading of the method declaration. The formal parameters are effectively initialised local variables.

Question 8.6   With call-by-value semantics, it is not possible for a method to affect its parameters. However, if the parameters are reference variables, the situation is different – see the next chapter.

Question 8.7   Overloading enables a method conceptually to accept different numbers and/or types of parameters, and carry out different operations upon them. This is achieved by writing more than one version of the method, with the same name, but different parameter lists.

Question 8.8   The more local the declaration, the less opportunity there is for the variable to be inadvertently changed by the program. This makes errors less likely, and facilitates easier debugging.

Question 8.9

1 **True** Individual algorithms are structured using selection and repetition constructs, but programs comprising more than one algorithm will implement each algorithm as a separate method.

2 **False** Returning a value is optional; methods can also operate via side effects such as writing to the screen or changing global variables.

3 **False** Static methods from other classes can be called by using the class name, followed by a dot, followed by the method name. Non-static methods are associated with objects; more on this later.

4 **True** – but see the next chapter for a way to circumvent this where necessary.

5 **False** Formal parameters are those declared in brackets in the method heading. Their values can be changed, but they only exist within the method, and are destroyed when the method terminates.

6 **True** Formal parameters have the same status as variables declared within the method, but they are initialised to the values of the corresponding actual parameters when the method is called.

7 **True** If you find when writing a method, that it appears to be doing two or more separate tasks, then you should consider splitting it into more than one method.

8 **False** A method call can only be a parameter to another method if the parameter method returns a value of the appropriate type.

9 **True** This reduces the possibility of the variable inadvertently being altered by the program, and makes the program easier to understand and debug.

10 **False** It is possible, as long as the two versions have parameter lists that differ in the number and/ or type of their parameters. This is known as method overloading.

8.9 Feedback on activities

Activity 8.1: Table of squares   Here is a solution using method *square1()*:

```java
public class Squares
{
   public static void square1(int y)
   {
      System.out.println((y * y));
   }

   public static void main(String[] args)
   {
      System.out.println("Number Square");

      for (int i = 1; i <= 10; i++)
      {
         System.out.print(i + "   ");
         square1(i);
      }
   }
}
```

Here is a solution using method *square2()*:

```java
public class Squares
{
   public static int square2(int y)
   {
      return y * y;
   }

   public static void main(String[] args)
   {
      System.out.println("Number Square");

      for (int i = 1; i <= 10; i++)
      {
         System.out.println(i + "   " + square2(i));
      }
   }
}
```

On each iteration of the loop, the first program prints the value of the counter followed by some spaces. It then calls the *square1()* method, passing it the value of the counter. The method prints the square, and returns the cursor to a new line ready for the next iteration.

```java
System.out.print(i + "   ");
square1(i);
```

On each iteration of the loop, the second program prints a String comprising the counter value concatenated with some spaces, concatenated with the result of the call to the *square2()* method (which is an integer).

```java
System.out.println(i + "   " + square2(i));
```

Activity 8.2: Factorial revisited The following program is one solution:

```java
import javax.swing.JOptionPane;

public class FactProg
{
    public static int factorial(int n)
    {
        int fact = 1;

        while (n > 0)
        {
            fact *= n;
            n--;
        }

        return fact;
    }


    public static void main (String[] args)
    {
        String numStr;
        int n;

        do
        {
            numStr = JOptionPane.showInputDialog(
                "Enter a value for n; -1 to finish ");
            n = Integer.parseInt(numStr);

            if (n != -1)
                JOptionPane.showMessageDialog(null,
                    n + "! = " + factorial(n));
        } while (n != -1);

        System.exit(0);
    }
}
```

Activity 8.3: Temperature conversion revisited The following is a possible solution.

```java
public static double celsiusToFahrenheit(int tempInC)
{
    final double FACTOR = 9.0/5.0;
    // ratio of F degree to C degree
    final double SHIFT = 32; // 0 C = 32 F

    double tempInF = tempInC * FACTOR + SHIFT;

    return tempInF;
}
```

Activity 8.4: Romance   Here is a possible solution:

```java
public class Loves
{

    public static void romance(String str1, String str2, boolean likes)
    {
        if (likes)
            System.out.println(str1);
        else
            System.out.println(str1 + str2);
    }


    public static void main (String[] args)
    {
        String s = "I love you";
        String t = " - NOT! ";
        boolean decision = true;

        romance(s, t, decision);

        decision = false;

        romance(s, t, decision);
    }

}
```

Activity 8.5: Pythagoras   The square on the hypotenuse is the sum of the squares on the other two sides: but you remembered that from school, didn't you?

The following method is a possible solution:

```java
public static double hypotenuse(int side1, int side2)
{
    return Math.sqrt( (double) (square2(side1) + square2(side2)) );
}
```

Note the use of casting to convert the integer expression into a *double* value; this is because the *sqrt()* method expects a *double* as a parameter.

Activity 8.6: Line drawing   Here is a possible solution:

```java
public static void drawLine(int n)
{
    for (int stCount = 1; stCount <= n; stCount++)
        System.out.print("*");
}
```

Activity 8.7: More versatile line drawing   Here is a possible solution:

```
public static void drawLine(int n, char symbol)
{
   for (int stCount = 1; stCount <= n; stCount++)
     System.out.print(symbol);
}
```

Activity 8.8: Drawing a triangle   Here is a possible solution:

```
public static void drawTriangle(int n)
{
   int noOfSpaces = n - 1;
   // Number required for first row
   int noOfStars = 1;
   // Number required for the first row

   for (int rows = 1; rows <= n; rows++)
   {
      // Draw line of spaces
      drawLine(noOfSpaces, " ");

      // Draw line of stars
      drawLine(noOfStars, "*");

      System.out.println(); // Go to new line

      noOfSpaces—; noOfStars += 2;
      // Change ready for next row
   }
}
```

Activity 8.9: A Christmas tree   Here is the program. Note the single-branch if statement in the drawTriangleIndented method, which ensures that the triangle is correctly indented.

```
public class Tree
{

   public static void drawLine(int n, char symbol)
   {
      for (int stCount = 1; stCount <= n; stCount++)
        System.out.print(symbol);
   }


   public static void drawTriangleIndented(int indent, int n)
   {
      int noOfSpaces = n - 1;
      // Number required for first row
      int noOfStars = 1;
      // Number required for the first row

      // Arrange to indent the triangle if necessary
      if (noOfSpaces < indent)
         noOfSpaces = indent;
```

```java
        for (int rows = 1; rows <= n; rows++)
        {
            // Draw line of spaces
            drawLine(noOfSpaces, " ");

            // Draw line of stars
            drawLine(noOfStars, "*");

            System.out.println();  // Go to new line

            noOfSpaces--;  noOfStars += 2;
            // Change ready for next row
        }
    }


    public static void drawBucket()
    {
        System.out.println("     *");
        System.out.println("     *");
        System.out.println(" *********");
        System.out.println("  *******");
        System.out.println("   *****");
    }


    public static void drawTree()
    {
        drawTriangleIndented(6, 3);
        drawTriangleIndented(6, 5);
        drawTriangleIndented(6, 7);
        drawBucket();
    }



    public static void main(String[] args)
    {
        drawTree();
    }
}
```

You might want to modify the methods again so that they return Strings rather than printing to the screen!

CHAPTER 9

Arrays

OVERVIEW

In the previous chapter you learned how to structure *instructions* in larger programs. We will now look at how to use Java *arrays* to structure the *data* used by your programs.

Learning outcomes   On completion of this chapter you should be able to:

- Recognise where arrays would be appropriate for solving a given programming problem

- Write programs that use arrays to solve problems

- Explain the programming concepts related to arrays and their implementation in Java

- Identify and correct errors in programs using arrays

- Analyse what a program containing arrays does, by dry running it.

9.1 Problem

You have collected the ages of 1,000 students and want to write a program to read them into the computer's memory and find the average age.

Here is the code to read in 1,000 numbers:

```
String s;

s = JOptionPane.showInputDialog("enter an age:");
int age0= Integer.parseInt(s);

s = JOptionPane.showInputDialog("enter an age:");
int age1= Integer.parseInt(s);
    .
    .
    .
s = JOptionPane.showInputDialog("enter an age:");
int age999= Integer.parseInt(s);
```

... and here is the code to find the average

```
double ave = (age0 + age1 + age2...
    .
    .
    .
    + age999)/ 1000.0;

JOptionPane.showMessageDialog(null, "Average age is " + ave);
```

Read it through again: what do you think of the above program?

Well, you would probably have found it quite hard to key in! Having lots of separate variables is very tedious – this program will be enormous.

It would be better if you could make one declaration to state that you require 1,000 integer variables, rather than 1,000 separate declarations of individual integer variables.

It would also be better if you could place the code to read one integer value into a loop, and somehow make the loop body code reference each of the 1,000 integer variables in turn, rather than repeat the integer reading code 1,000 times. Unfortunately, there is no way to do this with individual integer variables, because the only way to refer to each is by its name.

But there is a solution! It is time to learn about the *array*.

An array of integers is effectively a sequence of integer variables, which you can refer to individually by giving their position in the sequence.

A new plan: use an array
1 Read each value into a separate entry in an array
2 Initialise a total to 0
3 FOR i = 0 to 999
    add the ith age to the total
4 Output total/1000

Here is some code to read 1,000 integer values into an array called *ages*.

```
int[] ages = new int[1000];

String s;

for (int i = 0; i <= 999; i++)
{
    s = JOptionPane.showInputDialog("enter a no:");
        ages[i]= Integer.parseInt(s);
}
```

Here is some code to compute the average of the 1,000 numbers in the array.

```
int total = 0;

for (int i = 0; i <= 999; i++)
{
    total += ages[i];
}

double ave = total / 1000.0;

JOptionPane.showMessageDialog(null, "Average age is " + ave);
```

The following sections will go through this code piece by piece.

9.2 Declaring arrays

```
int[] ages = new int[1000];
```

This code declares an array reference variable called *ages*, creates an array of 1000 integer variables, and assigns the array to the reference variable.

An array is accessed via a *reference variable*. You have already seen reference variables in Chapter 4, where you learned that Java *Strings* are also accessed via reference variables.

Recap: reference variables

A reference variable does not contain its associated data, but contains a *reference* to the data (effectively the address where the data is stored in memory). You can represent the reference as an arrow, pointing to the data.

As we saw back in Chapter 4, a primitive type variable could be represented as:

```
int x;

x = 5;


x                    5
```

An array reference variable could be represented as:

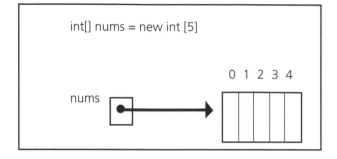

Here are some more array reference variable declarations.

```
int[] intArray;      // reference to an array of int

char[] charArray;  // reference to an array of char

double[] doubleArray; // reference to an array of double
```

You create an array object using the dynamic memory allocation operator *new*, followed by the type of the items to go in the array, and the number of items (size of the array) in square brackets. You associate the array with a reference variable using assignment.

For example:

```
intArray = new int[100];
```

creates an array object comprising 100 *int* variables and stores a reference to it in the reference variable *intArray*.

Automatic initialisation

When an array is created (sometimes called *allocating* the array), if it contains:

- **Numbers** – they are initialised to **zero**
- **Booleans** – they are initialised to **false**
- **References** – they are initialised to **null**.

9.3 Accessing array elements

As you can see from the diagram above, each box in an array has a number. The first box is number 0, the second box is number 1 and so on. Each of these numbers is known as the *subscript*, or *index* of an element of the array.

Array index

- The array index type must be integer.
- An array index starts at 0. This means that the index of the last element will be the number of elements in the array minus 1.

Look at the following declaration:

```
int[] heights = new int[20];
```

Pause to consider how many *elements* are in this array, and what the *index range* is.

Accessing an array element

You access an array element by giving the name of the array, followed by the index of the element in square brackets.

Examples

Given the array *heights* above:

```
heights[0] = 165;
// Places the number 165 in the first element of the array

heights[1] = 190;
// Places the number 190 in the second element of the array

heights[19] = 185;
// Places the number 185 in the last element of the array

System.out.println(heights[1]);
// Prints 190 on the screen

int i = 4;
System.out.println(heights[15 + i]);
// Prints 185 on the screen
```

Returning to the question at the top of this page about elements and index range: there are twenty elements, and the index range is from zero to nineteen.

9.4 Array processing with loops

A common requirement with arrays is to process each of the elements (or a range of elements) in turn. To do this, you can cause a loop counter to take each of the array index values in turn, and use this to process the corresponding array elements in the loop body.

Often we use a *for* loop when the range of indices to be processed is known in advance, and a *while* loop when the range is not known in advance.

Here is the code from above, to read in 1,000 ages

```
for (int i = 0; i <= 999; i++)
{
   s = JOptionPane.showInputDialog("enter an age:");
   ages[i]= Integer.parseInt(s);
}
```

The loop control variable *i* is used as an array index value for the array *ages* in the loop body. The loop will iterate 1,000 times, and read in 1,000 integer values, filling the array. This is still rather tedious, but you will see an easier way of getting large quantities of data into your programs when we cover *files* in Chapter 10.

Here, once again, is the code to compute the average of the 1,000 numbers in the array.

```
int total = 0;

for (int i = 0; i <= 999; i++)
{
    total += ages[i];
}

double ave = total / 1000.0;

JOptionPane.showMessageDialog(null, "Average age is " + ave);
```

The loop pattern is exactly the same as above, with the loop control variable used as the array index value, but this time the task performed by the loop is to add each successive value from the array to an initially zero total. When the loop terminates, this total is used to compute the average age.

Length

Associated with every array is an integer attribute called *length*. It is accessed by giving the name of the array reference variable, followed by a dot, followed by the word *length*. This attribute always contains the number of elements in its associated array – that is, the length of an array *a* is the value of the expression:

```
a.length
```

In section 9.3, what would the value of the following expression be?

```
heights.length
```

The answer is: 20.

This is useful when the program has to process an array, but does not know how many elements the array has.

For example, the above code to read in the ages could be modified as follows.

```
for (int i = 0; i <= ages.length - 1; i++)
{
    s = JOptionPane.showInputDialog("enter an age:");
    ages[i]= Integer.parseInt(s);
}
```

This makes the array-processing code more generally applicable. The code does not need to know how long the array is, so the array size can be changed and the code will still work.

It is also good practice to use a named constant to represent the size of an array when the array is declared; for example

```
final int SIZE = 1000;
int[] ages = new int[SIZE];
```

If you want the program to operate on a different-size array, you simply change the named constant.

Activity 9.1

Exam marks

Assuming that the numbers in an array called *marks* are exam marks, write Java code to compute the number of students who failed the exam (i.e. got a mark of less than 40).

Activity 9.2

Palindrome testing

Write a program to check whether an array *nums,* of single-digit numbers, is a palindrome (i.e. looks the same backwards as it does forwards).

Examples of numbers which are palindromes:

```
1234321
48984
1111111111
7392937
```

Activity 9.3

Partially full arrays

Sometimes you have to read an unknown quantity of data into an array. The issues here are:

- There may be *more* data items than there are elements in the array – the program must stop reading data when the array is full

- There may be *fewer* data items than there are elements in the array. You should keep track of how full the array is, to assist in future processing of the array.

Modify the first part of the 'average age' code to read in an unknown number of ages.

9.5 More on array reference variables

Once an array is created, it is fixed in size. However, a reference variable may be set to point to a different array at any time.

Consider what will happen when the following code is executed.

```java
int[] a = new int[5];
int[] b = new int[4];
a = new int[2];
b = a;
```

The figure shows the state after execution of the first two statements

```
int[] a = new int[5];
int[] b = new int[4];
```

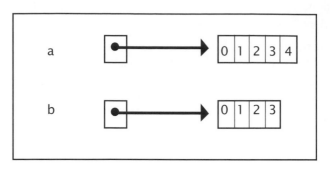

The next figure shows the state after execution of the statement

```
a = new int[2];
```

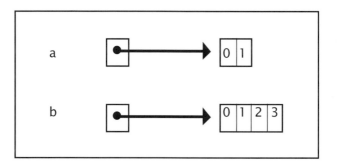

The array previously referenced by *a* is destroyed, and the memory it occupied is freed up for future use, by the Java run time system. This is known as 'garbage collection'.

The next picture shows the state after execution of the statement

```
b = a;
```

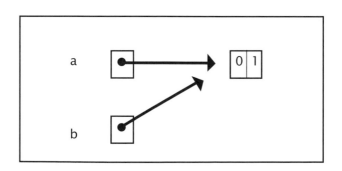

The assignment copies the value in reference variable *a* (a reference to the two-element array) into reference variable *b*, which means that the array now effectively has two names! Again, the array previously referenced by *b* is garbage-collected.

Dry running programs containing arrays

As with previous Java constructs, dry running is a good way to understand and debug programs containing arrays.

The principles are the same as before; you construct a table with significant line numbers down the side and variable names and tests across the top.

As always, the best way to learn is by trying it, so have a go at the following activities.

Activity 9.4

Dry running exercise

Dry run the following method.

```java
public static void printEvens()
{
    String output = "";

    final int SIZE = 4;                      // L1
    int[] evens = new int[SIZE];             // L2
    int i;                                   // L3

    for (i = 0; i < evens.length; i++)       // L4
    {
        evens[i] = 2 * (i + 1);              // L5
    }

    for (i = 0; i < SIZE; i++)               // L6
    {
        output += i +"\t"+ evens[i] + "\n";  // L7
    }

    JOptionPane.showMessageDialog(null, output);
}
```

Initialiser lists

When you create an array of integers, Java automatically initialises them to zero.

If you wish to initialise them to some other value, you can use a loop like this.

```java
// initialise all ages to 21

for (int i = 0; i <= 999; i++)
{
    ages[i]= 21;
}
```

However, for smaller arrays, there is a convenient shorthand. Look at the following code segment and consider what you think it does:

```java
int[] ages = {19, 27, 18, 18, 95, 14, 20, 19, 22, 37};
```

This segment creates an array of ten integers, initialised to the values shown (i.e. the first one is 19, the second one is 27 etc), and stores a reference to it in the array reference variable *ages*.

Note that you do not need to use *new* here – it is called automatically.

Clearly this would not be appropriate for very large arrays, but it is handy for smaller ones.

Activity 9.5

More dry running

Dry run the following program and answer the questions that follow.

```java
public static void main(String[] args)
{
    int[] numberset = {40, 5, 9, 7, 8, 300};                    //L1

    JOptionPane.showMessageDialog(
        null, "" + (numberset[2]+5));                           //L2

    JOptionPane.showMessageDialog(
        null, "" + (numberset[3]*100));                         //L3

    for (i = 0; i < 6; i++)
    {
        numberset[i] = numberset[i] + 2000;                     //L4
    }

    System.exit(0);
}
```

If the value of a variable cannot be known, write *UNKNOWN* as the answer.

1 What are the values of the elements in the array *numberset* when the line commented L1 is executed?

2 What are the values of the elements in the array *numberset* when the line commented L2 is executed?

3 What is printed to the screen when the line commented L2 is executed?

4 What is printed to the screen when the line commented L3 is executed?

5 What is the contents of *numberset* after the *for* loop commented L4 has executed?

Activity 9.6

Array initialisation

Write Java code to declare and initialise an array to contain the values of the 5-times table from zero times five to ten times five.

9.6 Reference parameters

Primitive type parameters (i.e. of types such as *int*, *char* and *double*) are passed to methods using call-by-value semantics (see the previous chapter).

Objects, including arrays, cannot be passed directly as parameters to methods; instead we pass the value of the object's *reference variable*, using call-by-value semantics. In other words, the value of the reference variable used as an actual parameter in the method call is copied into the corresponding formal parameter declared in the method heading.

The value stored in an object reference variable is a reference to (the address of) an object. In other words, the object is referred to using the actual parameter reference variable outside the method, and by the formal parameter reference variable inside the method. This allows the method to manipulate the object directly. This mechanism of effectively 'passing' the object to the method by passing a reference to the object is known as 'call-by-reference' semantics.

This has the advantage of *efficiency* – if an array were passed as a parameter directly using call by value, then a copy would be made, which could be wasteful if the array were very large or the method were called many times.

However, there is a danger. Suppose you do not want a method to be able to change the values stored in an array passed as a parameter, but merely to *use* these values. Unfortunately, there is no way that a program can prevent a method from changing an array passed to it.

Look at the following code, and see if you can work out what happens when it is executed.

```java
public static void incArray(int[] b)
{
   for (int i = 0; i < b.length; i++)
      ++b[i];
}

public static void inc(int n)
{
   n++;
}

public static void main(String[] args)
{
   int[] fibs = {1, 1, 2, 3, 5};
   incArray(fibs);
   inc(fibs[4]);
}
```

In this program, the *main()* method declares and initialises the array *fibs* to contain the first five Fibonacci numbers. The array reference variable is passed to method *incArray()* by the method call

    incArray(fibs);

which effectively passes the array by reference.

This means that the formal parameter reference variable *b* declared in the method heading actually refers to the same array as reference variable *fibs* in *main()*. The method increments every element value in the array. The primitive-type array element *fibs[4]*, which is the fifth element in the array, is passed by value to method *inc()* by the method call

    inc(fibs[4]);

which copies the value 6 into the formal parameter *n* declared in the method heading. *n* is then incremented by the method, but this has no effect upon the original parameter to the method because primitive types are passed by value.

Activity 9.7

Fibonacci series

Write a method to compute the first 40 terms in the Fibonacci series and store them in an array passed as a parameter. You may assume that the array has 41 elements, and store the terms in the elements indexed 1 to 40.

Activity 9.8

Fibonacci table

Write a method which takes as a parameter an array containing the first 40 Fibonacci numbers as above, and prints a table as follows.

Term	Fib Number
1	1
2	1
3	2
4	3
.	.
.	.
.	.
40	102334155

9.7 Summary

- Arrays are a means for storing lots of data items of the same type together under a single name
- Individual array elements are accessed using an integer index
- You often process arrays using loops, to visit each element in turn
- Arrays are created using *new*, and accessed via *reference variables*
- Arrays are passed to methods as parameters, by passing their reference variables.

9.8 Review questions

 Question 9.1 Fill in the blanks in the following:

1 The elements of an array are related by the fact that they have the same _____.

2 The number used to refer to a particular element of an array is called its _____.

3 A _____ should be used to declare the size of an array because it makes the program more scalable.

Question 9.2 State whether the following are *true* or *false*:

1 A single array can store many different types of values.

2 An array index should normally be of data type *double*.

Question 9.3 Answer the following questions regarding an array called *fractions*.

1 Declare a variable called *ARRAYSIZE* initialised to the value 10.

2 Declare the array *fractions* with *ARRAYSIZE* elements of type *double* and initialise the elements to 0.0

3 Name the fourth element from the beginning of the array.

4 Name the array element with index 4.

5 Assign the value 1.667 to array element 9.

6 Assign the value 3.333 to the seventh element of the array.

Question 9.4 What, if anything, is wrong (there may be more than one mistake) with the following statements? Give a correct version.

1 int[] n = {'a', 'b', 'c'};

2 int[] ages = {4;7;8};

3 int[] temperatures = new double[10];

Question 9.5 What is wrong with the following method? Give a correct version.

```
public static void f2()
{
    int a = 42;
    int[] ages = {19, 27, 18, 18, 95, 14, 20, 19, 22, 37};

    for (int i = 0; i <= 10; i++)
    {
        ages[i] += a;
    }
}
```

? **Question 9.6** Answer *true* or *false* to each of the following:

1 Arrays are created using *new*.

2 You access an individual array element using its index.

3 An array index can be of any primitive type.

4 The index of the first element of any array is 1.

5 Array elements contain random values, until you assign values to them.

6 The following creates an array of 10 elements.

int[] thing = {10};

7 If *a* and *b* are array reference variables which are currently referencing arrays, the assignment *a = b;* produces a single array with, effectively, two names.

8 Arrays are passed as parameters to methods using 'call-by-value' semantics.

9 The variable *length* contains the index of the last element in the corresponding array.

10 When processing a partially full array, it is good practice to store some extra data along with the array.

9.9 Answers to review questions

Question 9.1

1 type.

2 index, or subscript.

3 constant.

Question 9.2

1 **false**, an array can only store values of a single type.

2 **false**, an array index should normally be an integer constant or integer expression.

Question 9.3

1 final int ARRAYSIZE = 10;

2 double[] fractions = new double[ARRAYSIZE];

NOTE elements automatically initialised to 0.0 when *new* is used.

3 fractions[3];

4 fractions[4];

5 fractions[9] = 1.667;

6 fractions[6] = 3.333;

Question 9.4

1 Elements declared as ints; initialisers are chars.

2 Use commas, not semicolons, to separate initialiser values, such as
      int[] ages = {4,7,8};

3 The Array object is array of *double*, but the reference variable refers to arrays of *int*.

Question 9.5

The *for* loop counts past the end of the array: this should read i < 10 and not i <= 10.

Question 9.6

1 **True** *new* creates the array, and assignment is used to store a reference to the array in a reference variable, effectively giving the array a name.

2 **True** You give the array name with the index in square brackets.

3 **False** The index must be of type int.

4 **False** The first index is always 0.

5 **False** Array elements are automatically initialised: numbers to zero, booleans to *false* and references to *null*.

6 **False** This is an initialiser list with one value, which creates an array of one element containing the number 10.

7 **True** *b* contains a reference to an array, and the assignment copies this into *a*, so that *a* and *b* both contain a reference to the same array.

8 **False** Well, sort of! Array reference variables are passed using call-by-value, which means the arrays themselves are passed using 'call by reference' semantics. This means that the method can access the parameter array directly.

9 **False** *length* contains the number of elements in the array, which is 1 more than the highest index value, because indices start at 0.

10 True It is good practice to use a value stored in an integer variable to record an indication of how full the array is. Often the index of the next free element is stored. This will be used to control any loop required to access the existing 'occupied' elements, and to add more data if required.

9.10 Feedback on activities

Activity 9.1: Exam marks   The following is a possible solution:

```
int failCount = 0;

for (int i = 0; i < marks.length; i++ )
{
    if (marks[i] < 40)
        failCount++;
}

System.out.println("Number of fails is " + failCount);
```

Activity 9.2: Palindrome testing   You can achieve this by setting one variable to the index of the first element in the array, and another to the index of the last element in the array. You can then use a loop to compare the elements at these positions, which should be the same if the array contains a palindrome, then increment the lower variable and decrement the upper variable, compare the elements at these positions, and so on until *either*

- you find two elements which aren't the same (the number isn't a palindrome) *or*

- the two indices meet or cross over (you have checked the whole array, and it is a palindrome.

The following code uses *boolean* variables to contain the current values of these two conditions, and these are used in the *while* loop test.

```
int i = 0;
int j = nums.length - 1;

boolean isPal = true;
boolean finished = false;

while ((isPal) && (!finished))
{
    isPal = (nums[i] == nums[j]);
    i++; j—;
    finished = (i >= j);
}

if (isPal)
    System.out.println("It is a palindrome");
else
    System.out.println("It is not a palindrome");
```

Note that the test in

```
finished = (i >= j);
```

uses the >= operator. If the array has an even number of elements, then the values of i and j will eventually cross over, but if the array has an odd number of elements, you can stop when the two indices become the same.

Activity 9.3: Partially full arrays   Here is a possible solution.

```
int i = 0;

String s = JOptionPane.showInputDialog("enter an age, -1 to stop:");
int n = Integer.parseInt(s);

while ((i <= ages.length - 1) && (n != -1))
{
   ages[i] = n;
   s = JOptionPane.showInputDialog("enter an age, -1 to stop:");
   int n = Integer.parseInt(s);
   i++;
}

int nextFree = i;
// nextFree is index of next free element in array
```

The *while* loop terminates either when the array is full, or when the user enters the sentinel −1 to indicate the end of the data.

The variable *nextFree* keeps track of the next free element in the array, which will enable the program to add more ages later. Of course, the program would first have to check whether

```
nextFree == ages.length
```

which would indicate that the array was full.

Activity 9.4: Dry running exercise

1 In the table which follows, U means the variable exists but the value is undefined.

2 Note that *int* array elements are automatically initialised to 0.

line	SIZE	evens [0]	evens [1]	evens [2]	evens [3]	i	I < SIZE	2*(i+1)	Print to screen
L1	4								
L2	4	**0**	**0**	**0**	**0**				
L3	4	0	0	0	0	**U**			
L4	4	0	0	0	0	**0**	0<4? YES		
L5	4	2	0	0	0	0		**2**	
L4	4	2	0	0	0	1	1<4? YES		
L5	4	2	4	0	0	1		**4**	
L4	4	2	4	0	0	2	2<4? YES		
L5	4	2	4	6	0	2		**6**	
L4	4	2	4	6	0	3	3<4? YES		
L5	4	2	4	6	8	3		**8**	
L4	4	2	4	6	8	4	**4<4? NO**		
L6	4	2	4	6	8	0	**0<4? YES**		
L7	4	2	4	6	8	0			0 2
L6	4	2	4	6	8	1	**1<4? YES**		
L7	4	2	4	6	8	1			1 4
L6	4	2	4	6	8	2	**2<4? YES**		
L7	4	2	4	6	8	2			2 6
L6	4	2	4	6	8	3	**3<4? YES**		
L7	4	2	4	6	8	3			3 8
L6	4	2	4	6	8	4	**4<4? NO**		

Activity 9.5: More dry running

1 Array contains 40 5 9 7 8 300

2 Array contains 40 5 9 7 8 300

3 Output is 14

4 Array contains 40 5 9 7 8 300; output is 700

5 Array contains 2040 2005 2009 2007 2008 2300.

Activity 9.6: Array initialisation   You can use either of two methods. Either way, you will place the value of zero times five in the element with index 0, one times five in the element with index 1, two times five in the element with index 2 etc.

You need an array with eleven elements.

Method 1: Use a loop

```
final int SIZE = 11;

int[] table = new int[SIZE];

// initialise to 5 times table

for (int i = 0; i < table.length; i++)
{
    table[i]= i * 5;
}
```

Method 2: Use an initialiser list

```
int[] table = {0,5,10,15,20,25,30,35,40,45,50};
```

Activity 9.7: Fibonacci series   Note that this method uses *length* to control the loop termination, and therefore will fill an array of any length with Fibonacci numbers.

```
public static void calcFibs(int[] fibTable)
{
    fibTable[1] = 1;
    fibTable[2] = 1;
    // Note that fibTable[0] is not used as you do not
    // usually refer to the 0th term in a series.

    for (int i = 3; i < fibTable.length; i++)
    {
        fibTable[i] = fibTable[i - 1] + fibTable[i - 2];
    }
}
```

Activity 9.8: Fibonacci table   The following method will work.

```
public static void printFibs(int[] fibTable)
{
    // initialise output String with table headings
    String output = "Term\tFib Number\n";

    for (int term = 0; term < fibTable.length; term++)
        output += term + "\t" + fibTable[term ] + "\n";

    System.out.println(output);
}
```

This method uses the technique of generating an output String by successive concatenation.

One final point: Fibonacci numbers grow rather rapidly, and will cause integer overflow when they get too big. Overflow occurs when the integer generated is too big for the available memory; a number will be stored, but it will be the wrong number. Try placing this method and the one to generate the Fibonacci numbers in a program, and change the number of terms generated and printed, to find the point at which the overflow occurs. The following main method could be used for this purpose.

```java
public static void main(String[] args)
{
    final int SIZE = 41;
    int[] fibby = new int[SIZE];

    // Keep trying bigger array sizes until the
    // fibonacci numbers overflow

    calcFibs(fibby);

    printFibs(fibby);

    System.exit(0);
}
```

CHAPTER 10

Files

OVERVIEW

Java arrays are capable of storing large amounts of data in your programs. However, data stored in arrays is lost when the program terminates. This chapter shows you how to save your data in files on a disk so that it can be used again the next time the program runs.

Learning outcomes   On completion of this chapter you should be able to:

- Write programs that store data permanently in files on disk and read data from such files into the program for processing

- Explain the programming concepts used in file-handling programs and their implementation in Java.

10.1 Motivation

A problem

Suppose you write a program to read in 200 exam marks and store them in an array, then work out the average mark and print it out. You run the program and enter the marks. The marks are now in the array. The program prints the average and terminates.

... another problem

Now you write another program which reads in 200 exam marks and stores them in an array, then works out and prints the highest and lowest mark. You run the program and enter the marks. The marks are now in the array. The program prints the results and terminates.

... and yet another problem

Now you write another program which reads in 200 exam marks and stores them in an array, then works out and prints the number of fails (marks less than 40). You run the program and enter the marks. The marks are now in the array. The program prints the results and terminates.

Have you noticed a problem? Every time you run a program, you have to enter the same 200 exam marks. This is incredibly tedious and time-wasting.

Reading data from files

To avoid typing in 200 numbers every time you run a program, you could put the numbers in a *file* on the computer's disk. You could then get each program to read the numbers from the file rather than from the keyboard.

What exactly is a file? This can defined as a collection of information that can be stored on a disk; the disk could be a:

- Hard disk
- Floppy disk
- Zip disk
- CD-ROM
- Flash drive.

There are lots of different sorts of file; for example:

- Word documents
- Excel spreadsheets
- Program source files (text)
- Executable program files
- Data files for programs.

10.2 Sequential access files

There are lots of different types of files which can be used by Java programs, but we will only discuss *sequential access* files of *characters*.

A sequential access file is one in which data is written to the file in sequence, one data item at a time. The data is read from the file in the same sequential order. In a file of characters, each data item is a single character (actually a two-byte Java Unicode character code). The file is modelled in Java as a *stream* of characters. To manipulate files, a program must create *objects* defined by classes in the *java.io* package. You will learn more about classes and objects, including how to define your own classes and create objects from them in Chapters 11 and 12. However, in this chapter we will simply be *using* objects of predefined classes to write characters into files and read characters from files. The objects we will create have methods associated with them to carry out the required file operations.

We will need to be able to associate our program with the name(s) of one or more files on a disk, stating for each file whether we will be *writing to* the file or *reading from* it.

We will then need to use commands to read or write data to and from the file(s). We will look at each of these operations in turn.

10.3 Writing to a file

To write data to a file on a disk you must carry out the following steps:

- Create a *FileWriter* object in the program to represent the file and link it to the file (possibly creating the file if it does not already exist)
- Create a *BufferedWriter* object to collect characters together before they are sent to the file and connect it to the *FileWriter* object
- Create a *PrintWriter* object that converts values of different types into a stream of characters and connect it to the *BufferedWriter* object
- Write the data to the file by passing it to the *PrintWriter* object
- *Close* the file, releasing it for others to use.

You can create a *FileWriter* object as follows:

```
FileWriter outputFile = new FileWriter("wombat.txt");
```

This creates an object of class *FileWriter*, and stores a reference to it in the reference variable *outputFile*. This object is associated with a real file on the disk called wombat.txt, by way of passing the name of the real file as a parameter to the *FileWriter* object when the latter is created using *new* as shown (we will say more about the details of this mechanism in Chapters 11 and 12).

Now the reference variable *outputFile* is a name you can use within the program to refer to the real file on the disk. It may be thought of as a pipe connecting the program to the file, through which a stream of characters may flow to the file.

Note that if wombat.txt did not already exist, then it would be created by the above statement, and if it did already exist, then writing new data into it would erase any existing data it contained. If instead, we wanted to add new data to the *end* of the existing data in the file, then we could have opened the file as follows:

```
FileWriter outputFile = new FileWriter("wombat.txt", true);
```

Here, a second parameter, the *boolean* value *true*, has been supplied, which indicates that the file is to be opened in order to append new data to the end of the existing data.

We must now create a *BufferedWriter* object, as follows.

```
BufferedWriter outputBuffer
   = new BufferedWriter(outputFile);
```

This creates an object of class *BufferedWriter* and stores a reference to it in the reference variable *outputBuffer*. This object is connected to *outputFile* by way of passing the name of the latter as a parameter to the *BuffereredWriter* object when the latter is created using *new* as shown.

A *BufferedWriter* object receives a stream of characters, and passes them along to the *FileWriter* object. Sending characters to a file one at a time is very slow. The purpose of the *BufferedWriter* object is to collect a series of characters, then send them to the file all at once. This is much more efficient than sending the characters one at a time. The characters sit in the buffer and are sent to the file when the buffer is full. An analogy is that of borrowing books from a library. If you wanted four books, you would probably take them all out at once, rather than fetching them one at a time as you finish each book.

The final step is to create a *PrintWriter* object, as follows:

```
PrintWriter printStream
   = new PrintWriter(outputBuffer);
```

This creates an object of class *PrintWriter*, and stores a reference to it in the reference variable *printStream*. This object is connected to *outputBuffer* by way of passing the name of the latter as a parameter to the *PrintWriter* object when the latter is created using *new* as shown.

The *PrintWriter* object incorporates facilities which can be used to manage the conversion of Strings, integers etc into streams of characters to be sent to the buffer, and then to the file. You have effectively created a pipeline of objects, which process the data as it moves from the program to the file on disk.

You must now send your data along this pipeline.

You can send output from your programs to the *screen* using:

```
System.out.println()
```

which produces output in the *command window*. *System.out* is the *standard output object,* and *println()* is a method of this object, for writing Strings to the command window.

The *PrintWriter* object *printStream* is the analogous object for writing to your file. *PrintWriter* objects also have a method called *println()*. For example:

```
printStream.println("Hello");
```

will write the String *Hello* followed by a *newline* character into the file *wombat.txt*.

The *println()* method converts the String into a stream of characters that are collected together in the *BufferedWriter* object *outputBuffer* before being passed on via the *FileWriter* object *outputFile* to the actual file *wombat.txt*.

Here are some examples:

```
printStream.println("Hello");
printStream.println("Hello");
printStream.println("Hello");
```

writes into the file *Hello* followed by a *newline* character, three times. You can picture this as three lines of text as follows

```
Hello
Hello
Hello
```

but it is important to realise that the file is simply a sequence of characters, some of which are *newline* characters. Similarly, the effect of

```
printStream.println(42);
printStream.println("is the answer");
```

could be visualised as writing the following into the file

```
42
is the answer
```

but again, this exists in the file as a sequence of characters, two of which are *newline* characters.

Whatever value is supplied as a parameter to *println()*, the String equivalent of that value is written into the file.

Finally you close the *PrintWriter*, *BufferedWriter* and *FileWriter* down, which flushes any characters still waiting in the buffer into the file (if the buffer had not just been emptied, the characters would still wait there) and freeing the file for others to use.

This is done using the *PrintWriter* method *close()*, which automatically closes the buffer and file to which it is connected:

```
printStream.close();
```

In the command window, you can now use the DOS *type* command to view the contents of the data file as follows:

```
C:> type wombat.txt
```

If your program had used the instructions:

```
printStream.println("Hello");
printStream.println("Hello");
printStream.println("Hello");
```

to put data into the file, then the above command would display on the screen

```
Hello
Hello
Hello
```

You could also view the file using Notepad, Word or similar text-editing programs.

10.4 Reading from a file

To read data from a file on a disk you must carry out the following steps:

- Create a *FileReader* object in the program to represent the file and link it to the file
- Create a *BufferedReader* object to collect characters together before they are sent to the program, and connect it to the file
- Read the data from the file
- Close the file, releasing it for others to use.

You can create a *FileReader* object as follows:

    FileReader inputFile = new FileReader("wombat.txt");

This creates an object of class *FileReader*, and stores a reference to it in the reference variable *inputFile*. This object is associated with a real file on the disk called wombat.txt, by way of passing the name of the real file as a parameter to the *FileReader* oject when the latter is created using *new* as shown.

A *FileReader* object performs, not surprisingly, the opposite function to a *FileWriter* object – it is set up to get data out of a file, as opposed to putting data into the file. The above statement opens the file wombat.txt so you can read data from it.

 You must now create a *BufferedReader* object, as follows:

    BufferedReader inputBuffer
      = new BufferedReader(inputFile);

This creates an object of class *BufferedReader* and stores a reference to it in the reference variable *inputBuffer*. This object is connected to the *inputFile* object by way of passing the name of the latter as a parameter to the *BuffereredReader* object when the latter is created using *new* as shown.

A *BufferedReader* object receives a stream of characters from the file, and stores them in a buffer until they are needed by the program.

The above has set up the pipeline for reading from the file. You now want to start reading the data.

A *BufferedReader* object has a method called *readLine()*. When the program wishes to read in some data from the file, it can call this method.

    String line1 = inputBuffer.readLine();

The call to *readLine()* causes a stream of characters to be read from the file, up to and including the next *newline* character stored there. This stream of single characters is converted into a String object, which is returned by the *readLine()* method. In the above statement, this String has been stored in the String variable *line1*.

Finally, the file should be closed using:

     inputBuffer.close();

This closes the connection to the file as before. Note that this *close()* method is part of the *BufferedReader* object, whereas when we were writing to a file we used the *close()* method from the *PrintWriter* object.

10.5 The exam marks problem

We now have the tools to improve upon the exam marks processing programs just discussed. First we need a program to input the marks from the user and write them into a file.

We can store the marks into the file, one per line, using a loop which gets each mark from the user, then writes it into the file, terminating when the user enters some sentinel value such as -1, which could not be a valid exam mark. Here is the code:

```
String input = JOptionPane.showInputDialog("Enter a number, -1 to stop: ");
int num = Integer.parseInt(input);

while (num != -1)
{
    printStream.println(num);
    input = JOptionPane.showInputDialog("Enter a number, -1 to stop:");
    num = Integer.parseInt(input);
}
```

Activity 10.1

Reading marks

Each program for processing the exam marks needs some code to read the 200 marks from the file into an array. Write this code.

With this code in each of the exam marks processing programs, the programs can now work out the average, find the highest and lowest marks, count the fails, etc. by processing the array. You could try writing these programs as an exercise.

10.6 Reading from files of unknown size

For the solution to Activity 10.1, you were able to assume that there were precisely 200 lines in the file, and therefore you could use a *for* loop to read one line at a time. However, there are often times when a program must read all items from a file but does not know beforehand how many items are in the file. In such cases, you must use a non-deterministic loop which tests for the end of the file and stops when it is reached.

For example, suppose we want to find the average mark in a file full of exam marks, but we do not know how many exam marks are in the file. We must read the marks one by one and add each in turn to a running total. At the same time we must keep a count of how many marks have been read from the file. The program is as follows:

```java
// Finding the average mark in a file of exam marks
// Assumes marks were entered into the file one per line

import javax.swing.JOptionPane;
import java.io.*;  // This package contains our file handling classes

public class ExamAverage
{

    public static void main(String[] args) throws IOException
    {
        String fileName = JOptionPane.showInputDialog("Please enter filename");

        FileReader inputFile = new FileReader(fileName);
        BufferedReader inputBuffer = new BufferedReader(inputFile);

        double total = 0.0;
        int count = 0;

        String numString = inputBuffer.readLine();

        while (numString != null)
        {
            total += Double.parseDouble(numString);
            count++;
            numString = inputBuffer.readLine();
        }

        double average = total / count;

        JOptionPane.showMessageDialog(null,
            "The average mark in file " + fileName + " is: " + average);

        inputBuffer.close();

        System.exit(0);
    }
}
```

This program demonstrates some new ideas. The *while loop* test

        (numString != null)

is testing the value returned by the *readLine()* method, which is stored in *numString* on each iteration of the loop. When *readLine()* is invoked at the end of a file, it returns *null*, which enables us to test for when the end of the file has been reached, and therefore to process a file for which the size is not known in advance.

You will also note that the user is prompted for the name of the file to be processed, which is stored in a String and passed to our *FileReader* object. This makes the program more flexible as it can now be used with any appropriate file without us having to edit the program code to change the filename.

You may also have noticed the words

    throws IOException

on the end of the *main()* method header. *Exceptions* are a Java way to enable a running program to handle appropriately those conditions where the program encounters an error, thus preventing the error from causing the program to crash. For example, if the file being opened for reading did not exist, then the *FileReader* object cannot be created and a *FileNotFoundException* object is *thrown* (i.e. generated) to indicate this error. Similarly, if it was not possible to read from the file, an *IOException* object is thrown. (Actually a *FileNotFoundException* is a specialised form of the *IOException* – more on this concept in Chapter 12.) We could add code to the above program which would *catch* (a Java keyword – you could read this as 'respond to') such exception objects, taking appropriate action (for example, output a message telling the user what kind of error had occurred).

Now, when a method uses code that may throw the above types of exception, the method is *obliged* by the Java compiler to either include the appropriate exception-handling code, or to itself throw the exception by including the suffix *throws IOException* in the method heading as above. If this is not done, the program will not compile. If the method was called from another method, then the latter method now has the responsibility to catch (respond to) the exception. However, as the above is the *main()* method, there is no calling method and the exception will not be dealt with; the program will crash. You could test this out by running the above program and typing in the name of a non-existent file. Although beyond the scope of this book, exceptions are a valuable tool for the Java programmer, being a clean and elegant way of dealing with potential problems for a running program.

10.7 Summary

- Files of characters may be created, written to and read from by Java programs, by creating 'pipelines' of special objects.

10.8 Review questions

Question 10.1   Why do we use files in Java?

Question 10.2   Can a file only be accessed by one program?

Question 10.3   What is the nature of the data stored in files?

Question 10.4   Why do we use a buffer when writing characters to a file?

Question 10.5   What is the purpose of a *PrintWriter* object?

Question 10.6   Answer true or false to each of the following:

1 A file is a place to store data we wish to persist after our program has terminated.

2 File handling is done using 'pipelines' of objects.

3 One cannot pass an object as a parameter to another object.

4 A *PrintWriter* object is used as a printer driver.

5 A buffer object holds only one character.

6 The *println()* method is only found in the standard output object.

7 A *FileReader* object is the logical representation within a program of a physical file on disk.

8 A file which is open for reading is closed by calling the method *close()* from the input buffer.

9 A file buffer is a means of improving efficiency when processing files.

10 The *readLine()* method is used to read data from a file.

10.9 Answers to review questions

Answer to question 10.1   Files provide persistent storage; that is, we can store our data even after the program has finished, and don't have to enter it at the keyboard every time we run a program.

Answer to question 10.2   No, a file can be used by one program, then another, and so on.

Answer to question 10.3   There are many different sorts of files with different types of data in them, but the files we have looked at in this chapter store only sequences of characters.

Answer to question 10.4   We do this for reasons of efficiency. The operation of writing data to a file takes much longer than moving data around in main memory, so it makes sense to collect many data items in a buffer, and write all of them at the same time.

Answer to question 10.5   The *PrintWriter* object converts different data formats into a stream of characters to send to the file.

Answer to question 10.6

1 true – The data survives when the program stops running.

2 true – The data passes between the program and the file along such pipelines.

3 false – This is precisely what we do in setting up the pipeline of file-handling objects.

4 false – A *PrintWriter* object manages the conversion of values of different Java types into streams of characters.

5 false – A buffer object holds a large number of characters which are all written to or read from a file in one operation.

6 false – *PrintWriter* objects also support a version of this method, for writing data into files.

7 true – The association is set up by passing the name of the real file as a parameter to the *FileReader* constructor method (see Chapter 11 for explanation of constructors).

8 true – The method breaks the link between the program and the physical file.

9 true – Data for transfer to or from the file is stored in the buffer, and at some point all the data in the buffer is transferred in one go.

10 true – The method returns a String comprising all the characters in the file up to the next new line character.

10.10 Feedback on activities

Activity 10.1 : Reading marks   The following code also uses a loop, and assumes that there will be precisely 200 marks to be read.

```
String str;
int[] marks = new int[200];

for (int i = 0; i <= 199; i++)
{
    str = inputBuffer.readLine();
    marks[i] = Integer.parseInt(str);
}
```

CHAPTER 11

Classes and objects

OVERVIEW

We have been creating objects for some time now – Strings and arrays are examples of objects. You will now learn to specify your own objects using classes, and look at the object-oriented approach to program construction.

Learning outcomes On completion of this chapter you should be able to:

- Explain what classes are, and their relationship to programs

- Describe how classes may used as building blocks in object-oriented programs

- Explain the relationship between objects and classes

- Explain how methods are used to implement object behaviour.

11.1 What is an object?

Remember, you have already met Strings and arrays, which are examples of objects. We create an object using the dynamic memory allocation operator *new*, and we effectively give it a name by storing a reference to it in a reference variable. We also used objects of the predefined classes *FileWriter*, *BufferedWriter*, *PrintWriter*, *FileReader* and *BufferedReader* in Chapter 10. But how are the characteristics of these objects specified, and can we specify and create new objects of our own design?

We certainly can, and this is the basis of object-oriented design and programming.

So far, we have considered a *class* to be a collection of methods, which work together by calling each other to solve a programming problem. Each method can contain variable declarations, which are local to (only exist within) that method. But there is more to classes: much more!

Classes can be used to specify blueprints for *objects*.

So what characterises an object?

An object (usually) encapsulates:

- **Attributes** (data)
- **Behaviours** (methods).

The attributes do not reside in any of the methods, but are shared by (are accessible to) all of them. Their values at any given time represent the *state* of the object at that time.

Consider the following objects; which attributes might be associated with them?

- A 2-dimensional co-ordinate point
- A glass which can hold up to 1 litre
- A square to be drawn on a graphics screen
- A car in a simulation of a traffic situation
- A person's personal details
- A timepiece (clock, watch).

For each of the above examples, you should have come up with something similar to these responses:

- The 2-dimensional co-ordinate point: Two real numbers (i.e. type *double*); the x and y co-ordinates
- The glass: a real number (*double*) representing the volume of liquid in the glass. Other attributes could be numbers representing the dimensions of the glass, and/ or its capacity
- A square: possibly the co-ordinates of two opposite corners (two points), a colour in which to draw the square (could be a String, for example), texture, line thickness, etc
- The car: possibly numbers representing speed, acceleration, direction of travel, angle of the front wheels, volume of fuel in the tank, etc
- The person's personal details: possibly name and address (Strings), salary (*double*), phone number, etc
- The timepiece: the current time could be represented by three integers to represent the hours, minutes and seconds.

Objects as components

Note that in the foregoing example, two *co-ordinate* point objects were used in the construction of a *square* object. This concept of one object containing others is a common relationship between objects, to which we will return in Chapter 12.

You could define a class to specify any one of these objects, and declare variables in the class (but not inside any of the methods of the class), to represent the attributes listed. Such classes do not have a *main()* method, because they are not being used in the same sense as the classes you have met so far. Rather, these classes are a means of specifying the attributes and behaviour of objects that you may use in your programs.

What about behaviours?

- Methods are used to implement the *behaviours* of the object (i.e. what it can do, or have done to it)
- Examples of the behaviours of an object could be changing the values of the attributes, reporting the values of attributes, outputting results of calculations.

What behaviours might you want the above objects to have? Think about this before you read on.

Exactly which behaviours we might want these objects to have depends on the context, but examples could be:

- **The co-ordinate point:** change the x or y co-ordinate, move to the origin, draw itself (if part of a graphics system)
- **The glass:** 'drink' a given quantity of the liquid, fill the glass, empty the glass
- **Square:** draw itself, rotate by a given angle, change size
- **Car:** accelerate, use some fuel, turn wheels left or right by a given amount, start or stop engine
- **Person:** change age, change salary, change telephone number
- **Timepiece:** change the time.

11.2 'Time' for an example

To illustrate these principles, let us write a class to define timepiece objects (watches and clocks). What data (attributes) will be needed?

Well, the first requirement is to represent a time! We could store this in three integer variables, to represent the hours, minutes and seconds respectively.

What behaviours (methods) will be needed?

This depends on what use the timepiece is going to be put to, but some possibilities are:

- Create a timepiece with a time associated with it
- Change the time associated with the timepiece
- Output the current time stored, in hours, minutes and seconds
- As above, but in seconds since midnight
- Tick tock (i.e. advance the time stored by one second).

Here is a first stab at the definition of a *Timepiece* class. Note that all the attributes (variables) have been declared, comma separated, on a single line. This shorthand is possible because all three are of the same type, *int*. Note also that the attributes are not declared inside any methods.

```java
public class Timepiece
{
    // Declaration of object attributes
    private int hrs, mins, secs;

    // Constructor method
    public Timepiece(int h, int m, int s)
    {
        hrs = h; mins = m; secs = s;
    }

    // Get methods

    public int getHrs()
    {
        return hrs;
    }

    public int getMins()
    {
        return mins;
    }

    public int getSecs()
    {
        return secs;
    }

    // Set methods

    public void setHrs(int h)
    {
        hrs = h;
    }

    public void setMins(int m)
    {
        mins = m;
    }

    public void setSecs(int s)
    {
        secs = s;
    }
}
```

We can now create *instances* of this class. These are called *objects* – just as a variable is an instance of a primitive type. Each object will represent one timepiece. Each object will have its own copy of the attributes *hrs, mins* and *secs*.

Attributes are also called *instance variables.* Instance variables have *class scope* i.e. they are accessible throughout the class. They are usually declared as *private*, which means that they can only be accessed by the methods of this class, and not by methods of other classes. This is very important, and we will return to it later.

Creating Timepiece objects

So how can we create *Timepiece* objects using this class?

You may have noticed that the *Timepiece* class has a method called *Timepiece()*. This method takes three integer parameters, and assigns their values to the three instance variables. You may also have noticed that this method has no return type, not even void. The *Timepiece()* method is an example of a *constructor method*.

Constructor methods

Characteristics:

- Constructor methods are invoked when a new object is created
- They have the same name as their class
- Parameters, if any, are often used to give initial values to instance variables
- Constructor methods sometimes do other processing associated with initialising a new object
- Constructor methods have no return value.

Calling a constructor method

A constructor method is called when you create (instantiate) an object of the associated class using *new*. Memory is allocated to hold the new object, then the appropriate constructor method is called.

You use the same kind of statement as you have already seen when creating array or String objects. For example

```
Timepiece myWatch = new Timepiece(10, 38, 16);
```

A new *Timepiece* object is created, and the assignment stores a reference to the object in the reference variable *myWatch* which effectively makes *myWatch* the name of the object. Note how the three integer parameters for the constructor method are provided. If the constructor did not assign initial values to the numerical attributes, they would be automatically initialised to 0 (note that this does not happen with local variables declared inside methods).

Using Timepiece objects

The following is a Java class which uses the *Timepiece* class to create two *Timepiece* objects.

```java
public class Time
{
   public static void main(String[] args)
   {
      int h = 4, m = 30, s = 45;

      Timepiece myWatch = new Timepiece(h, m, s);
      Timepiece myClock = new Timepiece(h, 75, 20);
      myWatch = myClock;
   }
}
```

Note the combined declaration and initialisation of the three *int* variables.

What does the following statement do?

```
myWatch = myClock;
```

The two objects and their reference variables can be represented as follows:

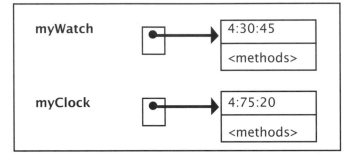

The assignment causes the reference stored in *myClock* to be copied into *myWatch*, as:

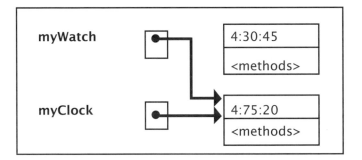

The effect is to give *two different* names to the *Timepiece* object representing 4 hrs 75 mins and 20 secs. The other *Timepiece* object no longer has any associated reference variables, and will be destroyed by the garbage collector.

Note: You are not copying the time by *myClock* into *myWatch*, as might be thought at first glance. You are actually making *myClock* and *myWatch* reference the same object!

What do you notice about the time by *myClock*?

The number of minutes represented is 75. Clearly, you should add 1 to the number of hours, and store 15 as the number of minutes. However, Java knows nothing about our intentions for these objects, and will allow us to store any three integers in the object instance variables.

11.3 Overloading constructors

We have already seen examples of overloading methods in Chapter 8. We can overload constructor methods by declaring different versions with different numbers and/or orders of parameters. Here are two alternative constructors for the *Timepiece* class.

1 A constructor which takes no parameters, and assigns the time 12:30:00 to the object instance variables.

```
public Timepiece()
{
    hrs = 12; mins = 30; secs = 0;
}
```

2 A constructor which takes a single parameter that represents the time as a number of seconds since midnight, and computes the corresponding values for the object instance variables using integer division and modulus (%).

```
public Timepiece(int s)
{
    hrs = s / 3600;
    mins = (s % 3600) / 60;
    secs = s % 60;
}
```

We can now create objects with statements such as:

- **Constructor 1:**
  Timepiece kitchenClock = new Timepiece();
- **Constructor 2:**
  Timepiece grandfatherClock = new Timepiece(3820);

and so on. The constructor method invoked depends on the type and number of parameters supplied when the object is created.

11.4 Get and set methods

Get methods are used to return the values of an object's attributes. For example

```
public int getHrs()
{
    return hrs;
}
```

They might also present the data in a different form. Here is another version of *getHrs()* which gives the hours on the 12-hour clock instead of the 24-hour clock.

```
public int getHrs()
{
    if (hrs > 12)
        return hrs -12;
    else
        return hrs;
}
```

Set methods are used to set the values of the object's attributes. For example:

```
public void setHrs(int h)
{
   hrs = h;
}
```

Such methods might also change the form in which the data is stored. For example, the following version of *setHrs()* takes a time from the 12-hour clock (am/pm represented by a *boolean* parameter), and sets the *hrs* attribute to the corresponding time from the 24-hour clock.

```
public void setHrs(int h, boolean isAM)
{
   if (isAM)
      hrs = h;
   else
      hrs = h + 12;
}
```

A set method may also do *validation* of the proposed new value for the attribute. Here is another version of *setHrs()* to illustrate this.

```
public void setHrs(int h)
{
   if ((h >= 0) && (h <= 23))
      hrs = h;
   else
      System.out.println("Hours must be between 0 and 23");
}
```

Predicate methods

It is often useful to have methods which you can use to test the truth value of some property of an object. Such methods must return a *boolean* value. For example, here is a method to test whether it is tea time (4 pm).

```
public boolean isTeaTime()
{
   return ((hrs == 16) && (mins == 0) && (secs == 0));
}
```

Calling the methods

All of the above methods could be placed in the *Timepiece* class, and any object created from this class would then possess them. But how can you call (invoke) the methods?

With static (class) methods, you used the name of the *class* with a dot and the method name. For example:

```
JOptionPane.showMessageDialog(null, "Hello");
```

When the key word *static* appears in a method header, this means that there is only one copy of the method, and it is associated with the class itself. This applied to all the methods we have used prior to this chapter. However, you will have noticed that the headers of the methods associated with the *Timepiece* class do not contain the word *static*. This means that in effect, every object of class *Timepiece* has its own copy of each method. Methods of classes which have been written for the purpose of creating objects (as opposed to the classes we have used prior to this chapter, which contained a *main()* method and sometimes other methods, and were not used to define the characteristics of objects) are usually defined as non-static. However, static methods are occasionally defined in such classes, in which case there will be only one copy of the method, which can be accessed by every object of that class. Such methods are useful for tasks such as counting the number of objects created etc.

With non-static methods, each object created from the class effectively has its own copy of the method. This means that, when you call a method, it is a method belonging to a particular object. To call such a method, you use the *object* name, dot and method name. For example:

```
myWatch.setHrs(14);
int hours = myClock.getHrs();

if (myWatch.isTeaTime() && myClock.isTeaTime())
    JOptionPane.showMessageDialog(null, "Both agree it's time for tea!");
```

In object-orientation parlance, calling a method belonging to an object is also known as *sending a message* to the object.

Tick tock

Write a method called *tickTock()* for the *Timepiece* class. This method should add one second to the time represented by a *Timepiece* object.

Pouring water

Write a class to specify *Glass* objects, where a *Glass* has as attributes a capacity and an amount of liquid currently in the *Glass*. Include a constructor method to create an empty *Glass* with a given capacity, *get* and *set* methods to get/ set the values of the capacity and the current amount of liquid in the *Glass*, and a method called *addLiquid()* which adds a given quantity of liquid to the *Glass*.

Now write a program to create two *Glass* objects, put some liquid into one, then empty it into the other.

11.5 Information hiding

An object of class *Timepiece* hides from any code that uses it the details of how it implements the time.

Such code can only access the object's *public* methods – known as the *interface* to the object. The details of how the methods are implemented are also hidden – other objects and classes only know about the *signatures* (headings) of the methods (i.e.the number and type of parameters required and the return type of each method).

You will recall from section 11.2 that this hiding of the instance variables representing the time is achieved by prefixing their declaration with the keyword *private*. (Note that methods can also be declared as *private*, which makes it impossible for them to be called from outside the class. This is useful if a method is required to be called only by one or more of the other methods of its own class.)

The value of each instance variable is usually accessed by calling an associated *get* method and the value may be changed only by calling an associated *set* method, as described in section 11.4. At this point you might be wondering what is the point of all this – surely if we declared the instance variables as *public* we would be able to access them in the same way as we access public methods, for example to change the value of *hrs* on *myWatch*

```
myWatch.hrs = 12;
```

rather than having to use a method like this

```
myWatch.setHrs(12);
```

This is true.

However, this *information hiding* is very useful. It allows us to carefully limit and control the interaction between different objects and classes, thus reducing the possibilities for inadvertent interaction. This is very important when developing large programs. Changes can be made to representations of attributes and implementation of methods in a class, and as long as the method headings do not change, any class or object using objects of the modified class need never know. They just call the methods as before, and get the results. The system operates on a need-to-know basis.

For example, you could change the way the time is represented in the *Timepiece* class, and as long as the headings (*signatures*) of the class's methods do not change, programs using *Timepiece* objects do not need to be modified.

To illustrate, suppose you decided to represent the attributes *hrs*, *mins* and *secs* using a 3-element array rather than as three separate variables:

```
private int[] time = new int[3];
```

where time[0] contains the hours, time[1] contains the minutes and time[2] contains the seconds.

You would then need to rewrite all the methods to operate on this new attribute data format, but you would not change the method headings (signatures). This means that none of the objects and classes using the *Timepiece* class need to be modified.

Here is an example of a method modified for the new attribute format.

```
public void setHrs(int h) // Heading unchanged
{
    if ((h >= 0) && (h <= 24))
        time[0] = h;
    else
        System.out.println("Hours must be between 0 and 23");
}
```

Activity 11.3

Information hiding

Suppose that you wish to represent the time in the *Timepiece* class as the number of seconds since midnight. You now need a single *int* attribute.

```
private int timeInSecs;
```

Write new versions of the *setHrs()* and *isTeaTime()* methods for the new attribute format. Remember: do not change the method signatures (headings), just their bodies.

To facilitate information hiding

- You declare instance variables as *private,* which means they cannot be accessed by methods of other classes/objects
- You declare as *public,* the methods that you want to be accessible to other classes and objects
- These methods form the *interface* between any object of this class and the rest of the program
- Note that sometimes you declare methods as *private*; you would do this when they are to be used only by other methods of the same class.

Methods and variables are declared as *static* when you want them to belong to a class only, and not to the objects of that class. If the class is used to create objects, these objects do *not* have their own copy of static methods and variables, but they do have access to the single copy in the class. These are also called *class* attributes and methods. You might use a class attribute to count the number of objects of the class which have been created, for example. The methods in all of the classes we wrote prior to this chapter were declared as *static*, because they were not used to specify objects.

11.6 The toString() method

There is a class called *Object* in package *java.lang*. This class defines 11 methods, including one called *toString()*. The *Object* class is automatically *inherited* by all Java classes (inheritance is an important aspect of object-oriented programming which will be explained in Chapter 12), which means that every Java class has these 11 methods.

However, the significant thing at this point is that you can *override* these inherited methods to create versions to use in your own classes. For example, the purpose of the *toString()* method is to return a String which somehow represents the associated object. A suitable overridden *toString()* method for the *Timepiece* class would be one which returns a String showing the time as represented by a *Timepiece* object, so the following method would be appropriate.

```
    public String toString()
    {
      return "\n" + hrs + " hours " + mins + " minutes and " + secs + " seconds";
    }
```

And now for the neat part...

We can call the *toString()* method in the same way as any other method in the *Timepiece* class. However, we can also now pass a *Timepiece* object to the *print()* or *println()* methods, or concatenate the object with a String; in other words, use the name of the object in a context where we would normally use a String. This causes the object's *toString()* method to be called automatically to return the String version of the object.

For example:

```
    JOptionPane.showMessageDialog(null,"The time by my watch is\n: " + myWatch);
```

This will print the following String in a dialog box:

> The time by my watch is:
> 4 hours 10 minutes and 18 seconds

11.7 Summary

- An object has a *state*, represented by the current values of its attributes (instance variables)
- An object has behaviours, represented by its methods
- Objects are specified using classes
- Objects are created using *new*, and initialised by special constructor methods which are called when the object is created.

11.8 Review questions

Question 11.1   How can you specify your own objects in Java?

Question 11.2   How can you create in your programs objects that you have specified yourself?

Question 11.3   What is the role of constructor methods in creating objects?

Question 11.4   Why might you overload constructor methods?

Question 11.5   How do you call the methods of an object you have created?

Question 11.6   Why do you usually declare attributes as *private* and methods as *public* in classes used to create objects?

Question 11.7   Answer *true* or *false* to each of the following:

1   All classes in Java must contain a *main()* method.

2   The behaviour of an object is what you can do to it and what it can do.

3 It is illegal to use one object in the definition of another.

4 Get and set methods are used to obtain and change the values of an object's attributes.

5 An object can only have one constructor method.

6 The constructor is called when an object is created.

7 You call an object's methods by using the name of the object's class, followed by a dot, followed by the method name and parameters, if any.

8 The *toString()* method makes an object into a String.

9 Attribute values represent the state of an object.

10 A predicate method returns a truth value.

11.9 Answers to review questions

Question 11.1 You must declare a class containing instance variables (non-static variables declared outside of all methods) to represent the attributes of each object, and methods which implement the behaviours of each object.

Question 11.2 You create such objects by using *new* and assigning the object to a reference variable of the appropriate type.

Question 11.3 Constructors are special methods with no return type specified. They are called when an object is created, and may be used for initialisation of the object attributes and other initial processing.

Question 11.4 Overloading constructor methods enables you to create your object with alternative data formats supplied as parameters (for example, the time in seconds instead of hours, minutes and seconds), or to initialise the object in different ways.

Question 11.5 You call the object's methods by giving the object name (actually the reference variable name), followed by a dot, followed by the method name and parameters if any.

Question 11.6 You do this to implement information hiding. You can change the representation of the attributes and implementation of the methods in any way you wish, as long as the methods have the same signatures (headings), and this will have no effect as far as any classes using the object are concerned.

Question 11.7

1 False Classes used to specify objects do not have a *main()* method.

2 True The behaviour is implemented using methods.

3 False This is very useful; for example, you might use a co-ordinate point object in the definition of a square object.

4 **True** The attributes themselves are not usually made accessible from outside the object, in order to implement information hiding.

5 **False** Constructors may be overloaded to provide several versions.

6 **True** The constructor is normally used to do initialisation of attributes and other initial processing.

7 **False** You can create many objects from one class. To invoke a method from a particular object, you give the *object* name, dot and method name (not the class name).

8 **False** The *toString()* method is inherited by every class, and returns a String. It is up to the programmer to write an implementation of the *toString()* method to return whatever String they feel is relevant for the objects of that class. Usually this will be some information about the state of the object (i.e. values of the attributes).

9 **True** For example, the attributes for a particular *Person* object might be name, height and eye colour with values "Fred", 175, "blue".

10 **True** Predicate methods are used to obtain truth-valued information about an object. For example, a *Person* object might have a method *isSmoker()* which returns *true* or *false* as appropriate.

11.10 Feedback on activities

Activity 11.1: Tick tock   This method must increment the *secs* attribute, but if this causes *secs* to become 60, then *secs* must be set to 0 and the *mins* attribute must be incremented. Similarly, if this causes *mins* to become 60, then *mins* must be set to 0 and *hrs* must be incremented. Finally, if this causes *hrs* to be 24, then you must set *hrs* to 0 – a new day has begun!

```java
public void TickTock()
{
   secs++;

   if (secs == 60)
   {
      secs = 0;
      mins++;
   }

   if (mins == 60)
   {
       mins = 0;
       hrs++;
   }

   if (hrs == 24)
       hrs = 0;
}
```

You can call the method for the *myClock* object as follows:

```java
myClock.TickTock()
```

Activity 11.2: Pouring water   Here is the class definition:

```
public class Glass
{
  private int capacity, contents;

  public Glass(int cap)
  {
    capacity = cap;
    contents = 0;
  }

  public int getCapacity()
  {
    return capacity;
  }

  public int getContents()
  {
    return contents;
  }

  public void setCapacity(int c)
  {
    capacity = c;
  }

  public void setContents(int c)
  {
    contents = c;
  }

  public void addLiquid(int quantity)
  {
    contents += quantity;
  }
}
```

Note that the above methods should also do some validation. For example, checking whether negative values are being allocated (although adding a negative quantity of liquid may be considered acceptable, as it is equivalent to removing some liquid), whether a given change will make the contents greater than the capacity, etc. You might want to modify the methods to deal with such cases.

...continued

Here is a class to use some *Glass* objects.

```java
public class Pouring
{
    public static void main(String[] args)
    {
        int liquid = 330; // 330ml of water

        Glass tumbler = new Glass(500); // capacity 500ml
        Glass bigOne = new Glass(1000); // capacity 1 litre

        // Put 250ml into the tumbler
        tumbler.setContents(250);

        // Pour contents of tumbler into big glass
        bigOne.addLiquid(tumbler.getContents());
        tumbler.setContents(0);
    }
}
```

Again, you should do some validation – for example, what happens if there is insufficient room in a glass for the liquid you add, etc.

Activity 11.3: Information hiding   To 'set the hours' in the new format, you must remove the existing 'hours' component from the time in seconds by taking the remainder after dividing by 3,600 (the number of seconds in an hour). You then add on the new hours component by multiplying the parameter by 3,600 and adding it to the above remainder.

```java
public void setHrs(int h)
{
    if ((h >= 0)&&(h <= 24))
        timeInSecs = (timeInSecs % 3600) + h * 3600;
    else
        System.out.println("Hours must be between 0 and 23");
}
```

The new *isTeaTime()* method returns *true* if and only if the time in seconds divides by 3,600 precisely 16 times i.e. with no remainder.

```java
public boolean isTeaTime()
{
    return ((timeInSecs / 3600 == 16) && (timeInSecs % 3600 == 0));
}
```

CHAPTER 12

More on classes

OVERVIEW

In the previous chapter you learned to specify your own objects by writing classes. In this chapter we will explore ways in which classes may be related to one another to form the building blocks for creating more useful programs.

Learning outcomes   On completion of this chapter you should be able to:

- Explain the meaning of *inheritance* and *composition*

- Describe how relationships (associations) between classes can be implemented

- Describe how the above enables code to be reused

- Explain the term *polymorphism*.

12.1 Composition

We touched upon the concept of class composition in Chapter 11 when we discussed the example of a *square* object on a graphics screen containing *co-ordinate point* objects to define its position on the screen. Composition (also known as *aggregation*) is the concept of a class having other classes as the types of one or more of its attributes.

Consider classes for defining the following objects; what additional classes might be useful in defining the attributes of these classes?

- A diary – class *Diary*
- A queue at a supermarket till – class *Queue*
- A model of a garden – class *Garden*
- A car – class *Car.*

For each of the above examples, you should have come up with answers similar to those given in order below:

- The *Diary* class: a *DiaryEntry* class, which might itself contain a *Date* class
- The *Queue* class: a *Person* class to represent each member of the queue
- The *Garden* class: a *Shed* class, *Barbecue* class, *Fountain* class, *Lawn* class etc
- The *Car* class: an *Engine* class, *Gearbox* class, *Passenger* class etc.

Note that the *Passenger* class used for the *Car* class might be the same as the *Person* class used for the *Queue* class, or it might be necessary to add new characteristics to the *Person* class in order to create a *Passenger* class. We will return to this concept later.

Note also that the *DiaryEntry* class would have to represent several different categories of diary entry such as meetings, appointments and reminders. We will also return to this issue later on.

Each of the above examples comes from the real world, but each might also be implemented in a computer program. The diary could be an online diary, the supermarket queue could be part of a simulation, the garden could be part of a computer-aided design package for landscape designers and the car could be part of a traffic simulation or design package.

Activity 12.1

Composition

Write a *DiaryEntry* class, which has an attribute of class *String* to describe the nature of the entry and an attribute of class *Date* to record the date of the entry. You will also need to write the *Date* class, which will require three attributes; namely *day*, *month* and *year*. Write a test program to create an object of class *DiaryEntry* and print out its attributes.

The concept of composition implements the so-called *has a* relationship between classes. In other words, you should implement an association between two classes *A* and *B* using *composition* if you can say that *A* has a *B*, or vice versa. For example, a car has an engine, a cooker has an oven.

12.2 Inheritance

You will recall from Chapter 11 that we discussed a class called *Object* in package *java.lang* which defines 11 methods, including one called *toString()*. We said that the *Object* class is automatically *inherited* by all Java classes, which means that every Java class has these 11 methods. We then looked at how we could override the *toString()* method in our *Timepiece* class to make it do something useful. We will now return to the concept of inheritance and explain it in more detail.

A class *A* can inherit from a class *B* by including the words *extends B* in the declaration of class *A* as follows.

```
public class A extends B
{
  .
  .
  .
}
```

This means that *A* will have all the attributes and methods of *B*. This is an important aspect of object-oriented programming. It allows classes developed for one application to be reused in another. If a class in the Java API or elsewhere is potentially useful but requires some extra attributes or methods, then we can define a new class which inherits the attributes and methods of the existing class and then add the necessary extra attributes and methods. If it is required that an existing method inherited from class *B* should be implemented differently in class *A*, then one can *override* the inherited method to create an appropriate version, as we did with the *toString()* method in Chapter 11 (the main purpose of the version of the *toString()* method in class *Object* is to specify that all Java classes are to *have* a *toString()* method. This can then be overridden as appropriate).

So if every class must inherit from class *Object*, then do we have to include something like

```
public class A extends Object
{
  .
  .
  .
}
```

in every class definition? The answer is no; every class implicitly inherits from *Object* without the need to include the words *extends Object*.

Now let us look at the above example of car passengers to illustrate the concept of inheritance. We noted that a class to represent car passengers might be the same as the *Person* class for the supermarket queue, or it might be necessary to add new characteristics to the *Person* class in order to create a *Passenger* class. Let us assume that we have a class *Person* which we have already been using in our supermarket queue simulation program. For simplicity we will say that the only attribute in the class *Person* is a String holding the person's name. We will also omit the usual set and get methods. The class is as follows:

```java
// Specifies a person's details

public class Person
{
    protected String name;
    // Note use of keyword protected instead of private
    // See below for explanation

    public Person()
    {
    }

    public Person(String nameIn)
    {
        name = nameIn;
    }

    public String toString()
    {
        return "Name " + name;
    }
}
```

Now let us assume that for our *Passenger* class, we require the *name* attribute of the *Person* class, but with an additional attribute to indicate whether or not the passenger is also the driver. The *Passenger* class must inherit the *name* attribute of the *Person* class and add the additional *boolean* attribute. The class is as follows:

```java
// Specifies a passenger's details

public class Passenger extends Person
{
    private boolean driving;

    public Passenger(String nameIn, boolean drivingIn)
    {
        name = nameIn;
        driving = drivingIn;
    }

    public boolean isDriver()
    {
        return driving;
    }

    public String toString()
    {
        String oput = "Name " + name;

        if (isDriver())
            oput += " is driving";
        else
            oput += " is not driving";

        return oput;
    }
}
```

Here is a small test program for these classes:

```java
// Tests the Person and Passenger classes

public class PassengerTest
{
    public static void main(String[] args)
    {
        Person p = new Person("John Smith");

        // toString() method of p invoked
        System.out.println(p);

        Passenger ps = new Passenger("Fred Bloggs", false);

        // toString() method of ps invoked
        System.out.println(ps);
    }
}
```

Note that the *name* attribute of class *Person* was declared as

```java
protected String name;
```

The keyword *protected* denotes that this attribute is visible within the class *Person* and within any classes that inherit *Person*. If we had used the keyword *private*, then *name* would not be available in the class *Passenger*.

In the constructor method for *Passenger*, we could alternatively have passed the parameter *nameIn*, which contains the value for the *Person name* attribute, directly to the *Person* constructor method by using the keyword *super* as follows:

```java
public Passenger(String nameIn, boolean drivingIn)
{
    super(nameIn);
    driving = drivingIn;
}
```

The use of *super* invokes the *Person* class constructor. *Person* is said to be the *superclass* of *Passenger*, and *Passenger* is said to be a *subclass* of *Person*. In fact, it would be perfectly possible to define a new class to extend *Passenger*, another class to extend that class and so on, creating a hierarchy of classes concerned with more and more specialised types of vehicle passenger. One can view such a hierarchy as a kind of family tree, with classes getting more specialised as you go down the tree. In fact, all classes in Java are part of one big hierarchy with the class *Object* sitting right at the top. A class *A* which directly or indirectly inherits from another class *B* is said to be a *descendant* of *B*, and *B* is said to be an *ancestor* of *A*.

The concept of inheritance implements the so-called *is a* relationship between classes. In other words, you should implement an association between two classes *A* and *B* using inheritance if you can say that an *A* is a *B*, or vice versa. For example, a car is a vehicle.

Consider the following pairs of classes; which pairs should be implemented using inheritance?

- *Animal* and *Cat*
- *Car* and *Motorbike*
- *Table* and *Chair*
- *Book* and *Page*
- *Boat* and *Canoe*

For each of the above examples, you should have come up with answers similar to those given in order below:

- Yes, because a cat is a type of animal.
- No, because a car is not a type of motorbike or vice versa. However, the car and the motorbike could both inherit characteristics from a common superclass which we could call *Vehicle*.
- No, because a table is not a type of chair or vice versa.
- No; this is an example of the composition relationship from section 12.1; a book has a page.
- Yes, because a canoe is a boat.

It is sometimes tempting to use inheritance to extend existing classes where the relation "is a" is not actually being implemented. For example, suppose we already had a *Mirror* class with attributes *height*, *width* and *frameMaterial* (wood, metal or plastic). We want to define a *Picture* class to represent pictures to hang on a wall. We could have *Picture* extend the *Mirror* class, because pictures will require each of the above attributes, but this is an incorrect use of inheritance, because a picture is not a type of mirror. It would be better to define a common ancestor class for *Mirror* and *Picture* to contain their common characteristics, or to place the above attributes in a class *FrameDetails* which could itself be the type of an attribute of the *Mirror* and *Picture* classes (composition).

Activity 12.2

Inheritance

The *DiaryEntry* class you wrote for Activity 12.1 is probably too general for use in a real online diary. For example, real diary entries might represent meetings, appointments or reminders. Write a *Meeting* class which inherits from *DiaryEntry* and adds a new attribute *noOfAttendees* to contain the number of people who will be coming to the meeting. Write a test program to create a *Meeting* object and print out the values of its attributes.

12.3 Abstract classes and polymorphism

A class which is a descendant of another class will be more specialised. For example, a class *EstateCar* might inherit all the characteristics of a class *Car*, but add additional characteristics such as load capacity. In this case it is likely that we will want to create objects of class *Car* and objects of class *EstateCar*. However, we sometimes write classes for which we will not want to create objects. For example, the classes *Car* and *Motorbike* might each inherit from a common ancestor class *Vehicle*. The latter might have a method to return the number of wheels, which is a characteristic shared by cars and motorbikes.

However, this method would be implemented differently in the *Car* class and the *Motorbike* class. The *Car* class could then add further attributes and methods specific to cars only, such as boot size and presence or otherwise of air conditioning. The *Motorbike* class might add attributes such as whether the bike is two- or four-stroke, whether or not it can take a pillion passenger etc.

We would then create objects of classes *Car* and *Motorbike*, but we would not want to create *Vehicle* objects, as class *Vehicle* is too general to represent any actual vehicle we might see on the road. It exists only to specify common characteristics to be inherited by other classes. We can specify that a class is not to be used for creating objects by using the *abstract* keyword. The abstract *Vehicle* class might look like this:

```
public abstract class Vehicle
{
    public abstract int getNumOfWheels();
}
```

Note that the method *getNumOfWheels()* is also specified as *abstract*, and that only the signature of the method is specified (i.e. it has no method body). The implementation of the method is left to the classes inheriting from *Vehicle*, and of course the method will be implemented differently in the *Car* and *Motorbike* classes respectively (Note that classes inheriting an abstract method are *required* to provide an implementation of the method). Here is a possible specification of the *Car* class:

```
public class Car extends Vehicle
{
    public int getNumOfWheels()
    {
        return 4;
    }
}
```

The *getNumOfWheels()* method from *Vehicle* has been overridden to return 4, an appropriate value for a car. In the *Motorbike* class, the method would be overridden to return the value 2.

The following is a small test program to try out the *Car* and *Vehicle* classes:

```
// Tests the Vehicle and Car classes

public class CarTest
{
    public static void main(String[] args)
    {
        Vehicle v = new Car();

        System.out.println(v.getNumOfWheels());
    }
}
```

The above is an example of *polymorphism*, which means *many forms*. We could define a number of further classes which extend the *Vehicle* class, for example *Bicycle*, *Tricycle*, *Monocycle*, *Train* and *Truck*. Each of these would implement the *getNumberOfWheels()* method differently. Suppose we then had an array of vehicles, and we wanted to loop through the array and print out the number of wheels of each vehicle. The code processing the array does not know *what* each vehicle is, but it does know that each has a *getNumberOfWheels()* method which, if invoked, will carry out the required task for that particular vehicle.

The method has the same signature in each vehicle object, because this was specified in the abstract class *Vehicle* from which each *concrete* class (*Car*, *Motorbike*, etc.) defining the objects was specialised. The array could be declared as follows:

```
Vehicle[] vehicleArray = new Vehicle[10];
```

Note that the array is of base type *Vehicle*. However, we can place objects of any subclass of *Vehicle* into our array. Assuming the array has been filled with a mixture of cars, bicycles, etc. (perhaps by a loop requesting each vehicle type from the user), the code to do the printing might look like this:

```
for (int i = 0; i < vehicleArray.length; i++)
    System.out.println(vehicleArray[i].getNumOfWheels());
```

You can see that polymorphism allows us to *generalise* our program – the array processing code simply sends the *getNumOfWheels()* message (i.e. method call) to each vehicle in the array, and this message is interpreted appropriately for each specific vehicle type. The array processing code does not even know the type of vehicle to which it is sending the message, but it trusts that each specific vehicle has an appropriate implementation of the *getNumOfWheels()* method. At some future time, we might decide to create further classes of transport which also extend the *Vehicle* class. As long as these new classes also implement the *getNumOfWheels()* method, objects of these new classes can be placed in the *Vehicle* array and will work seamlessly with the existing array processing code. This makes polymorphism a very useful tool in object-oriented programming.

Another example would be a collection of shape objects such as circles, rectangles and triangles to be drawn on a graphics screen. Each object would probably include a *draw()* method inherited from an abstract common ancestor class, which would be implemented appropriately in each specific shape class to draw objects of that class. For example, if a program asked a circle to draw itself, the *draw()* method invoked in the *Circle* class would be one that had overridden the version it inherited, to become a method to draw circles. Classes defining other shapes such as rectangles, triangles etc. would each have their own appropriate implementation of the inherited *draw()* method.

Another polymorphic feature of Java is the overloading of methods, which we have already seen. It is particularly useful to be able to overload constructor methods, so that we can initialise the objects we instantiate in different ways by supplying different parameters to the constructor. Another example is overloading of operators; for example the use of + to denote addition or String concatenation.

12.4 Summary

- Any class can have other classes as the types of its attributes; this is called *composition*
- A class *A* can be defined as extending another class *B*; this means that *A* *inherits* the attributes and methods of *B*
- Classes that are not designed to create objects are defined as *abstract*; such classes exist only to enable other classes to inherit and implement their abstract methods. This is an example of *polymorphism*
- Polymorphism enables the same method call to be used with a number of related objects and for each to respond in an appropriate manner.

This chapter and the previous one have given you a brief introduction to the concepts of object-oriented programming. If you continue your study of programming, you will inevitably learn much more about object orientation, which will enable you to tackle problem solving by programming in a more natural and intuitive way. You might even study other programming paradigms, such as functional or logic programming. Wherever your study of programming takes you, you should now have a good grasp of the basic concepts of procedural programming and a taste of object-oriented programming upon which you can build.

Have fun!

12.5 Review questions

Question 12.1   What is the difference between *composition* and *inheritance*?

Question 12.2   What is the difference between *overloading* and *overriding*?

Question 12.3   What is the advantage of polymorphism?

Question 12.4   What is an abstract class?

Question 12.5   What is the keyword *extends* used for?

Question 12.6   In what circumstances would you declare attributes as *protected* rather than *private*?

Question 12.7   Answer *true* or *false* to each of the following:

1 Inheritance implements the "has a" relationship between classes.

2 The term *composition* refers only to music classes.

3 A *superclass* is an extra-large class.

4 A method in a subclass must not have the same name as a method in its superclass.

5 Composition implements the "has a" relationship between classes.

6 The word *super* can be used to invoke a superclass constructor.

7 The ability of a family of related classes to each implement their own version of a method is an example of *polymorphism*.

8 It would be appropriate for a *Garden* class to extend a *Lawn* class.

9 It would be appropriate for a *Dog* class to extend a *Cat* class.

10 It would be appropriate for a *MobilePhone* class to have an attribute of type *KeyPad* where *KeyPad* is a class.

12.6 Answers to review questions

Question 12.1   *Composition* refers to the case where a class uses one or more classes as types for its attributes. *Inheritance* refers to the case where a class is a specialisation of another class. The former class 'inherits' the attributes and methods of the latter and adds new attributes and methods of its own.

Question 12.2   *Overloading* refers to the case where several versions of a given method are placed in a class, differing in their parameter lists and/ or return types. *Overriding* refers to the case where a method defined in a superclass is implemented in a different way in a subclass.

Question 12.3   The advantage of polymorphism is that it enables us to write more general programs. The same method call can be used with a number of objects of related classes and each object will interpret the message in a way appropriate to itself.

Question 12.4   An abstract class is a superclass from which objects cannot be instantiated. It contains method signatures for a set of methods which are required to be implemented by its subclasses.

Question 12.5   The keyword *extends* is used to specify that a class is a specialisation of (i.e. inherits from) another class.

Question 12.6   The keyword *private* is used to specify that the attribute or method to which it refers is only visible within the containing class. The keyword *protected* is similar except that it also allows the associated attribute or method to be visible in subclasses.

Question 12.7

1 **False** Inheritance implements the "is a" relationship.

2 **False** Composition is where a class uses another as an attribute type.

3 **False** A superclass is a class from which another class has inherited.

4 **False** A method in a subclass may override the corresponding superclass method by providing its own implementation.

5 **True** Composition is where one class has another as an attribute type.

6 **True** The superclass constructor is often invoked by the subclass constructor in this way.

7 **True** This is very useful in writing more generally applicable programs.

8 **False** A garden is not a kind of lawn, but a garden may contain a lawn. The correct relationship is composition.

9 **False** *Dog* and *Cat* could both inherit from, say, an abstract *Quadruped* class, but not from each other.

10 **True** A mobile phone "has a" keypad.

12.7 Feedback on activities

Activity 12.1: Composition The *Date* and *DiaryEntry* classes, together with a test program, are listed here:

```java
// Specifies a date as day month and year
public class Date
{
    private int day, month, year;

    public Date(int d, int m, int y)
    {
        day = d; month = m; year = y;
    }

    public String toString()
    {
        return day + "/" + month + "/" + year;
    }
}

// Specifies a diary entry as content and the date of the entry
// Makes use of the Date class
public class DiaryEntry
{
    private String entry;
    private Date dateOfEvent; // Date class used for attribute

    public DiaryEntry(String content, int d, int m, int y)
    {
        entry = content;
        dateOfEvent = new Date(d, m, y);
    }

    public String toString()
    {
        return "Event:\n" + entry + "\n" + "is scheduled for " +
            dateOfEvent;
    }
}

// Program to test the DiaryEntry and Date classes

import javax.swing.JOptionPane;

public class DiaryTest
{
    public static void main(String[] args)
    {
        String description = JOptionPane.showInputDialog(
            "Please enter description of event");

        DiaryEntry d = new DiaryEntry(description, 21, 3, 2005);

        System.out.println(d);

        System.exit(0);
    }
}
```

Activity 12.2: Inheritance   The classes and test program are given below.

```java
// Specifies a diary entry as content and the date of the entry
// Makes use of the Date class
public class DiaryEntry
{
    protected String entry;
    protected Date dateOfEvent;      // Date class used for attribute

    public DiaryEntry(String content, int d, int m, int y)
    {
        entry = content;
        dateOfEvent = new Date(d, m, y);
    }

    public String toString()
    {
        return "Event:\n" + entry + "\n" + "is scheduled for " +
            dateOfEvent;
    }
}


// Specifies a meeting by extending DiaryEntry class
// to add number of meeting attendees
public class Meeting extends DiaryEntry
{
    private int noOfAttendees;

    public Meeting(String content, int d, int m, int y, int present)
    {
        super(content, d, m, y);
        noOfAttendees = present;
    }

    public String toString()
    {
        return "Meeting " + super.toString() + "\nThere will be " +
            noOfAttendees + " attendees";
    }
}
```

```
// Program to test the Meeting class

import javax.swing.JOptionPane;

public class MeetingTest
{
    public static void main(String[] args)
    {
        String description = JOptionPane.showInputDialog(
            "Please enter description of meeting");

        String presentStr = JOptionPane.showInputDialog(
            "Please enter number of attendees");
        int present = Integer.parseInt(presentStr);

        Meeting m = new Meeting(description, 21, 3, 2005, present);

        System.out.println(m);

        System.exit(0);
    }
}
```

Note that the attributes of the *DiaryEntry* class have been declared as *protected* rather than *private*. This is to make them visible in the subclass *Meeting*.